David Batchelor

Concretos

Anomie

Detail from *Reef 02*, 2018, cast acrylic, concrete, dimensions variable

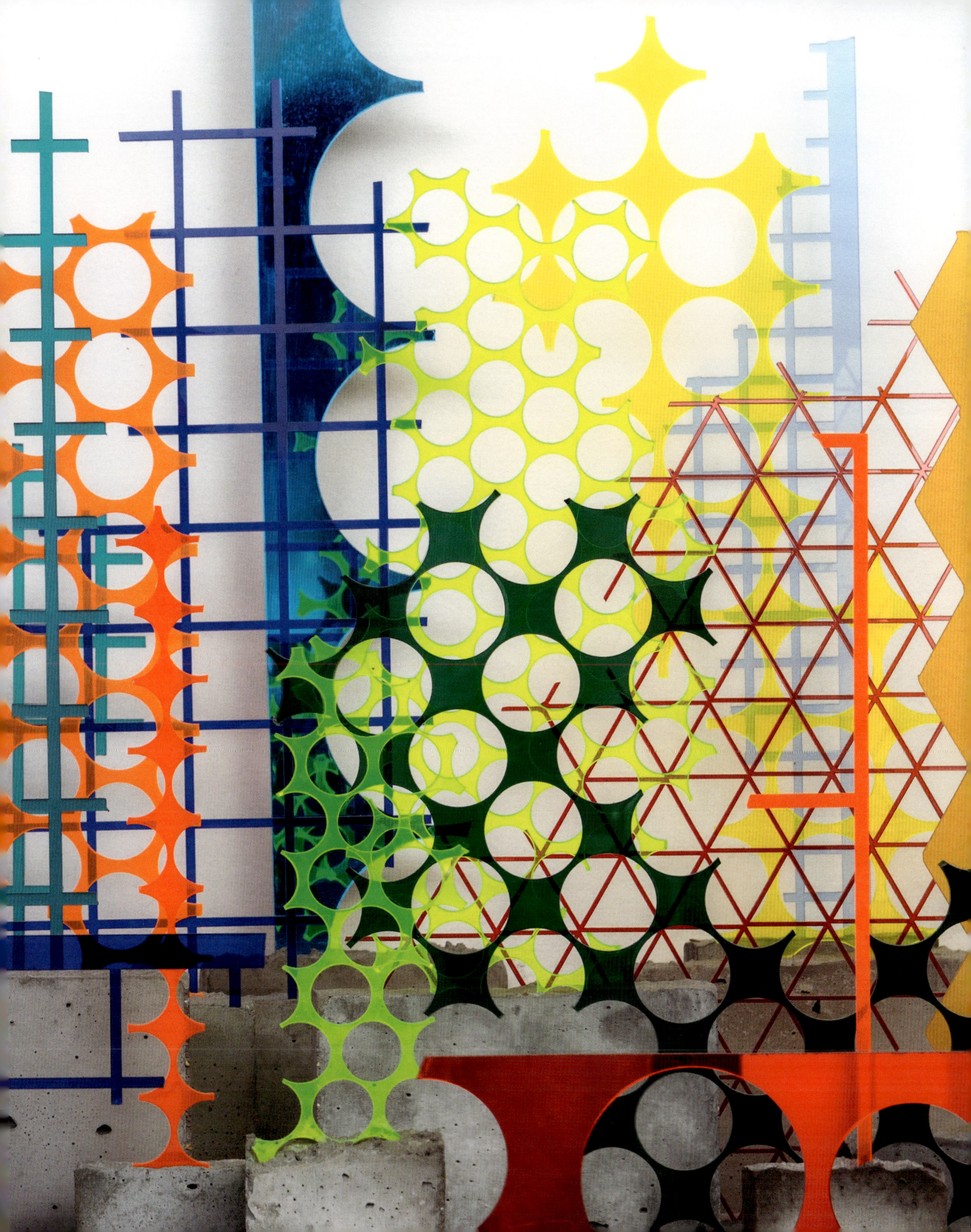

For VR71 with thanks

8
On Making Things
David Batchelor

16
Plates

132
The Pleasure Principle
Eleanor Nairne

136
The Neutral and the Active
Adrian Forty

143
Acknowledgements

On Making Things
David Batchelor

How to Make a Concreto

In the early summer of 2009, we travelled from our home in London to Sicily for a holiday. On arrival, we stayed for a few nights at a faded old grand hotel on the outskirts of Palermo, and one bright morning we decided to get a bus along the coast and spend the day at a well-known local beach. I can't recall much about the beach or many of the details of the day, but I do remember that at some point we walked along a street of houses a block or two back from

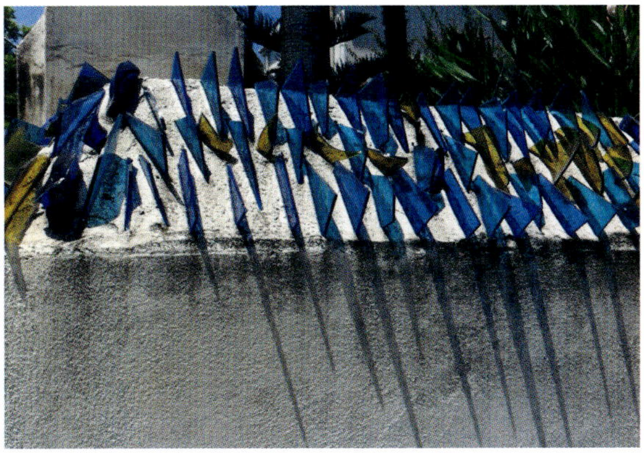

Palermo, 2019

the seafront. The houses may have been homes or holiday rentals, and one particular dwelling made me stop for a moment to look more closely. It was on a corner where two streets joined at ninety degrees, and a medium-height wall separated its garden from the pavement and the road. The house looked orderly if mostly ordinary; the woodwork was painted a seaside mid-blue, and the garden was neatly planted and well tended. It was the boundary wall that got my attention, which had shards of broken glass embedded in it. But it wasn't exactly this that made me stop and look, it was the unusual and particular way in which it had been done.

I have seen a thousand different medium-height walls in many different cities, their tops encrusted with similar shards of broken glass, and all done with the same purpose in mind. I don't usually pay much attention to these walls. Their execution is marked by a kind of aesthetic indifference that probably symbolises an equivalent indifference to the pain or injury they might cause to anyone who comes into contact with them. The glass comes from whatever broken bottles are at hand, and no obvious attention is paid to the choice of colours. Green usually predominates, and it is often punctuated by a smattering of clear, brown or sometimes blue. The distribution of colours looks arbitrary. These works are poorly executed and they are poorly maintained. Dirt and grime and debris accumulate between the glass uprights and in the cement indentations. All in all, they are unpleasant in several ways at once.

Which is what made this particular wall a few miles outside Palermo so unusual and so compelling. I have never seen any wall in which this potential for violent injury to the over-curious has been so thoughtfully executed. Each and every stage of its composition was marked by careful consideration – even, I hesitate to say, by love. First of all, the wall was well made and was finished with a neat sloping apex. Only the outward-facing edge of the apex had glass embedded in it. Most of the glass was cut to the same right-angled triangular shape and the same approximate size, which means it can't have come from broken bottles and must have been sourced with significantly more thought. Nearly every piece of glass was carefully aligned in two long neat rows. The edges, angles and orientation of each triangle were thoughtfully positioned and evenly matched. And then – and this is what first caught my attention – every piece of glass was either one of two shades of transparent blue or, occasionally, a light yellow-brown. (I was slightly thrown by the yellow-brown bits, which looked more like an afterthought, as if there wasn't quite enough blue to complete the job.) Finally, it was well maintained: on this wall everything was kept very *clean*. All in all, in the bright sunlight of a southern European summer, this angled wall of blue glass, with its long shimmering blue shadows, was, well, it was enough to make me stop and take a couple of photographs on my phone.

For many artists the street is a more or less constant source of ideas, hints and possibilities. That said, in my experience, many of its promises come to nothing when picked up and taken to another place and re-examined in a different light. Sometimes what looks good on the street only looks good on the street, and any attempt to move it simply kills it. But sometimes, if you are lucky, an image or an object or an idea survives the transition and it gains another life.

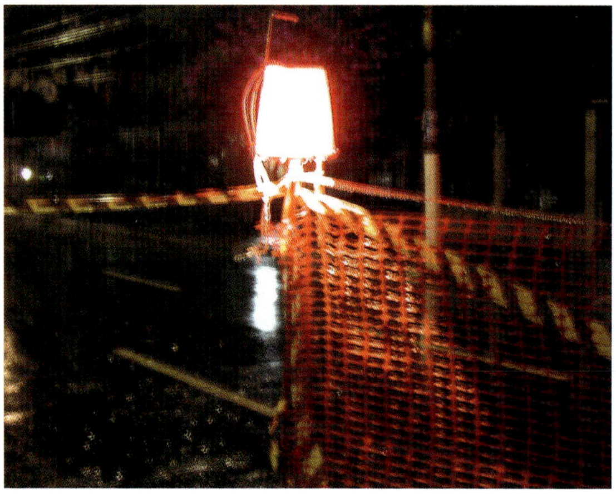

São Paulo, 2004

Some years ago, in the early 2000s, I was visiting São Paulo and installing a work for the city's contemporary art biennial. One evening I happened to walk down a street near my hotel and passed a fenced-off area behind which were some half-finished roadworks. It was dark and the site was deserted, but its perimeter fencing was marked out by a series of glowing red lights. At first this seemed entirely unremarkable: every roadworks I can remember or imagine has had red warning lights around it. But, unlike in most of Europe, where the lights would have to be of a particular type and a regulated size and a specified degree of luminescence, these lamps were simply a series of upturned red plastic buckets, each of which had a standard domestic lightbulb fixed into its base. I was immediately struck by the elegantly improvised look of these glowing semi-sculptures. Which is hardly a surprise for someone who was at the time involved in making large towers of illuminated lightboxes, and was increasingly preoccupied with the many types and the various places of colour in the modern city. So I took a few photos and decided, when I got back in the studio, that I would contrive some kind of chandelier made from individually illuminated coloured plastic containers. This is often how things begin.

By the end of the first decade of the new century, I was no less interested in how and where colour manifests itself in the city, but I had become more caught up with some rather technical questions about colour in sculpture and painting. In particular I was concerned with ways in which I could make colour not just a feature of a sculpture or painting, but its central and overriding subject. With illuminated work this is relatively straightforward, largely because the coloured light tends quite literally to put everything else – structure, support, materials – into the shade. It is less straightforward with non-illuminated colour, which will always have to negotiate its presence with those other elements of a work. I felt I was finding a way of making colour the primary focus of the work, and had in fact been doing something of the kind for some time before I realised what I had been doing. Since my first tentative experiments with it, now thirty years ago, my preferred way of presenting colour has been to isolate it. In one way or another, without entirely being aware of it, I found myself looking for ways to separate the experience of colour from other elements of the work. This is never quite possible, because colour is always tied to a medium or material of some sort, be that paint or metal, glass or plastic or light. But it can be made to look that way.

In the early 1990s I began placing rectangles of shiny coloured glass or plastic on simple horizontal grey steel shelves. Shortly after that I made a number of multi-part works in which flat panels of coloured plastic were inserted into the tops of found industrial dollies. And throughout the 1990s and 2000s I made an open-ended series of works on card or paper in which a central blob of colour – made from poured liquid paint, or paint sprayed from a can, or layers of adhesive tape – was seemingly balanced on a schematic, rectangular, black or grey base or plinth. In each case, I came to realise, a three- or two-dimensional block of vivid colour was supported by a simple neutral base, a base that was physically and materially distinct from the colour placed on it. This separation of colour from its support was, for me, the key to it becoming its own presence in the work.

It doesn't take a leap of the imagination to see that the wall outside Palermo with its sharp symmetrical ornamentation was doing exactly what I had been struggling to conceptualise in the studio for about a decade and a half. In 2011, I made my first *Concreto*. I found a stained-glass artist in North London who sold offcuts of coloured glass; I made a simple mould the same size as a standard house brick; and I bought some cement and sand from a builders' merchant near the studio. I broke

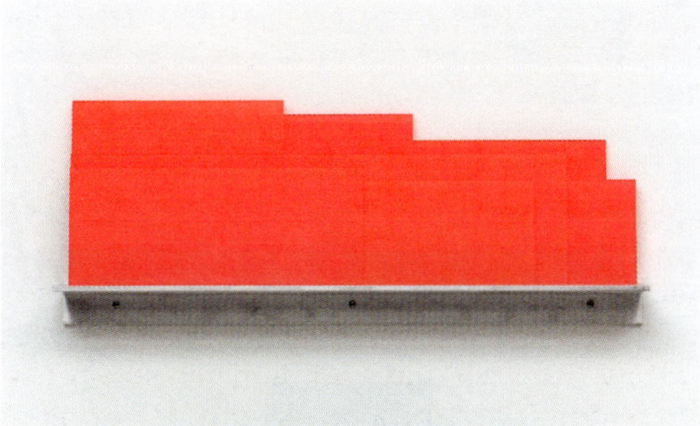

Shelf-Like 6, 1995, cast acrylic, fluorescent paint, aluminium, 39 x 120 x 12 cm

Atomic Drawing 09, 2010, adhesive tape, card, 35 x 21.5 cm

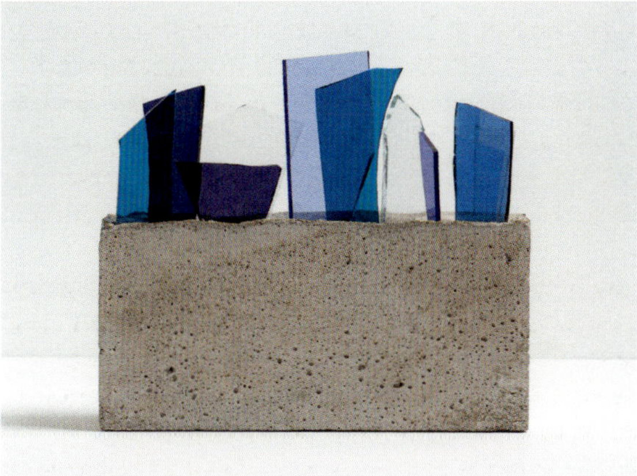

Concreto 1.0h/04, 2013, glass, concrete, 19 x 21 x 6.5 cm

up the glass (at first I tried cutting it but sometimes the shapes turned out better when I dropped it); I mixed the sand and cement with not quite the right amount of water; and as the concrete began to set I carefully placed several shards of glass into the mould. The next day, when the cement had set properly, I released the work from its former. After several attempts to get the concrete mix right, I began to experiment with making different-sized blocks (all multiples or divisions of the basic brick unit). After that I tried using plastic offcuts instead of glass; and I experimented with making compositions of multiple individual elements. Since then I have tried using found objects from the street and studio detritus. Some of these have ended up as free-standing works over three metres tall and some are half the size of a single brick. Over the past decade I have made a lot of *Concretos*, and I am still looking for their limits.

How to Make a Poem

In a 2019 radio interview, John Cooper Clarke suggested that all you need to make a poem is a pen, a piece of paper, and a capacity for idleness. As gnomic utterances go, this one is pretty good, not least because it appears to be entirely accurate. Exactly the same could be said for drawing, of course; and the same principle could be applied to many of the more basic and enduring forms of art: a few simple materials and a willingness to look at things in a certain, or, more to the point, in an uncertain way. I don't want to get drawn into discussing exactly what Clarke might have meant by 'idleness', but it is worth briefly dwelling on the notion. First of all, the term has a long and rather distinguished history that has been addressed since antiquity, in one form or another, by philosophers, moralists, social critics, novelists, poets, playwrights and artists. In the modern period this ranges at least from William Hogarth's engravings *Industry and Idleness*, published in 1747, to Bertrand Russell's essay 'In Praise of Idleness' of 1935. But it was in the nineteenth century that idleness really had its day, quite possibly as a counterpoint to the unprecedented growth in industry during those years. The notion of a detached individual – standing aside from the ebb and flow of commerce and from the cycles of production, labour and useful activity in general – became increasingly attractive to many Romantics and later decadents. Standing aside and doing nothing more than allowing yourself to look at the world in a non-instrumental way, in a way not governed by function or purpose but by pleasure – or poetry. Clearly doing nothing useful is not the same as doing nothing at all. Idling is an activity, after all, an activity that has been associated historically with reverie, daydreaming, reflection and meditation. It is also identified with inattention, inertia, lassitude, narcosis and stupefaction, and one of the pleasures of idling, perhaps, is that there is no clear or obvious boundary between its more or less virtuous forms. Idling may result in fresh ways of seeing the world and in novel insights, it may even be a precondition for such insights, but it may also lead nowhere at all.

Clarke cites Charles Baudelaire as one of the great nineteenth-century advocates of idling, although there are many others to choose from. The *flâneur* was Baudelaire's ideal idler: an acute observer of the inner workings of modern city life who, at the same time, is never quite a participant in it. A man – and, at the time, almost always a man – and a man of leisure – someone who for one reason or another didn't have to provide for himself by doing useful work – the idler appears a fairly privileged figure. That said, for Baudelaire and for Édouard Manet, the exemplary detached observer also included the drunk and the barmaid, the beggar and the prostitute. Arguably, in later years the figure became democratised, and idling has remained remarkably constant in the artistic imagination. From the Surrealists' love of undirected walking, to the Situationists' advocacy of the *dérive*, the artist was there throughout the twentieth century, attentively adrift in the daily life of the city.

How to Make a Painting, possibly

I watch *The Joy of Painting* on television. Bob Ross was not an idler. His half-hour oil painting lessons were a fixture of American television during the 1980s and early 1990s, and he was extraordinarily good at making fantastically odd pictures – over thirty thousand of them, and almost all dreamy unpopulated landscapes. The programmes were revived, I think, to inspire or at least to distract people during the Covid-19 pandemic lockdowns.

The strange and most compelling thing about Ross's paintings, apart from the speed with which he makes them, is they are simultaneously highly realistic and entirely fanciful. No existing landscape is ever referred to, no actual species of tree or grass, no known type of rock or formation of cloud is ever allowed to get in the way of his weirdly plausible vistas. Everything is wet-on-wet technique: there is the palette-knife-tree-trunk technique, the fan-brush-fluffy-cloud technique, the one-inch-flat-decorator's-brush-babbling-brook-over-stones technique, the endless quantities of sap green and van Dyke brown, and there is the bottom-right-hand-corner-signature-in-red technique. And then there is Ross himself, his huge palette eclipsed only by his even huger perm, and his mellifluous talk of happy clouds and cosy cabins and God-be-with-you sign-offs. And, all in all, it is incredibly pleasurable and even slightly magical to watch. The problem for me is that Ross is such a virtuoso in what he does, he makes it look impossible *not* to make your picture as accomplished as his. And yet, at the same time, I know if I tried to follow his tutorials, I would end up in such a rage of frustrated incompetence that after ten minutes I would vow never to pick up a paintbrush again.

I would like to put Bob Ross in a room with John Cooper Clarke. I think they would have a lot to say to each other: about art and entertainment, about performing poetry and painting, and about being popular and being taken seriously by your peers. But I doubt they would agree about how art is made and what it is made from. For Clarke art comes from idle observation; for Ross it comes from industrious technique. Clarke's slow Salford drawl makes you wonder whether he will ever get started; Ross's perky enthusiasm makes you wonder if he will ever stop. For Clarke it is all about the city: its details and margins as much as its centres and set-pieces; its cracks and its corners; its dead-ends and its deadbeats. And he looks the part: all snakeskin boots, thin black suits over a thinner white frame and a pallor celebrating a lifelong aversion to the gentle kiss of the morning sun. For Ross it is all about nature: robust and healthy and clean and good. And he looks the part too in his beard and his open-necked casual shirt and his practical loose-fitting jeans. Except it isn't quite that because while Ross clearly loved the natural world, there is little indication that any actual landscape was ever given

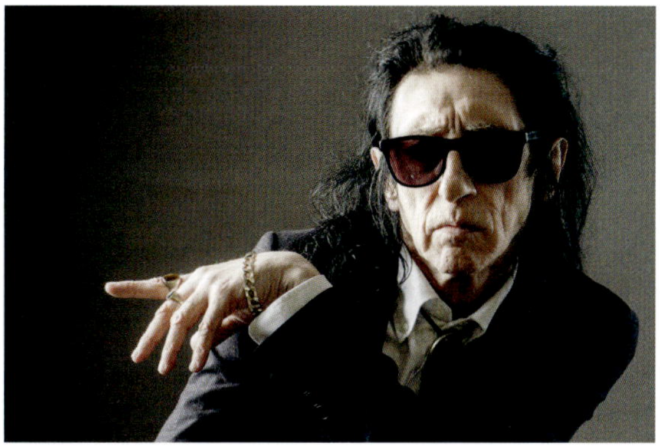

John Cooper Clarke

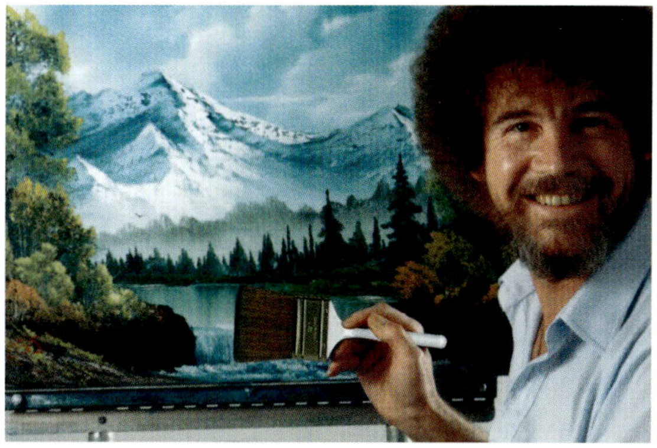

Bob Ross

the opportunity to intrude into his homely vistas. Nothing seems to get in the way of Ross's painting; his technique seems impervious either to objections from the outside world or to any nagging sense of inner doubt.

I don't think Ross sets out to make me feel inadequate and incompetent, but that is the general effect. His work also requires so much *stuff*: an easel and a canvas and a palette and several brushes and a dozen tubes of paint with unlikely names and so on. In my experience, buying a lot of equipment before you begin is not always a good way to get started. But perhaps that isn't the point. Perhaps the only thing that matters is to get started and see for yourself where it leads. And both John Cooper Clarke and Bob Ross offer suggestions about how to get started. You and I will never make a painting like Ross and you and I will never make a poem like Clarke. But, following their prompts and suggestions, we might just make something of our own.

On Making Things in a Pandemic, April 2020

[This part was written during the first mandatory lockdown of the coronavirus pandemic. I had been asked by the Yale/Mellon journal *British Art Studies* to write on the subject of 'Luxury and Crisis' in the decorative arts, and to discuss a particular work that related to these concerns.]

Everyone has been profoundly affected by the coronavirus pandemic, whether or not they themselves have become ill. For a great many people this has meant spending a lot more time alone. Solitude – how we might cope with it and what we might learn from it – has become an urgent topic in the media. I have read and listened to discussions by psychologists and philosophers, writers, religious commentators, educationalists and therapists. And I have seen many people turn in their solitude to making things. These things might be drawings or paintings, designs or clothes, music or gardens. One of the possible by-products of this health crisis that has become an economic and social crisis is that we will emerge to a more decorative world, or at least a more decorated world. And this, it seems to me, raises questions about the purpose of decoration, and about the uses of the apparently useless.

The UK may or may not cultivate a particularly utilitarian mind-set; it may or may not have developed a pragmatic culture that really values only that which serves an identifiable social or economic necessity; it may or may not regard all else as a luxury to be tolerated as and when time and money allow. But I don't think it makes sense to call these products of our solitude 'luxuries', even if many of them might fit the conventional definitions of the term. Covid-19 has brought with it some vivid reminders of other necessities: those of kindness and compassion, for example. And calmness: an ability to stand apart, if only momentarily, from the turmoil and to reflect. It seems to me that any activity that contributes to this quality of reflective calmness needs to be embraced as a joyful necessity, rather than tolerated as a dispensable luxury. In this, the decorative arts are no different from fine art or music or literature.

We can never know why early *Homo sapiens* and Neanderthals felt compelled to decorate their environments and adorn the objects around them with abstract shapes and schematic figures, and I am not at all sure we understand what compels us to do it now. But, given we do do it now and always have done it in the past, it is probably safe to assume it answers a need of some kind, and a fairly basic one at that. That need might be pleasure. Pleasure is complex (ask Epicurus or Freud) and I can't begin to address it properly here. But surely the considered pleasures of making things and sharing the results of this making are, at the very least, a necessary counterbalance to the more routine and often stressful necessities of everyday life, Covid-induced or otherwise.

The quilts made by Arrange Whatever Pieces Come Your Way are vibrantly beautiful examples of these pleasures. The title given to the project by Sheelagh Boyce and Annabelle Harty, initiated in 2016, says something about the ethos of their quilt making, and it says something about the traditions of quilting from which they draw. For me, these are contemporary versions of a tradition that transcends the academic distinction between the decorative and the fine arts. In being made from pre-existing swatches and bolts of fabric – shirts, jackets, kimonos, etc – they also address other pleasures and necessities, and in particular those of reusing, reframing and revaluing discarded materials of a culture that affords itself the luxury of waste.

On Still Making Things in a Pandemic, February 2022

At the time of writing the Covid-19 pandemic has lasted over two years. The social, personal, medical, political and economic effects have been overwhelming and, for many, quite devastating. We hear about death every day, although the fact that over two hundred people are still dying from coronavirus every twenty-four hours in England passes almost without comment. Perhaps this is because it is mercifully fewer than the thousand and more daily deaths that were recorded in an earlier phase of the crisis. Over the months, many of us have become amateur statisticians of death. We are bombarded each and every day by numbers and figures and graphs, all of which, in one way or another, seek to show us where we are in the virus's game-plan; whether things are as bad as they

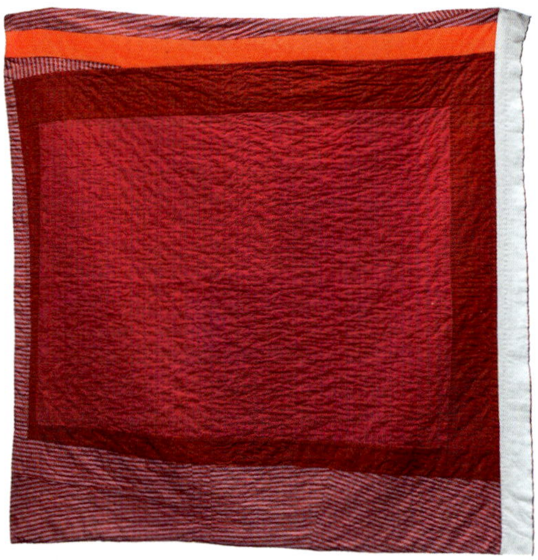

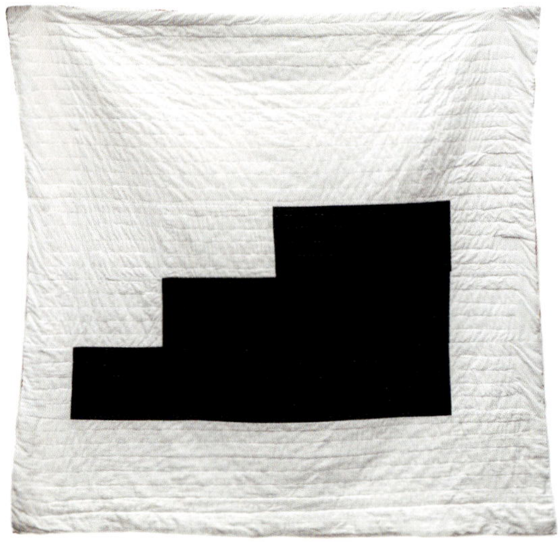

Arrange Whatever Pieces Come Your Way, *Quilt 8*, 2018 (front and back), cotton, bamboo, 115 x 115 cm

seem, or better, or worse; whether we are emerging from a crisis or falling deeper into it; whether we should feel hope or despair. At one point I began to hear the chilling phrase 'excess deaths' a lot. It refers to the number of people dying above and beyond the statistically normal death rate, and is thus considered a fairly accurate measure of deaths caused by coronavirus. I don't hear the phrase so much now, perhaps because it was considered too callously brutal for the early evening news round-ups. But every day in too many ways we are reminded of the constant presence of death.

In art we have the *memento mori*. The term and its purpose – to remind the viewer of the inevitability of death, even and perhaps especially in the presence of great plentitude and comfort – have been features of art since antiquity. In painting and sculpture, a *memento mori* traditionally takes the form of a skull, sometimes with additional bones, placed somewhere within a larger overall composition. But there are many other emblems of impermanence, some of which are more subtle than others. These range from the hourglass to a candle by way of a wilting flower to a spot of mould on a piece of fruit. Today, I feel like saying, every white plastic lateral flow test device and every spike in every graphic visualisation of the pandemic is a *memento mori*. But at the same time I am aware, in spite of the current crisis, that most people's lives in the West are generally less precarious than they were at any time in the past. So perhaps the *memento mori* hasn't been made entirely redundant by recent events.

That said, I have never been entirely persuaded by these symbolic reminders of the impermanence of everything. One reason, perhaps, is a general absence of any sense of permanence that would make it necessary to be reminded of its opposite. Over 150 years ago, Baudelaire (him again) talked of the entire experience of modernity in terms of 'the fugitive, the ephemeral and the contingent'. This feeling of radical uncertainty and instability was what it meant to be modern, and every puff of industrial smoke and every reflection on a shiny patent leather shoe was its emblem. In this sense, then, perhaps modernity itself is a *memento mori*, as every element and emblem of the modern is also an emblem of its and our impermanence.

In the same year, 1863, in an essay on the work of Eugène Delacroix, Baudelaire reported that the painter likened the piano-playing of Chopin to the singing of 'a brightly coloured bird, hovering over the horrors of a bottomless pit'. It is a striking image but it is also, arguably, a reversal of the conventional terms of a *memento mori*. Here, rather than some larger picture containing within it a coded reminder of death, the work of art itself is surrounded by the darkness of the abyss. The work is thus, in itself, more a reminder of life than of death: more a *memento vivere* than a *memento mori*. And it doesn't have to take the form of a sublime improvisation by Chopin. My feeling is you don't have to look far to find such reminders, not least because any work of art, before it is anything else, is precisely this. Any voluntary act of making, whatever its form or subject or purpose, however permanent or impermanent or beautiful or banal its results, is a *memento vivere*. The value of making things became vividly clear during the enforced solitude of lockdown, as I suggested above: among the many daily reminders of darkness and death, there were also many reminders of life. Each one a small victory among many defeats, perhaps, but each one enough, sometimes, to make those defeats a little more bearable.

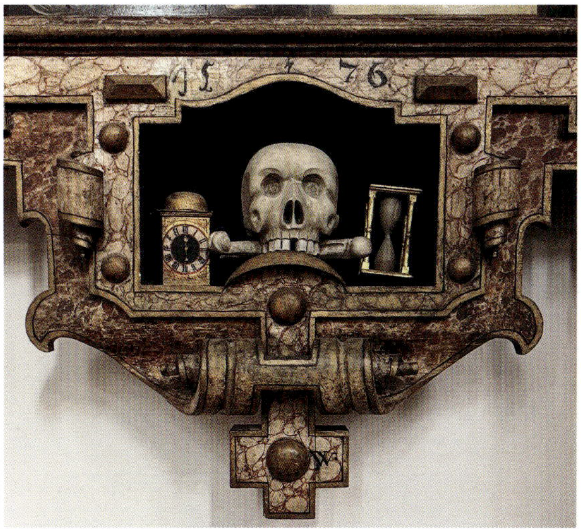
Anon, Munich Cathedral

Cons

Neo-Cons

Alt-Cons

Geo-Cons

Neo-Neo-Cons

I-Cons

Ex-Cons

2012 –

The first *Concretos* were all made with shards of coloured glass embedded in a simple concrete base. The moulds for the earliest works were the size of a single standard house brick. Later and larger works were made using moulds the size of 2, 4, 6, 8 or 10 bricks.

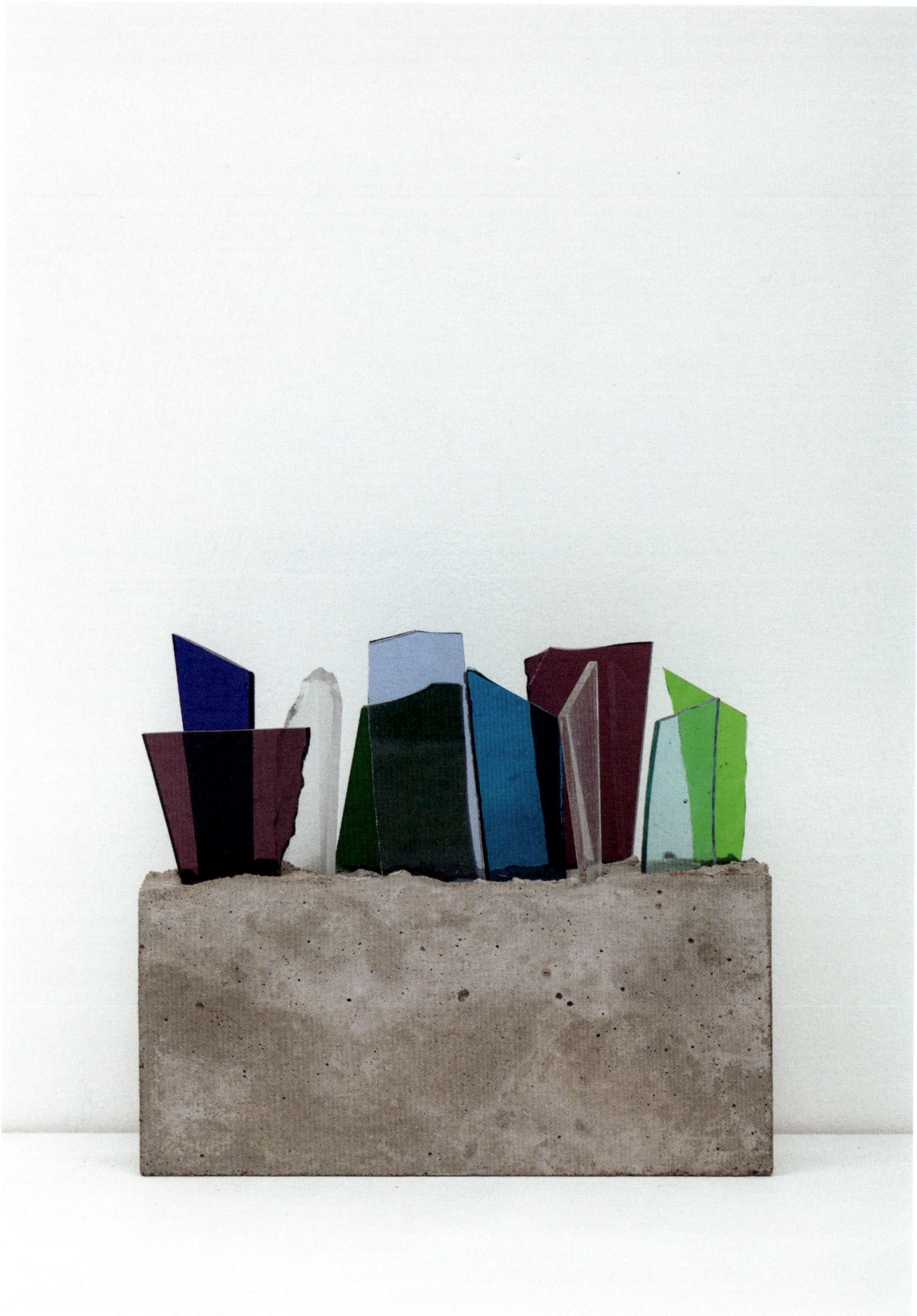

Concreto 1.0h/01, 2012
Glass, concrete
20.5 x 21.5 x 6.5 cm

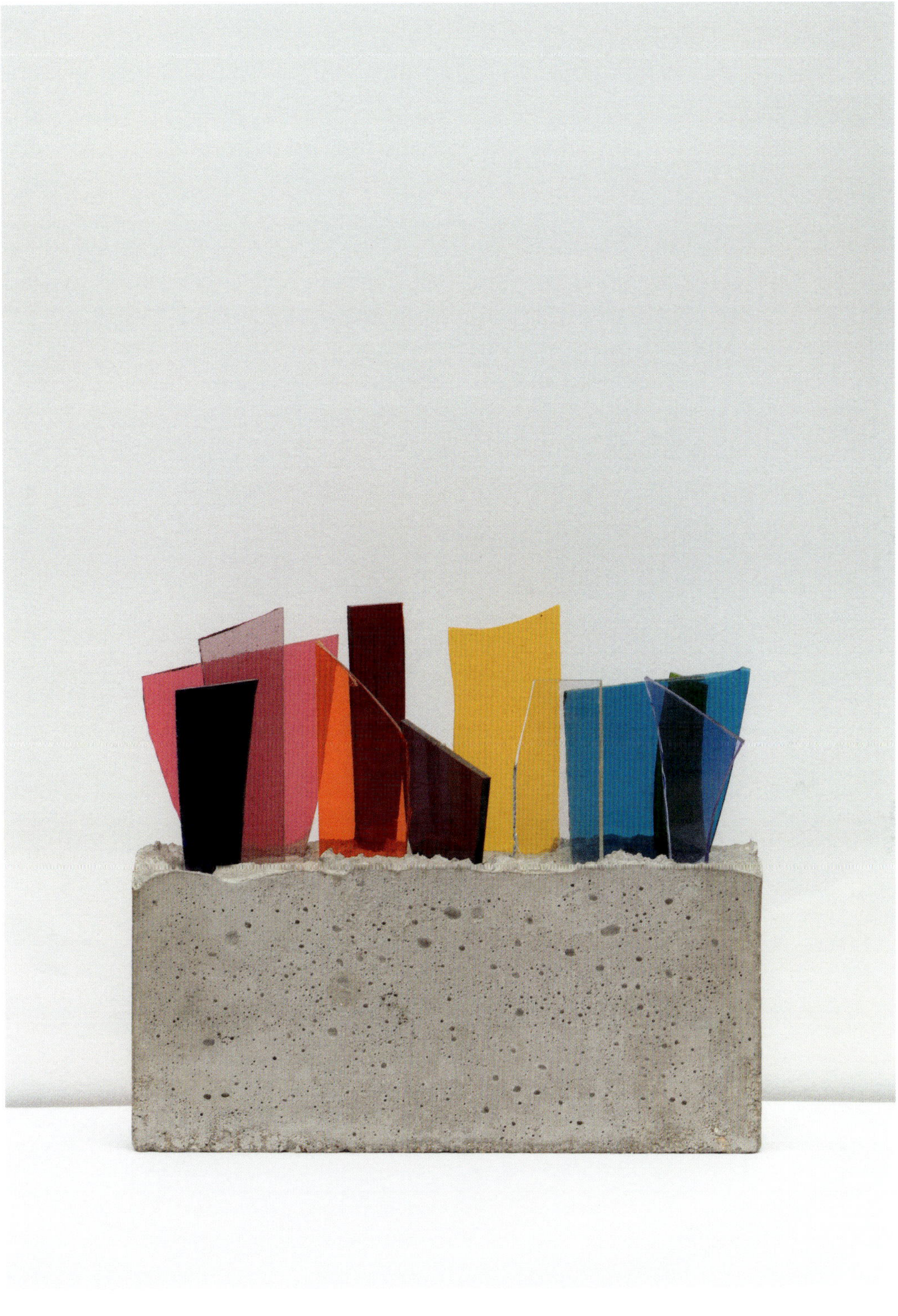

Concreto 1.0h/14, 2014
Glass, concrete
19 x 21.5 x 6.5 cm

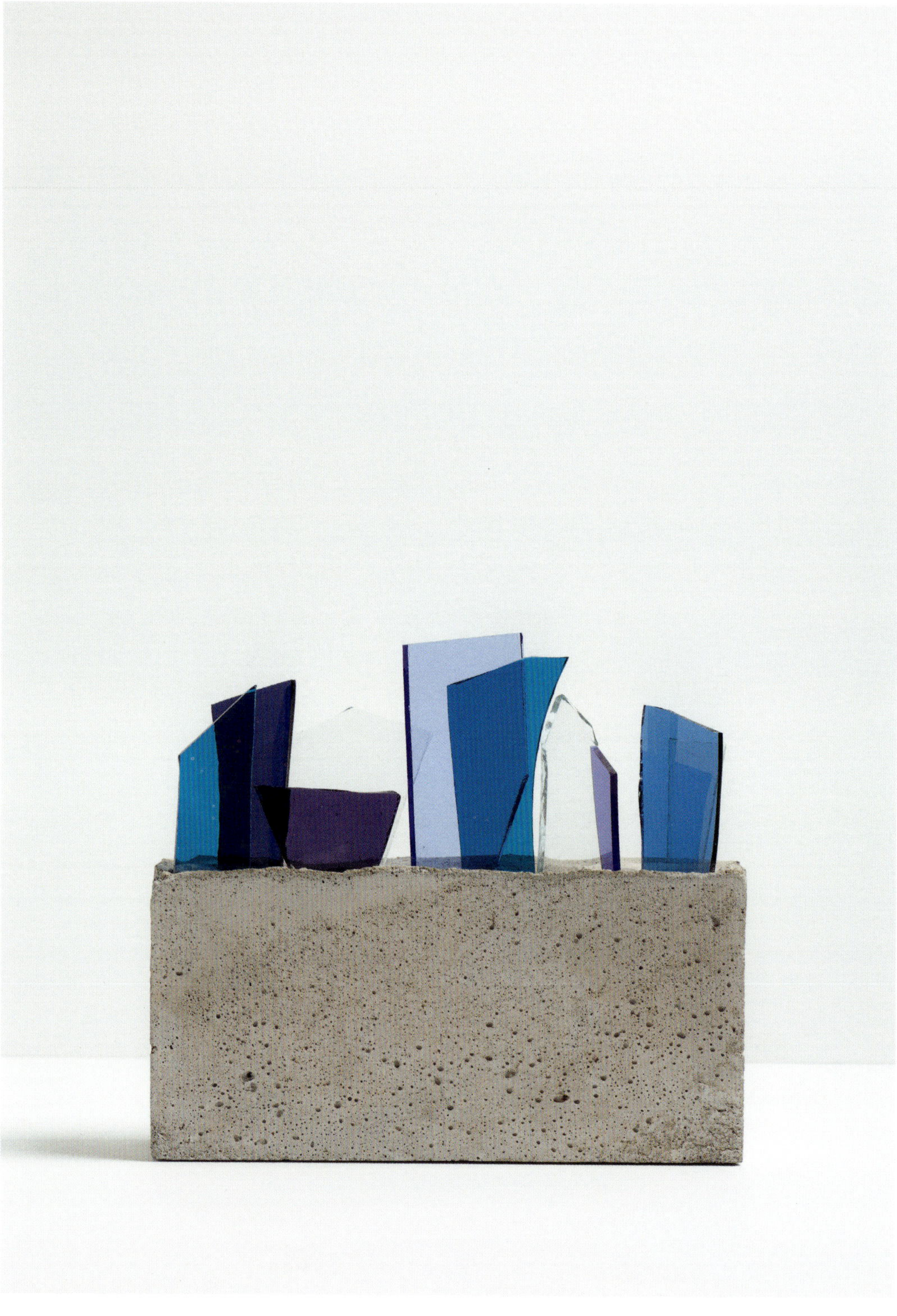

Concreto 2.0h/02, 2013
Glass, concrete
20 x 21.5 x 6.5 cm

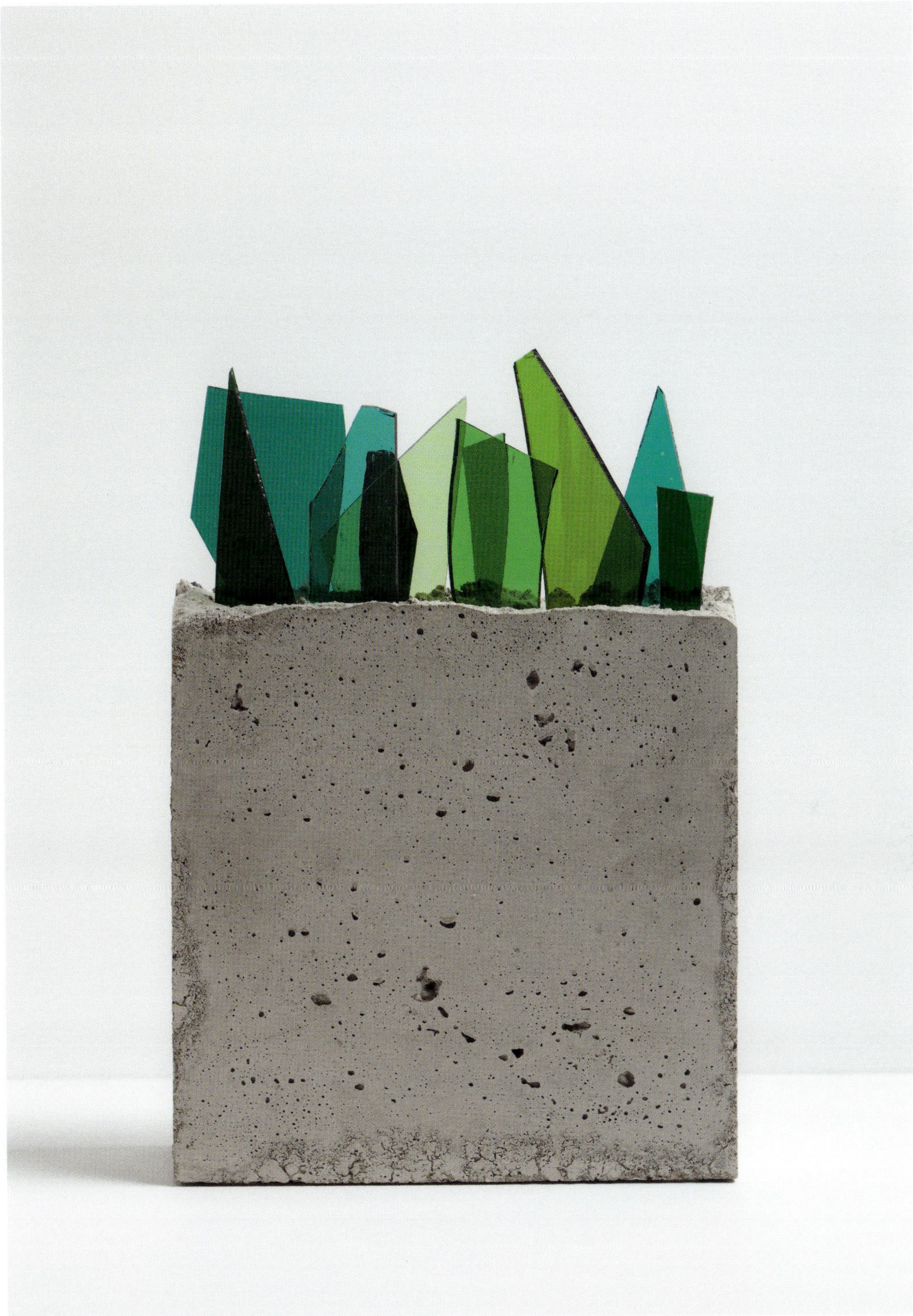

Concreto 2.0h/03, 2013
Glass, concrete
29.5 x 21.5 x 6.5 cm

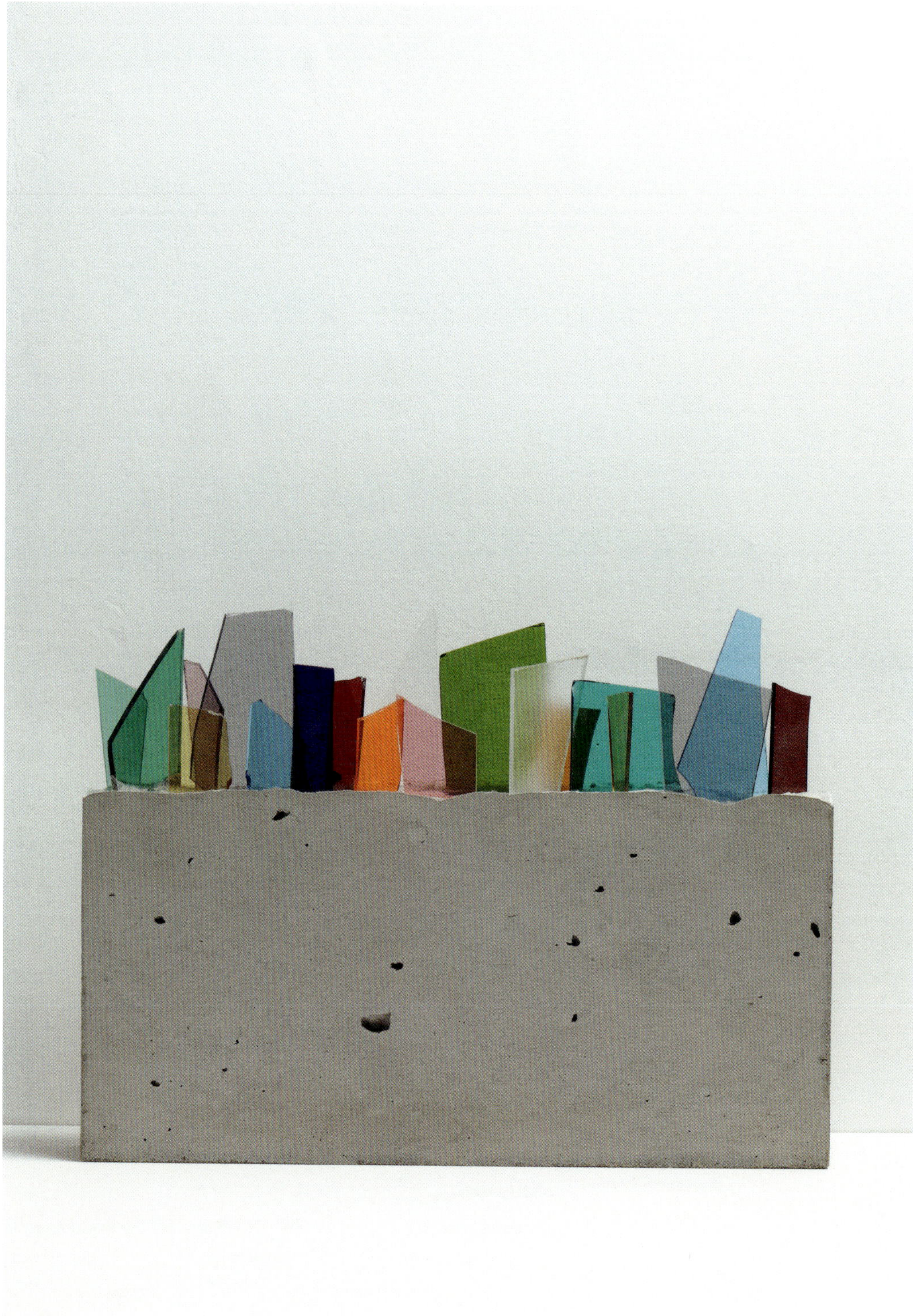

Concreto 4.0/04, 2015
Glass, concrete
32 x 42 x 6.5 cm

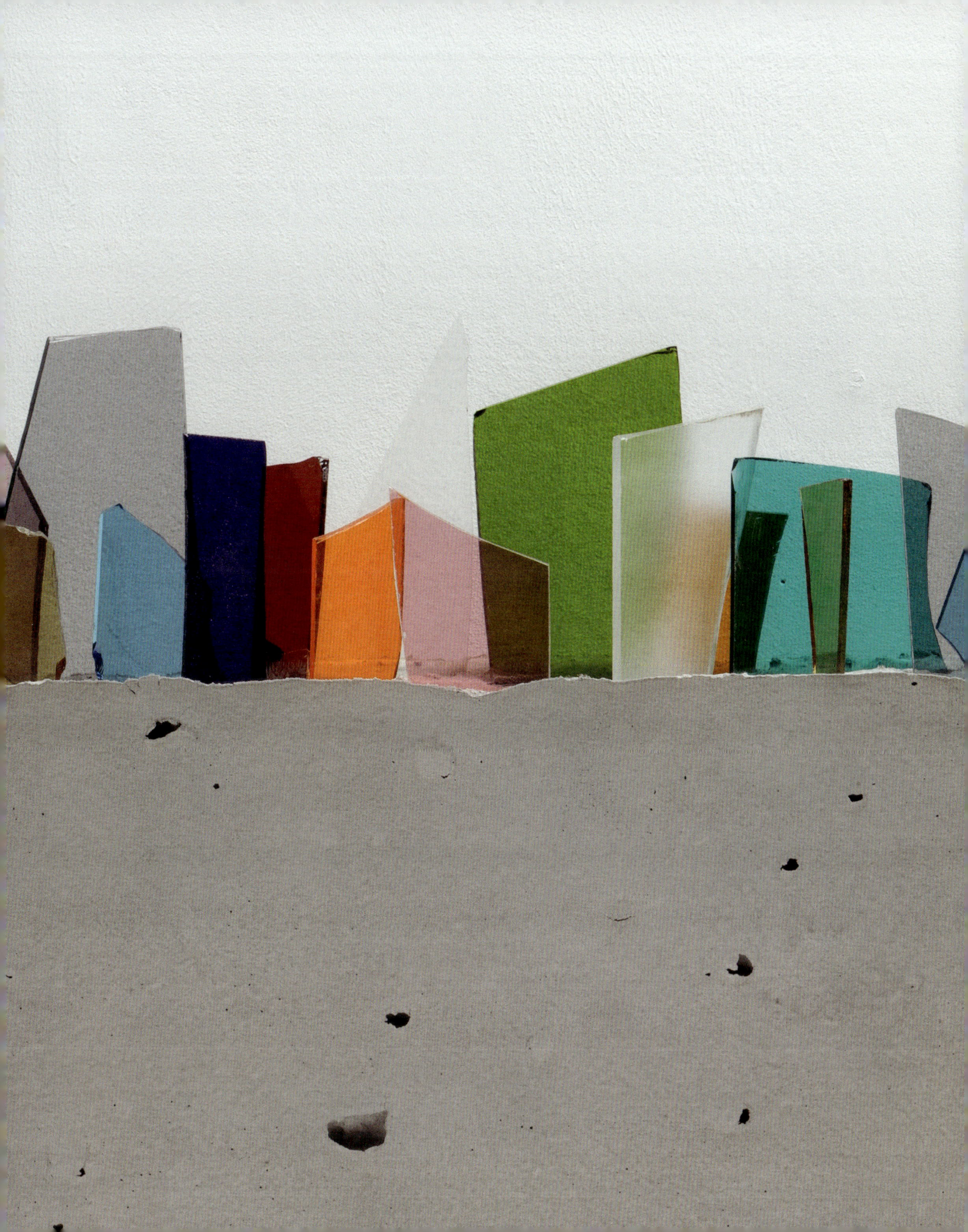

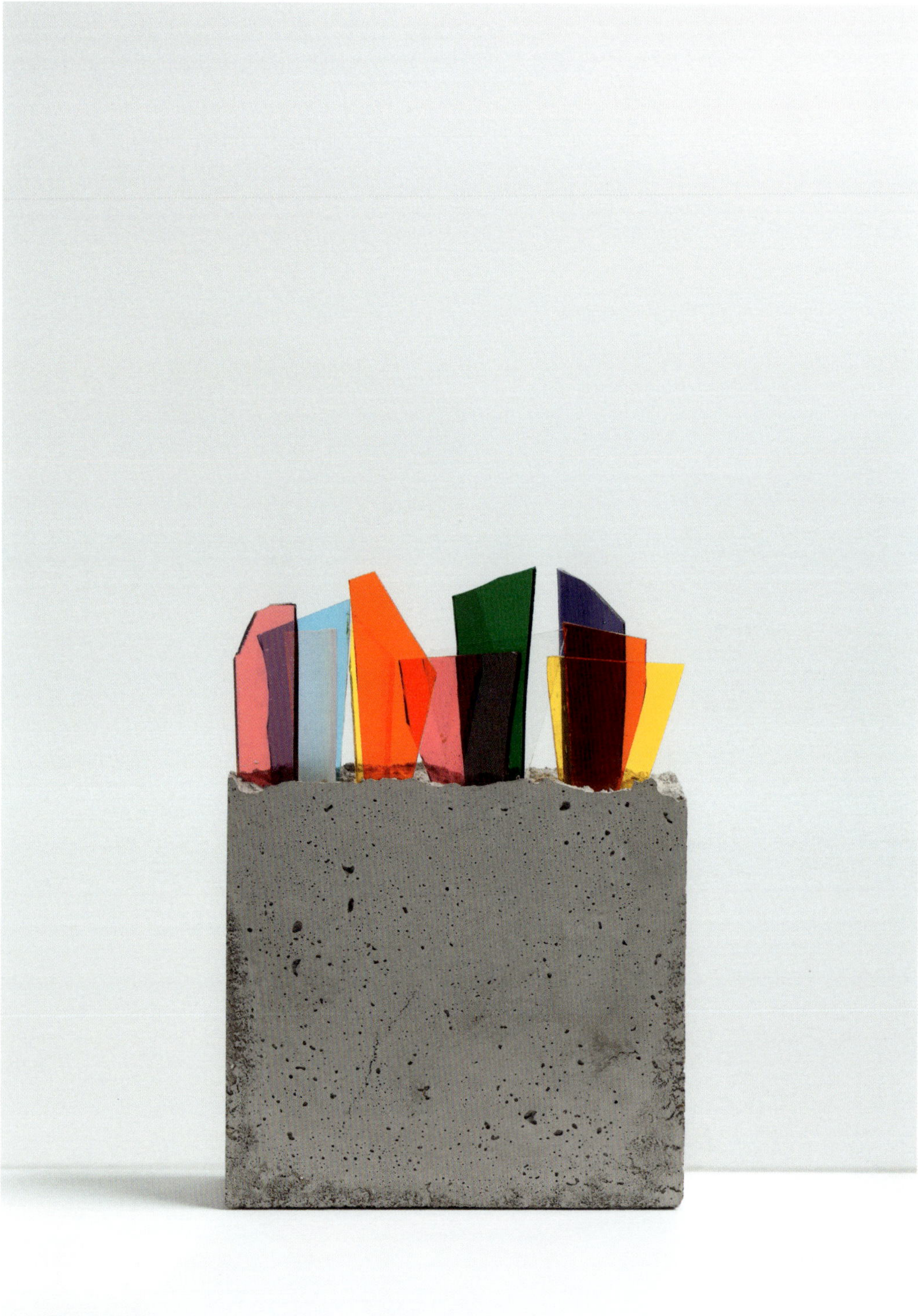

Concreto 2.0h/06, 2014
Glass, concrete
29.5 x 20 x 6.5 cm

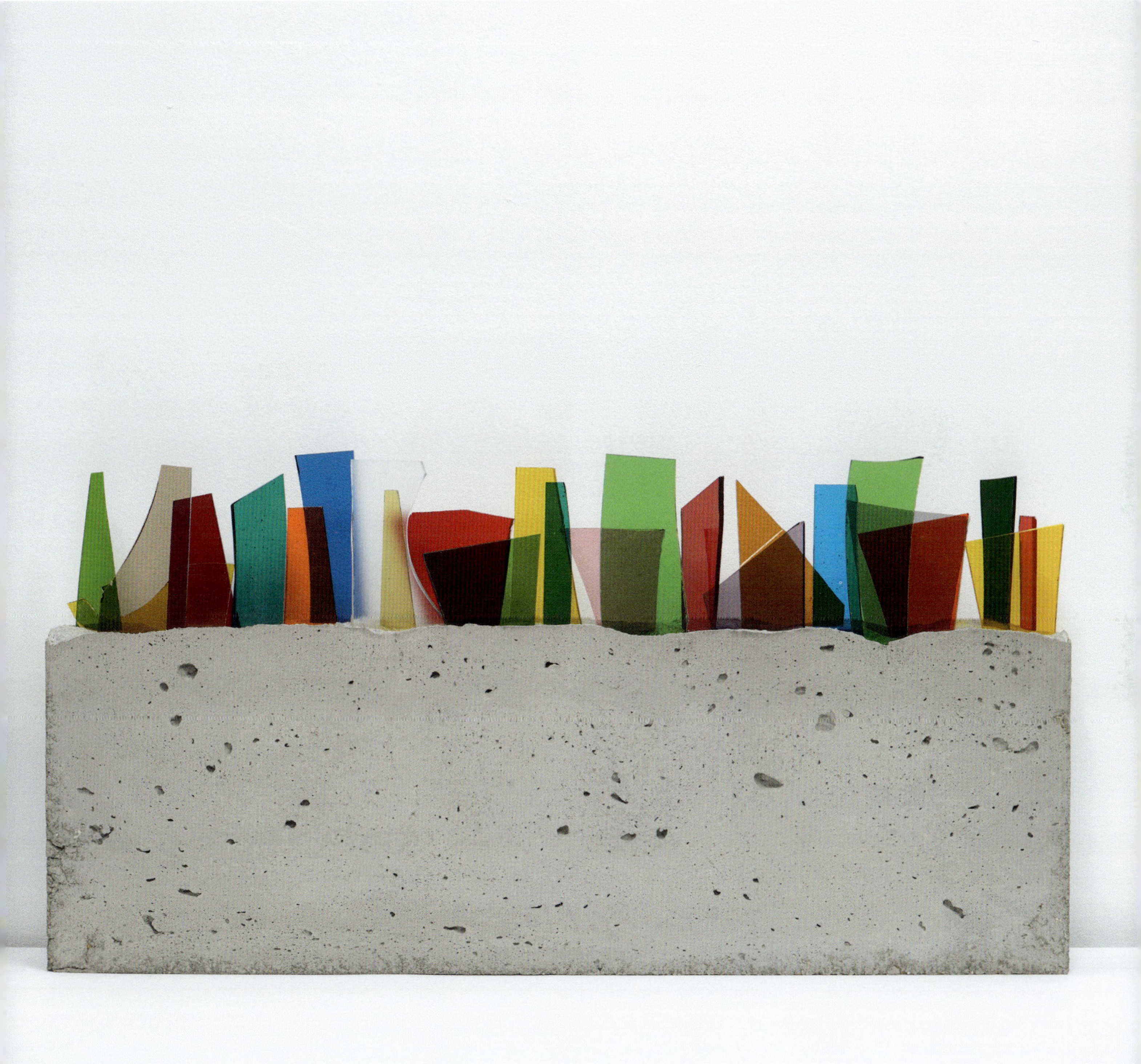

Concreto 6.0/01, 2019
Glass, concrete
30.5 x 60 x 6 cm

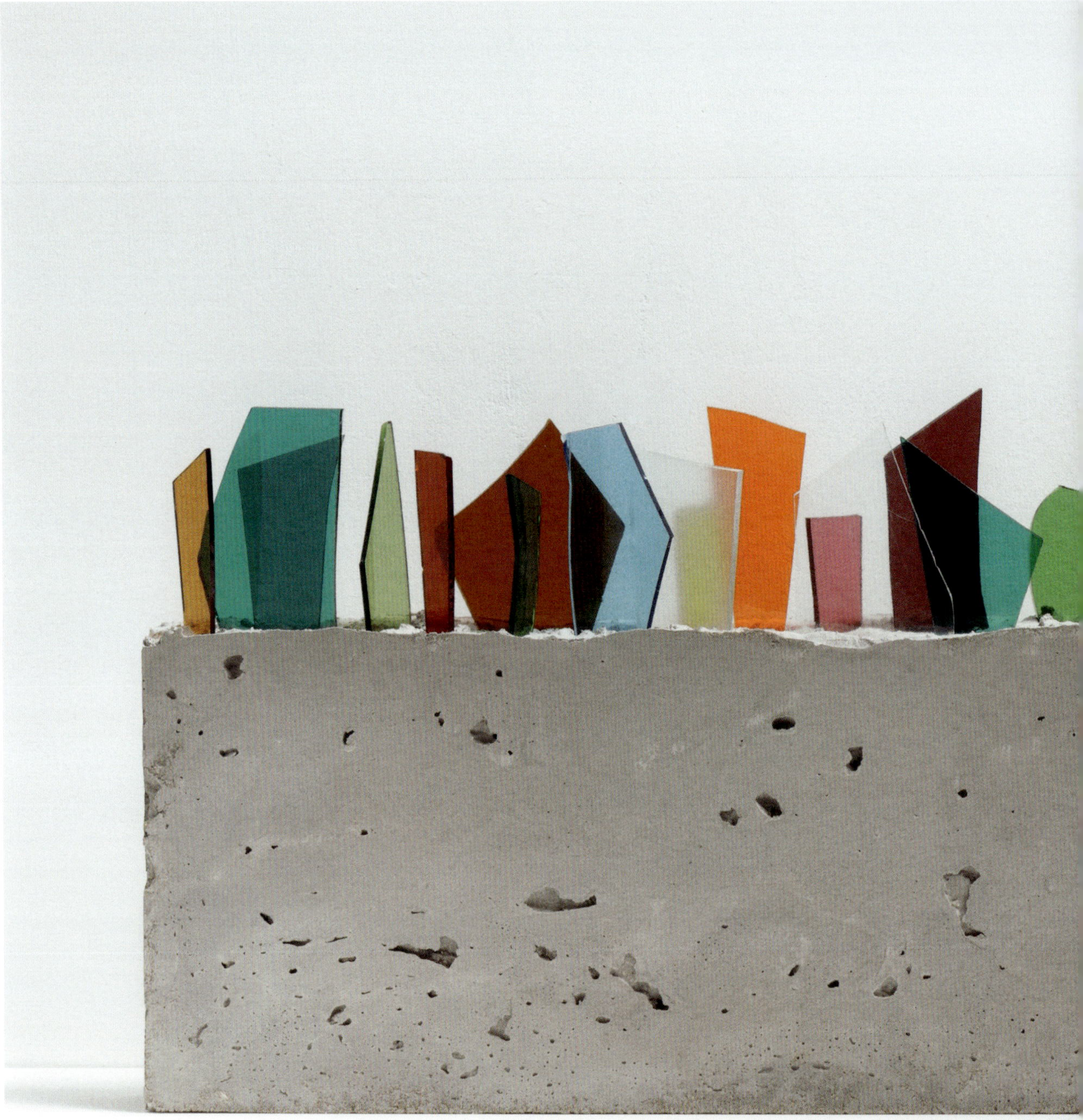

Concreto 8.0/01, 2017
Glass, concrete
30 x 79.5 x 6 cm

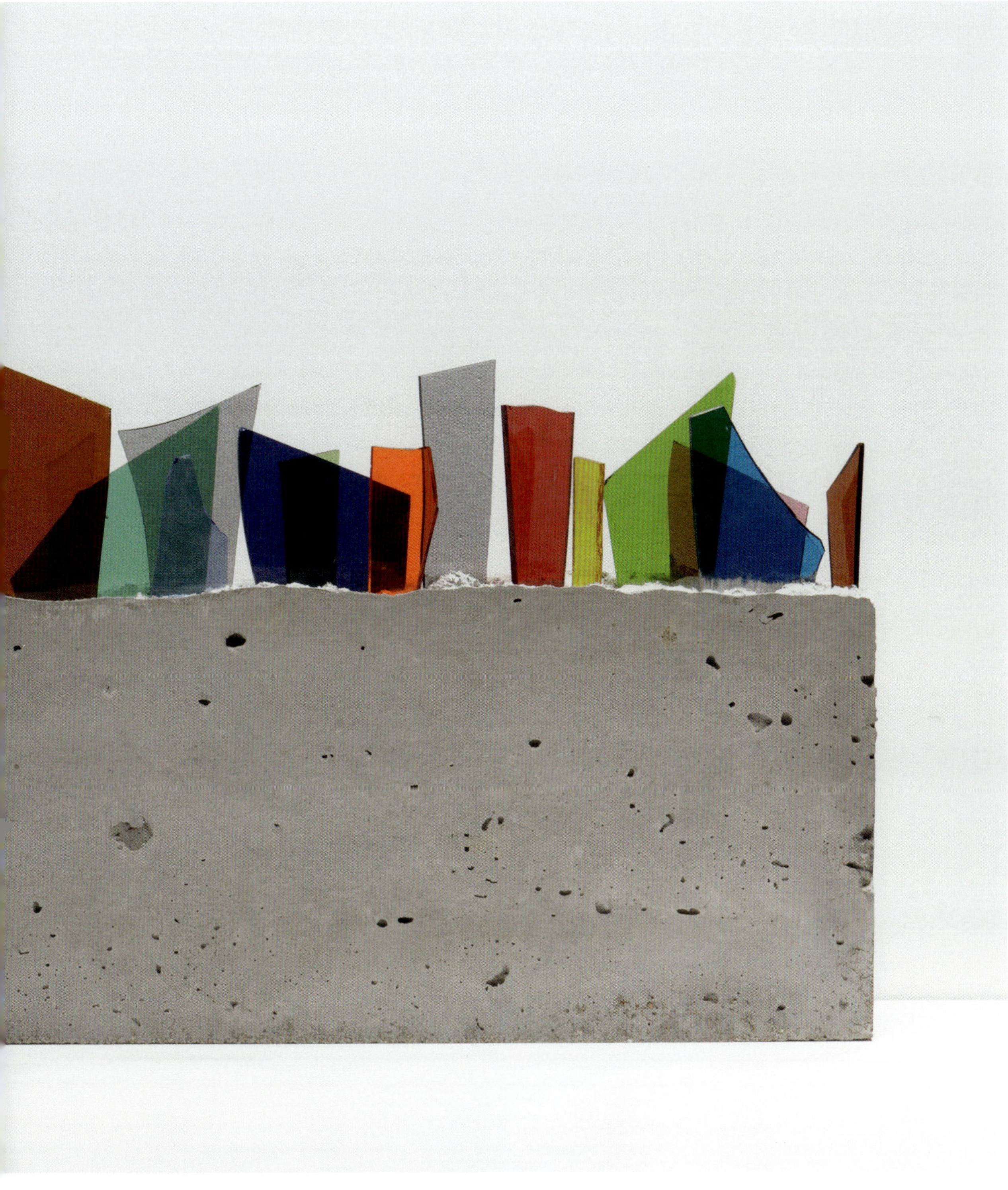

Cons
Neo-Cons
Alt-Cons
Geo-Cons
Neo-Neo-Cons
I-Cons
Ex-Cons

2016 –

The first *Neo-Concretos* were made with offcuts of coloured acrylic I found when I was moving studio in 2016. The individual units are placed in clusters of up to 100, to produce layers of overlapping transparent colours and perforated shapes.

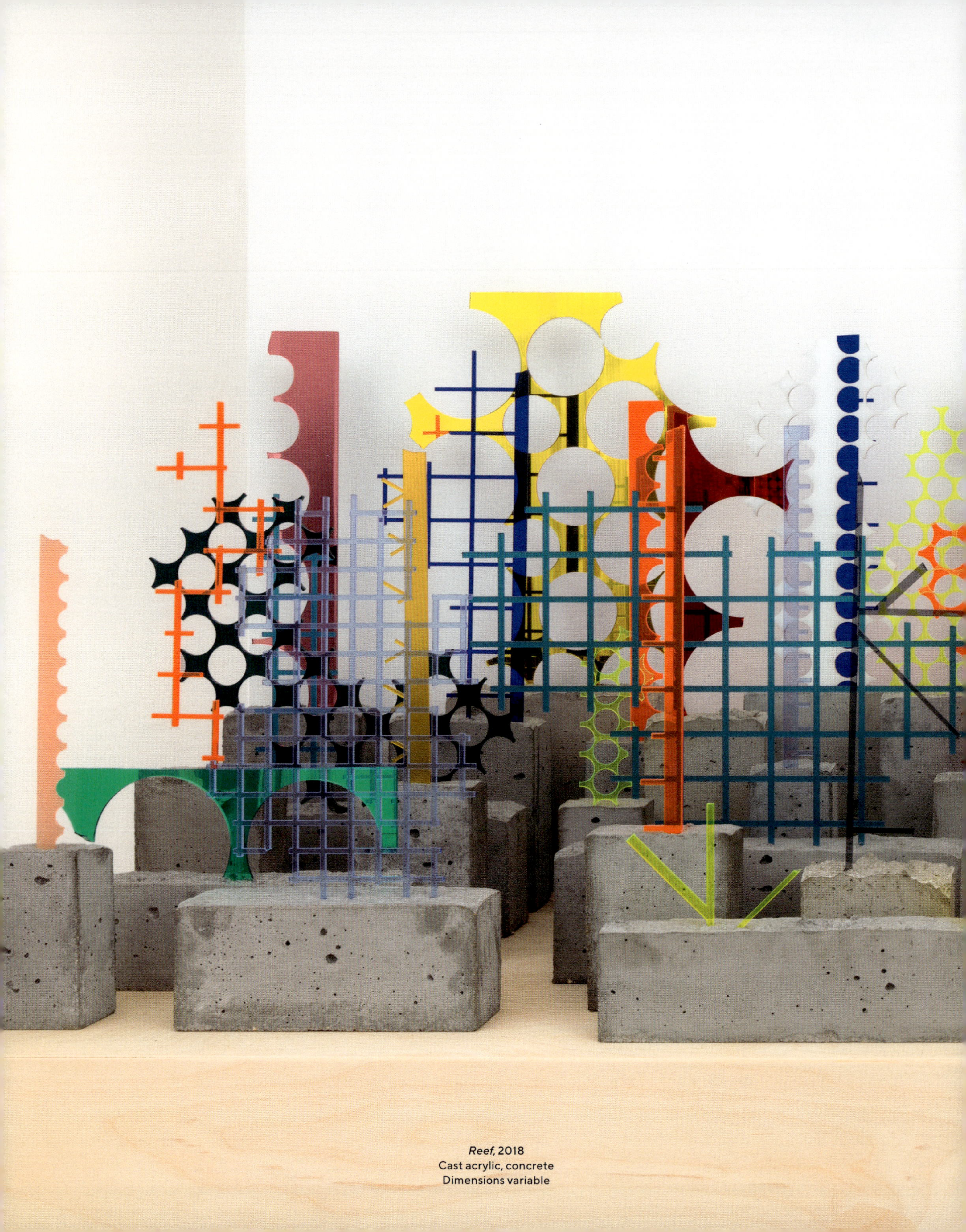

Reef, 2018
Cast acrylic, concrete
Dimensions variable

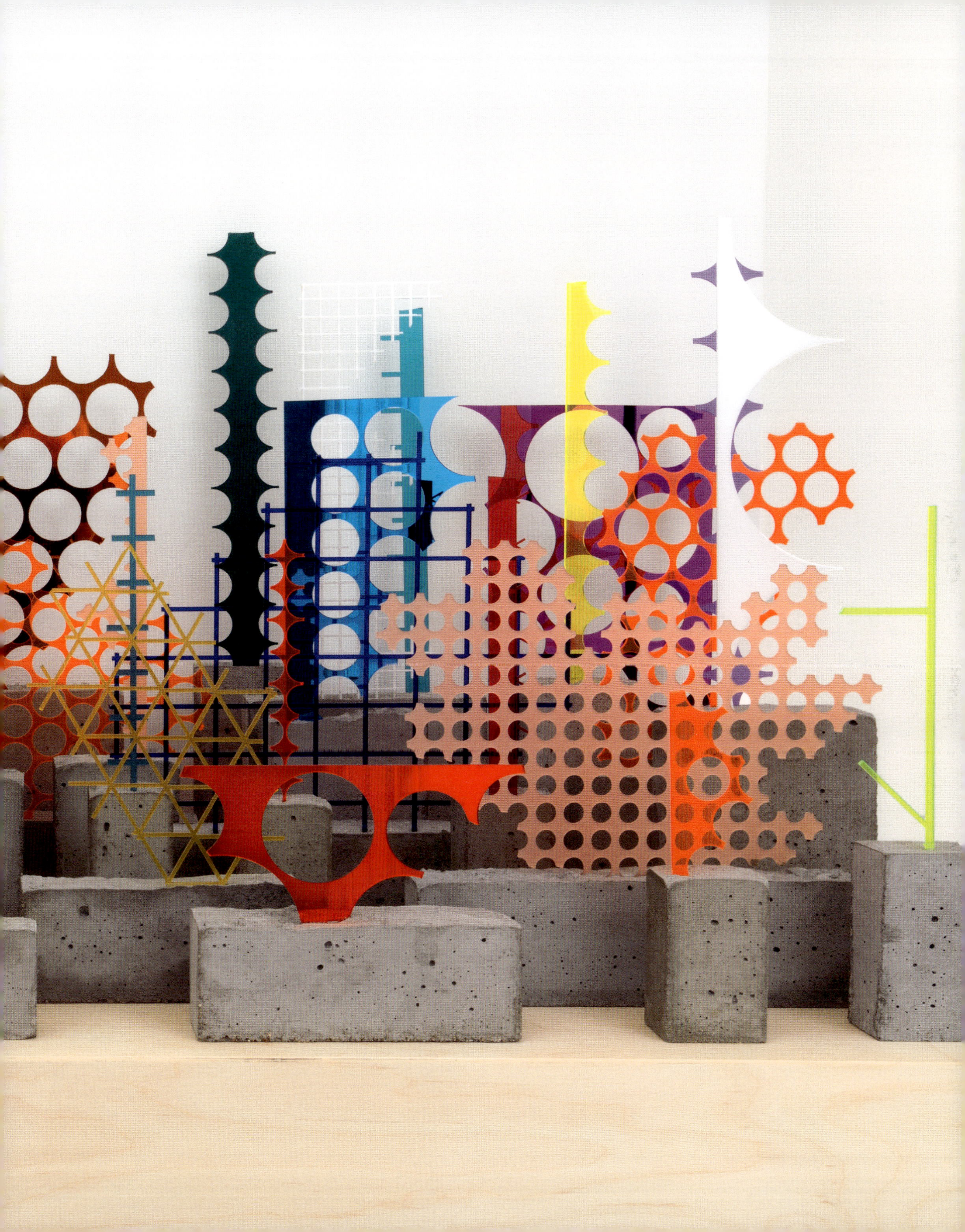

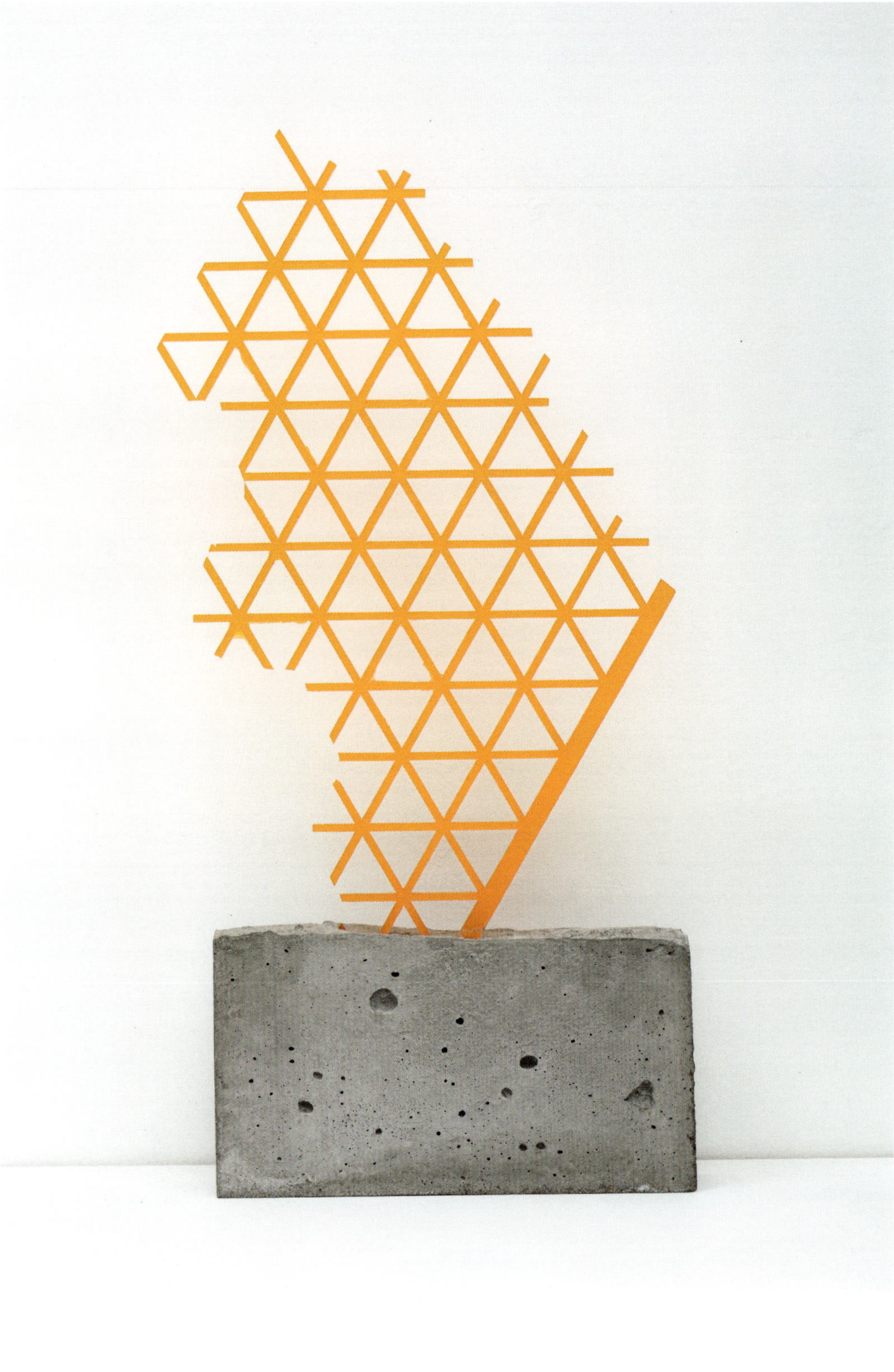

Neo-Concreto 132, 2017
Cast acrylic, concrete
52.5 x 25 x 6 cm

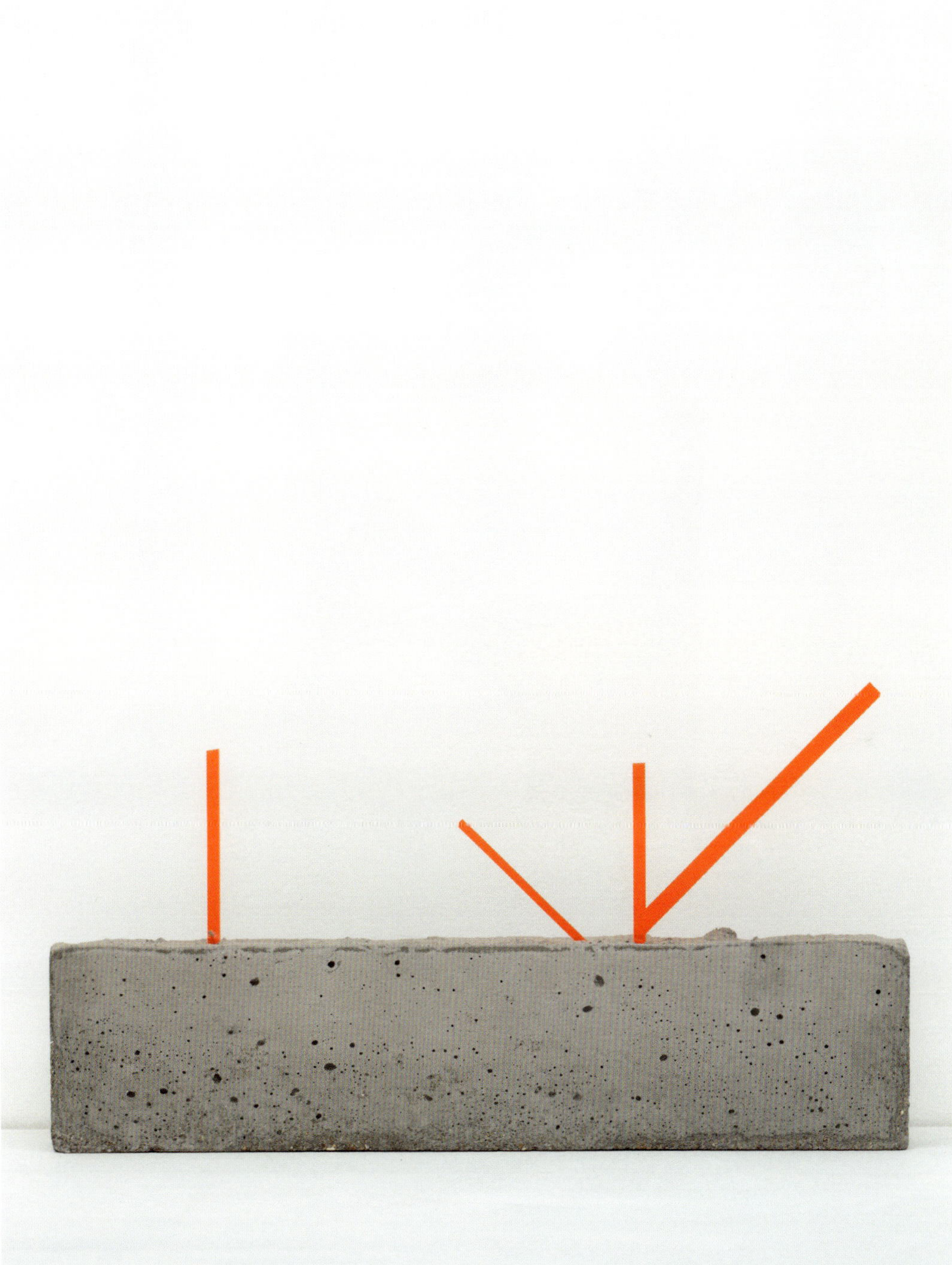

Neo-Concreto 22, 2016
Cast acrylic, concrete
15 x 32 x 5 cm

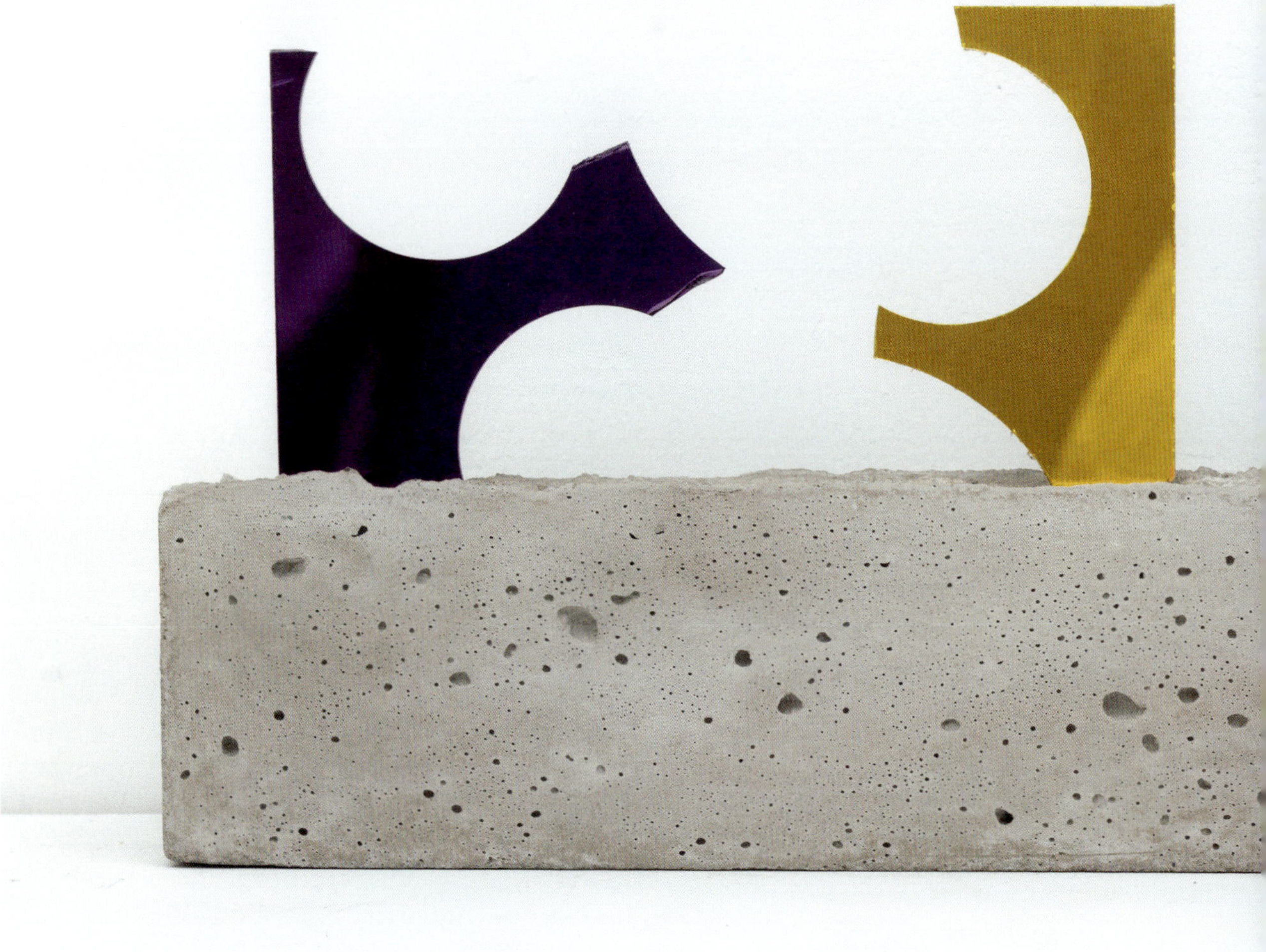

Neo-Concreto 10, 2016
Cast acrylic, concrete
17.5 x 45.8 x 6 cm

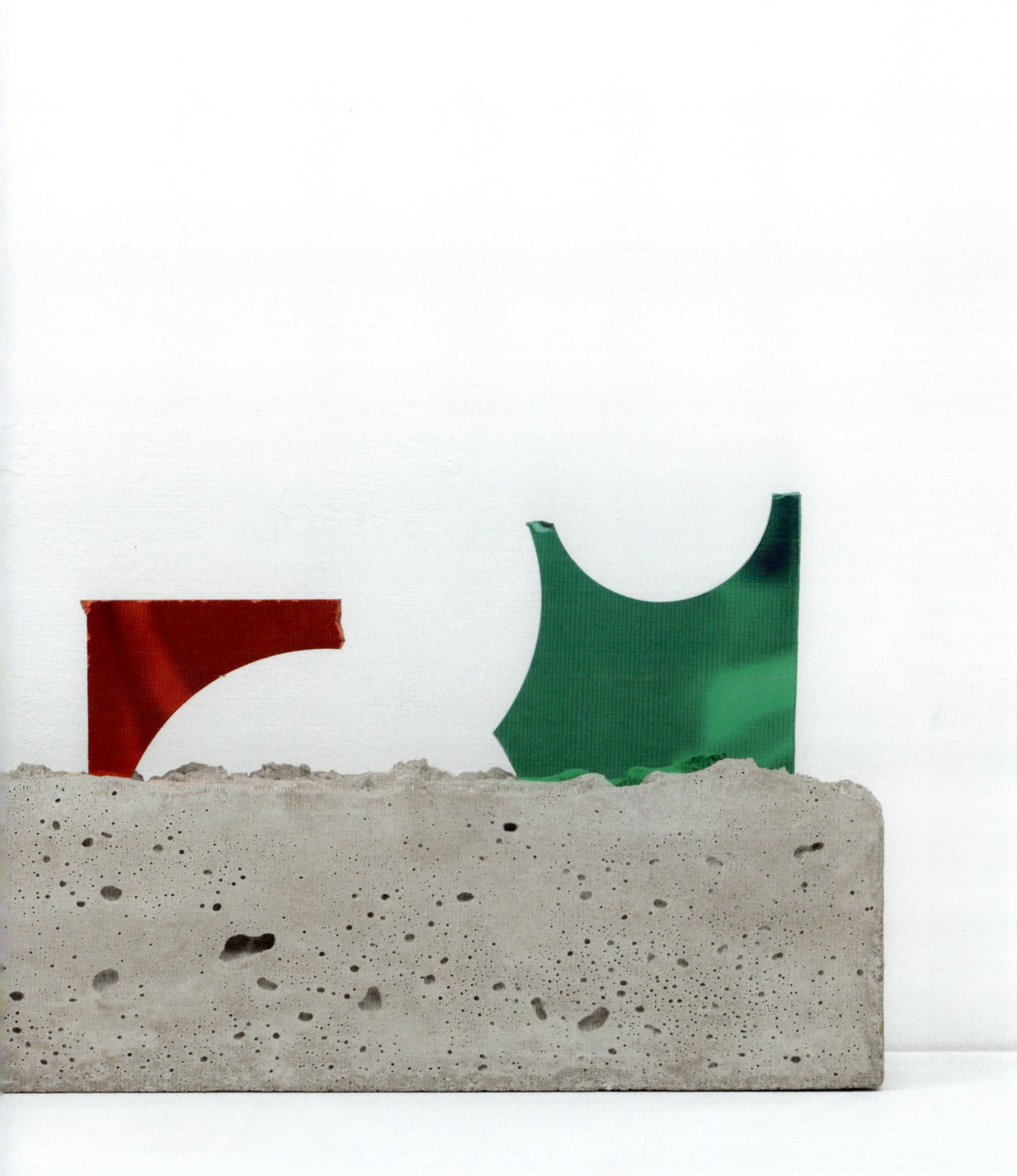

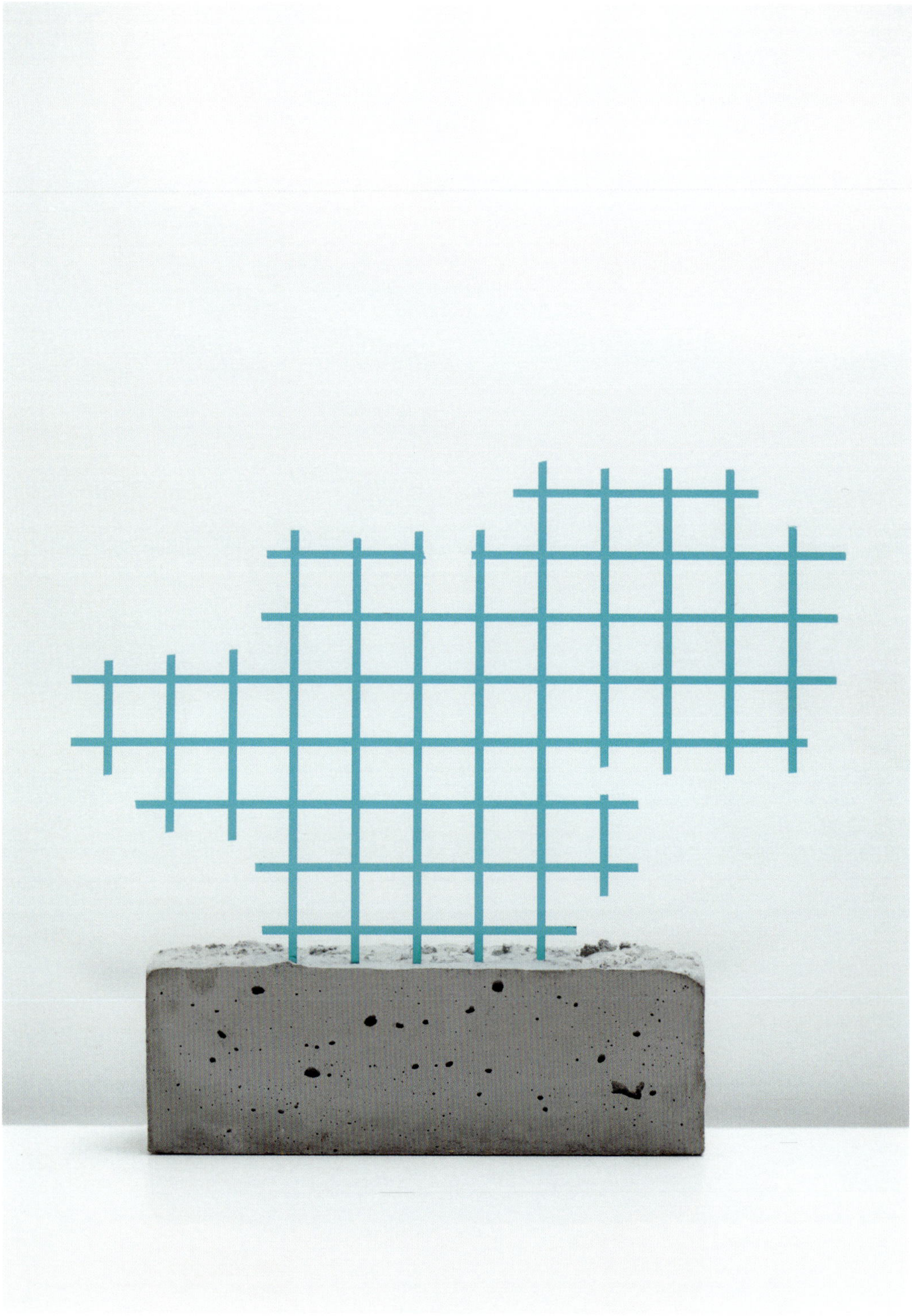

Neo-Concreto 42, 2016
Cast acrylic, concrete
35 x 38 x 6 cm

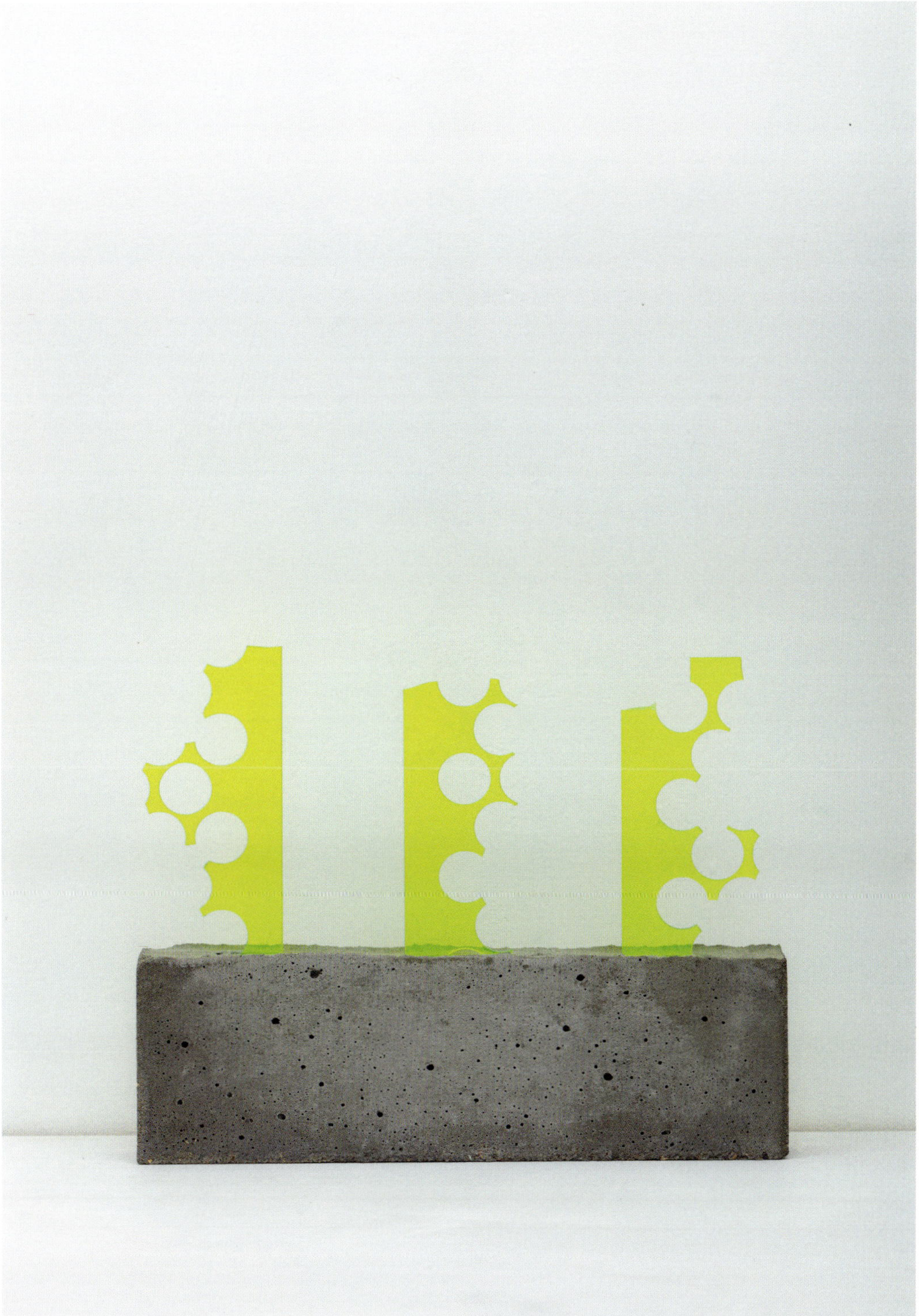

Neo-Concreto 102, 2016
Cast acrylic, concrete
21 x 26 x 5 cm

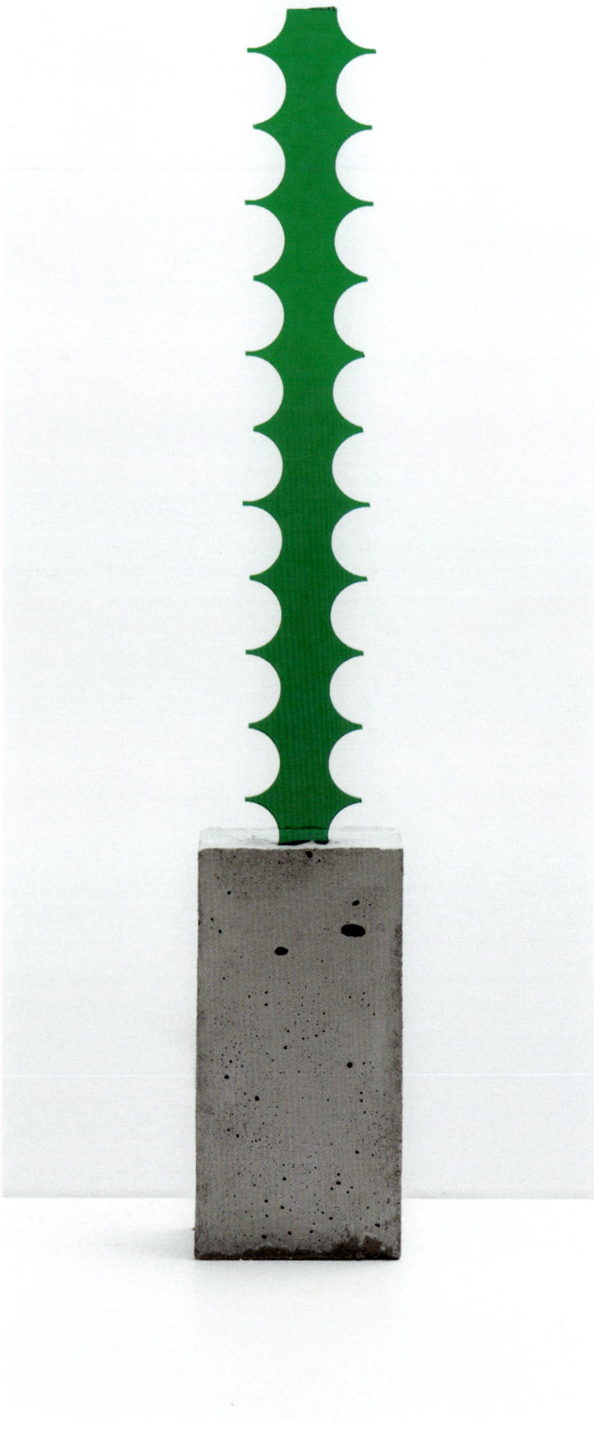

Neo-Concreto 99, 2016
Cast acrylic, concrete
63 x 10.2 x 6.5 cm

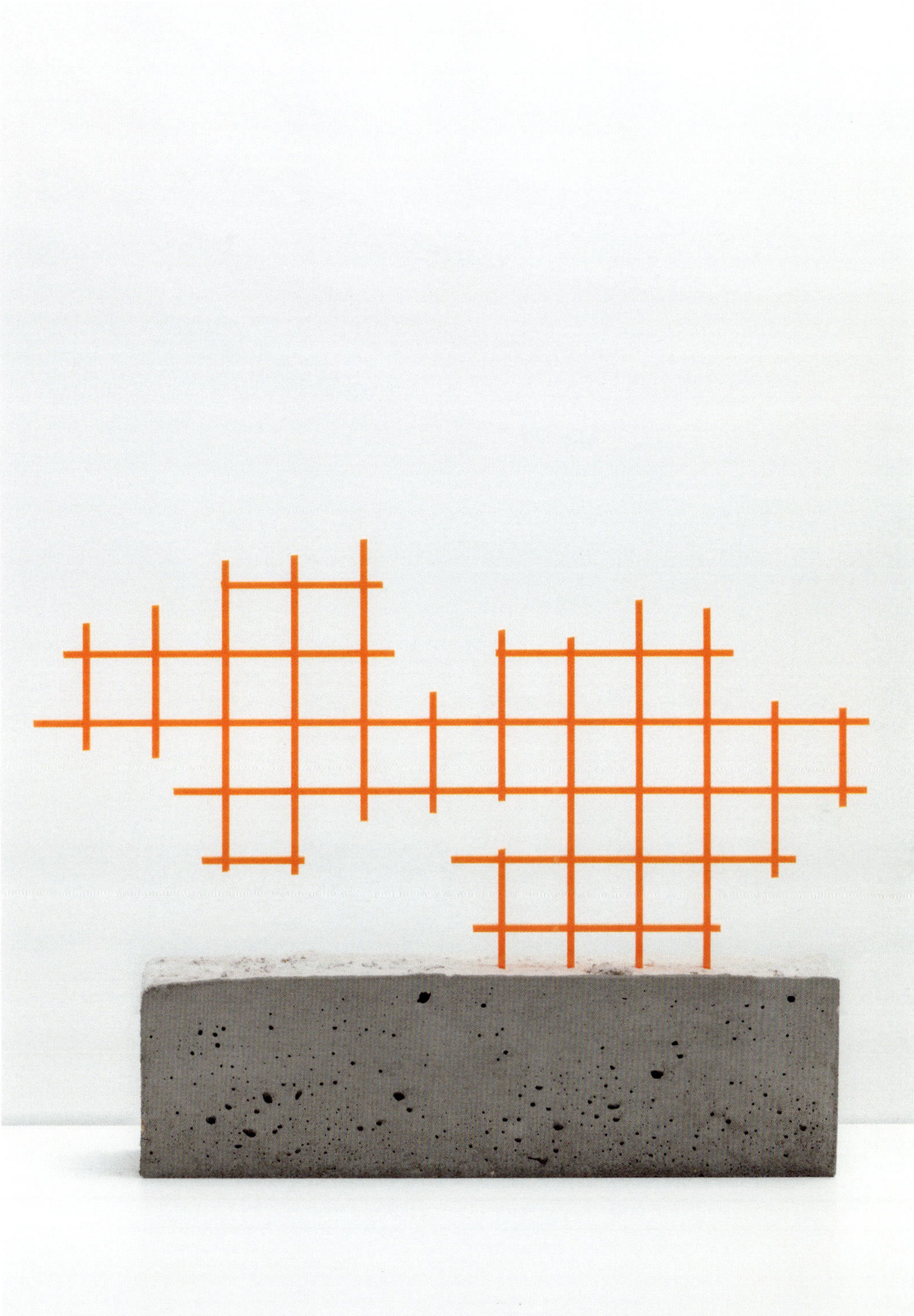

Neo-Concreto 90, 2016
Cast acrylic, concrete
31 x 41.5 x 5.5 cm

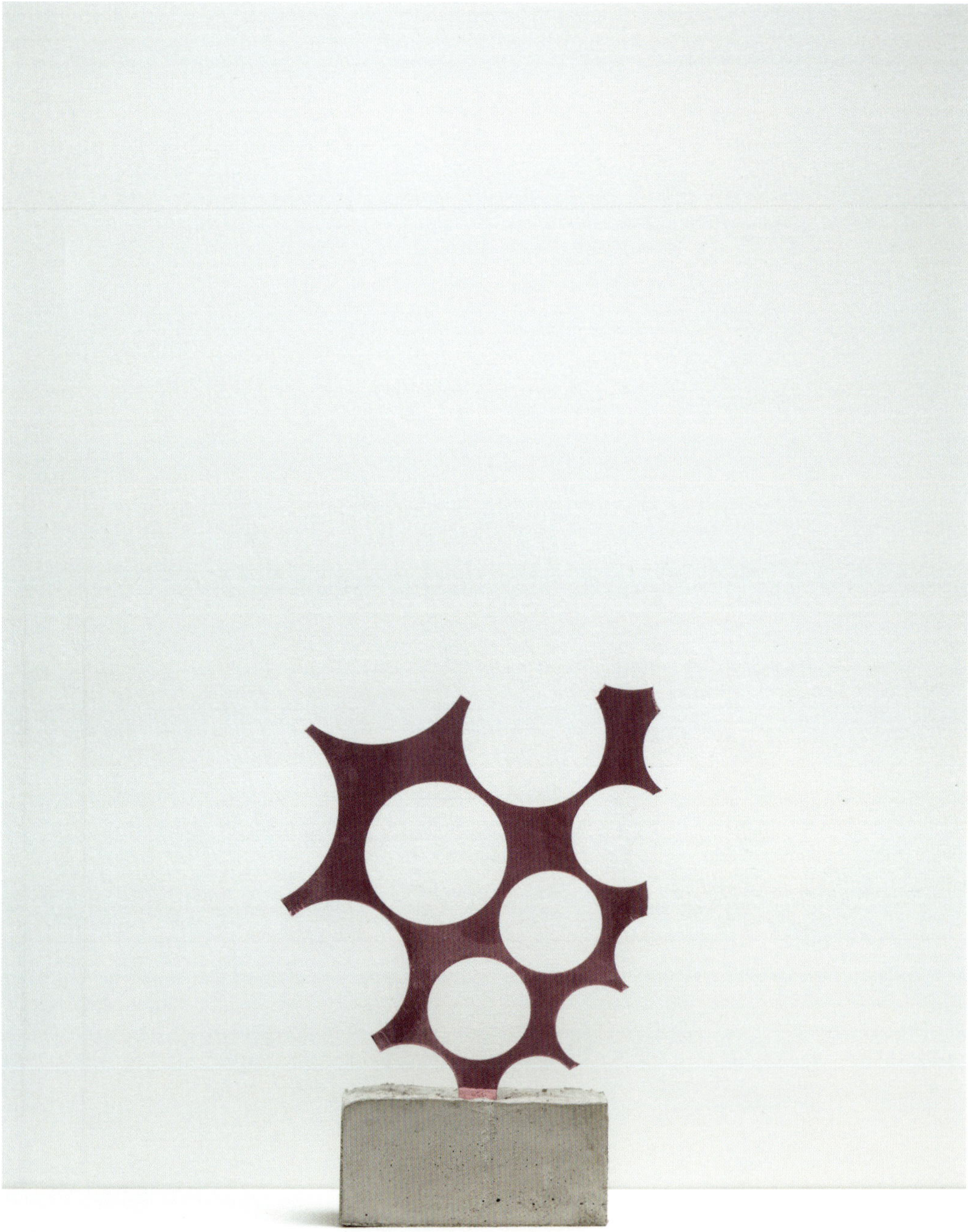

Neo-Concreto 131, 2017
Cast acrylic, concrete
26.5 x 18.5 x 5 cm

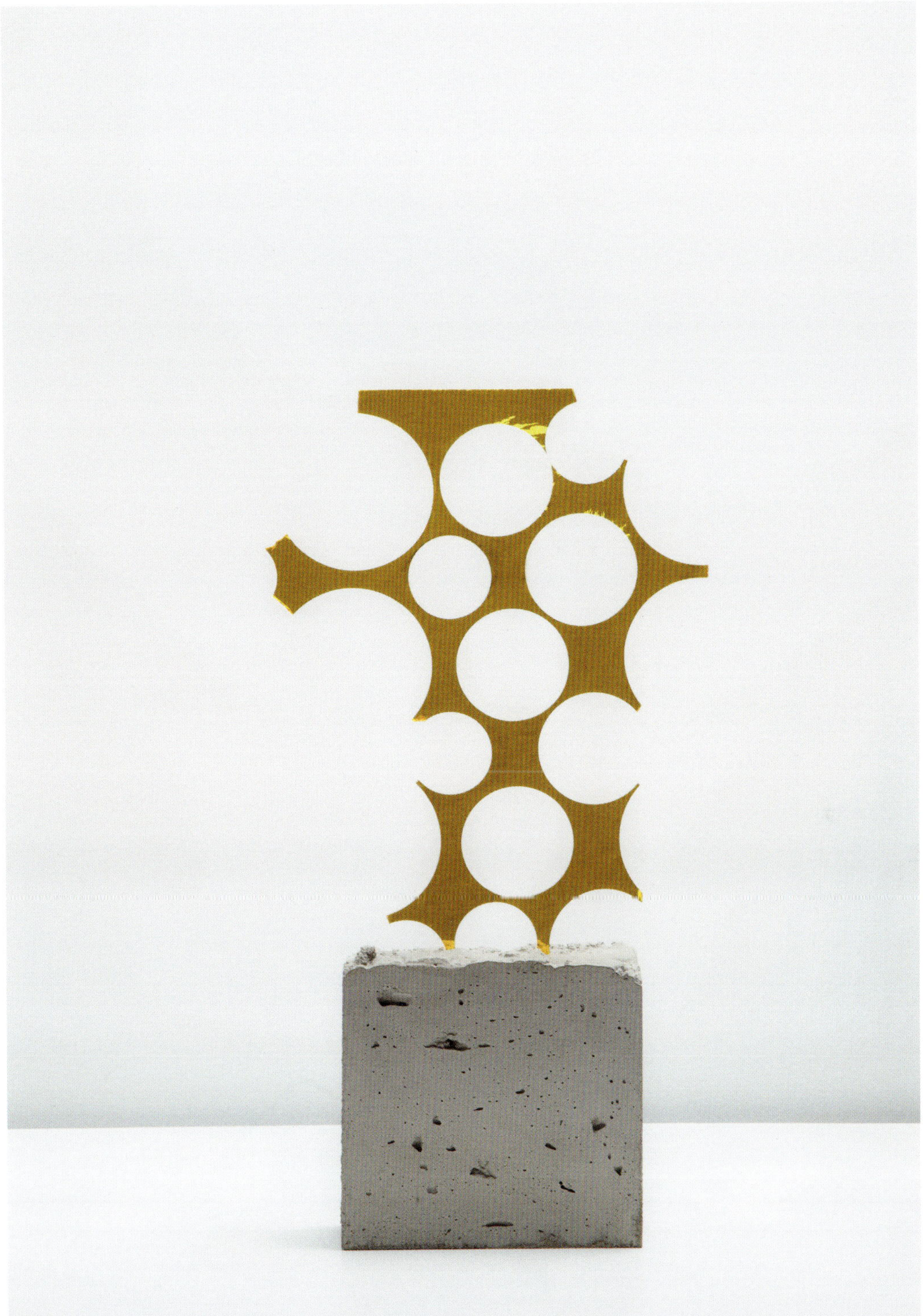

Neo-Concreto 01, 2016
Cast acrylic, concrete
57.5 x 20 x 7 cm

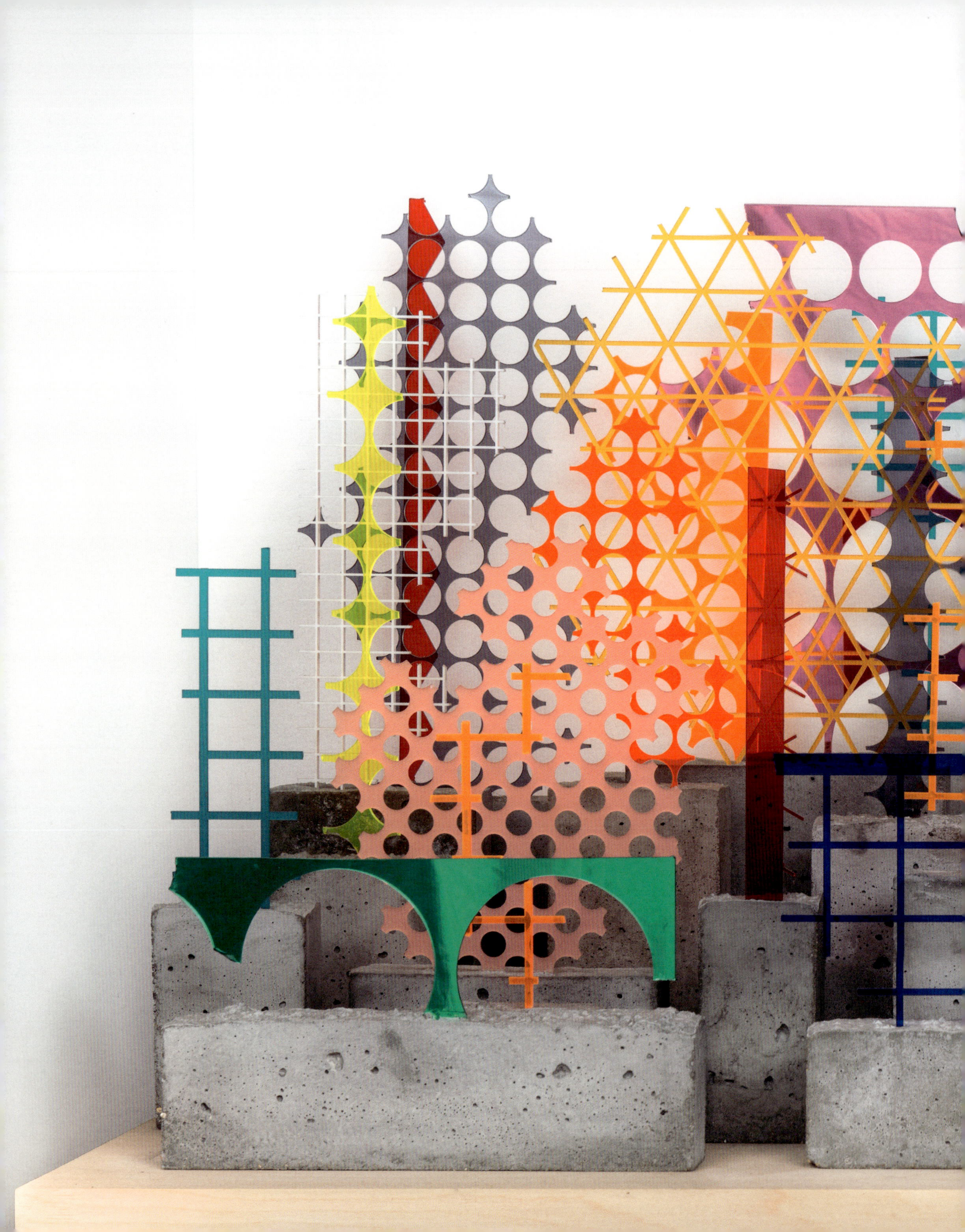

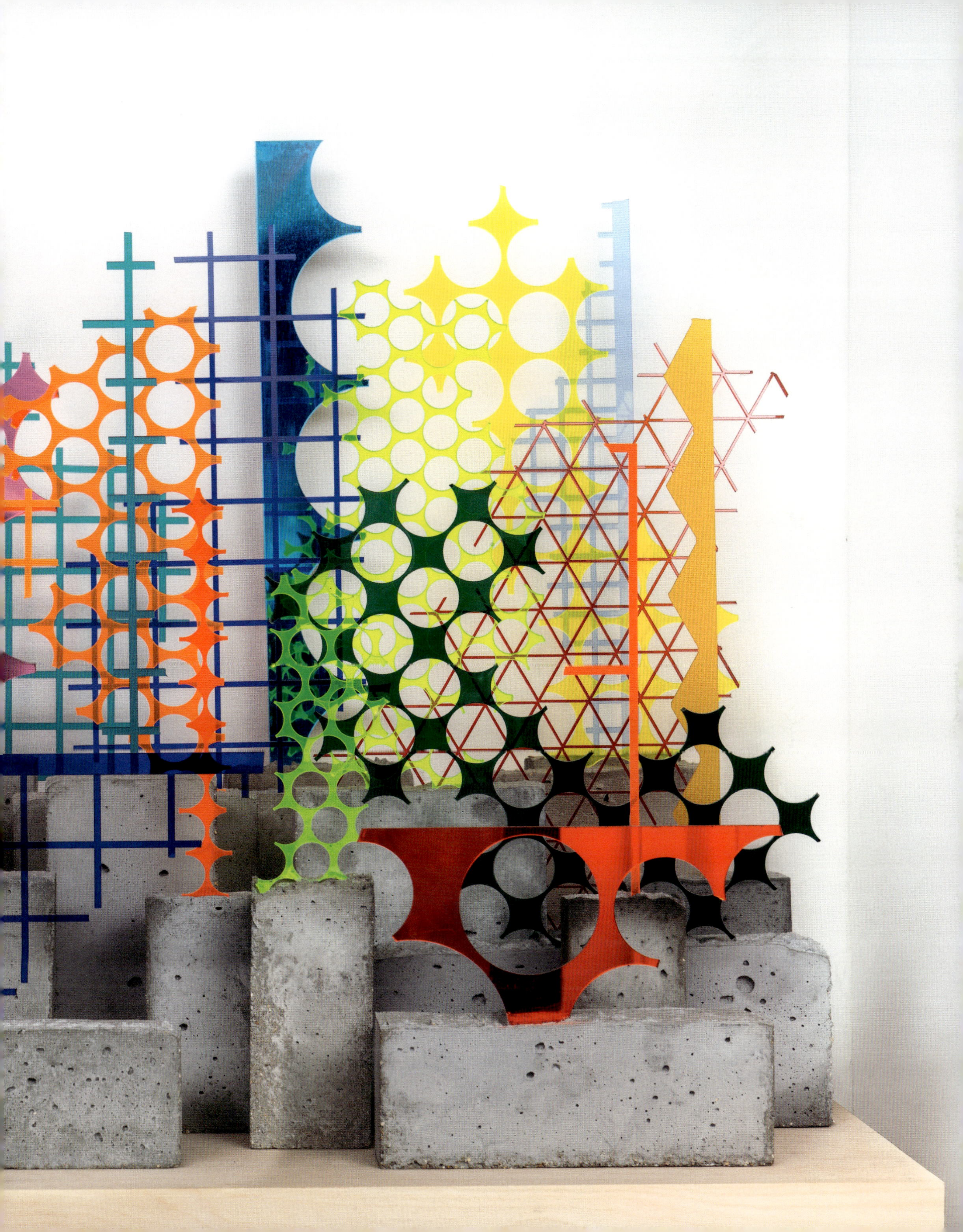

Previous pages:
Reef 02, 2018
Cast acrylic, concrete
Dimensions variable

Cons
Neo-Cons
Alt-Cons
Geo-Cons
Neo-Neo-Cons
I-Cons
Ex-Cons

2017 –

The upper section of an *Alt-Concreto* is often an object found in the street or in the corner of the studio. To date they have included rusty steel mesh, folding wooden rulers, set squares, French curves, a collection of beaded necklaces, a plastic fan and a painted wooden skeleton.

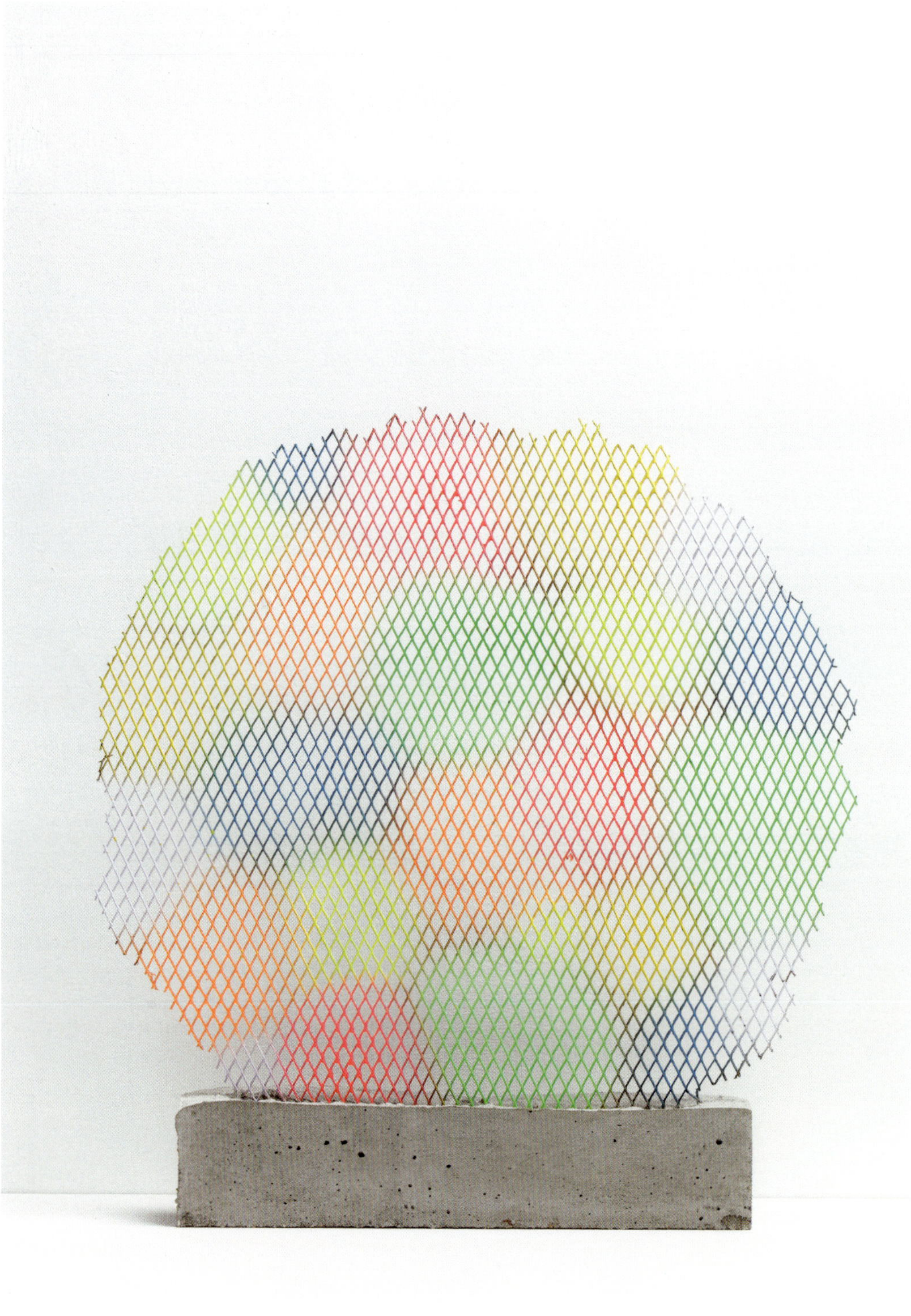

Alt-Concreto 03, 2017
Steel mesh, spray paint, concrete
43 x 39 x 5 cm

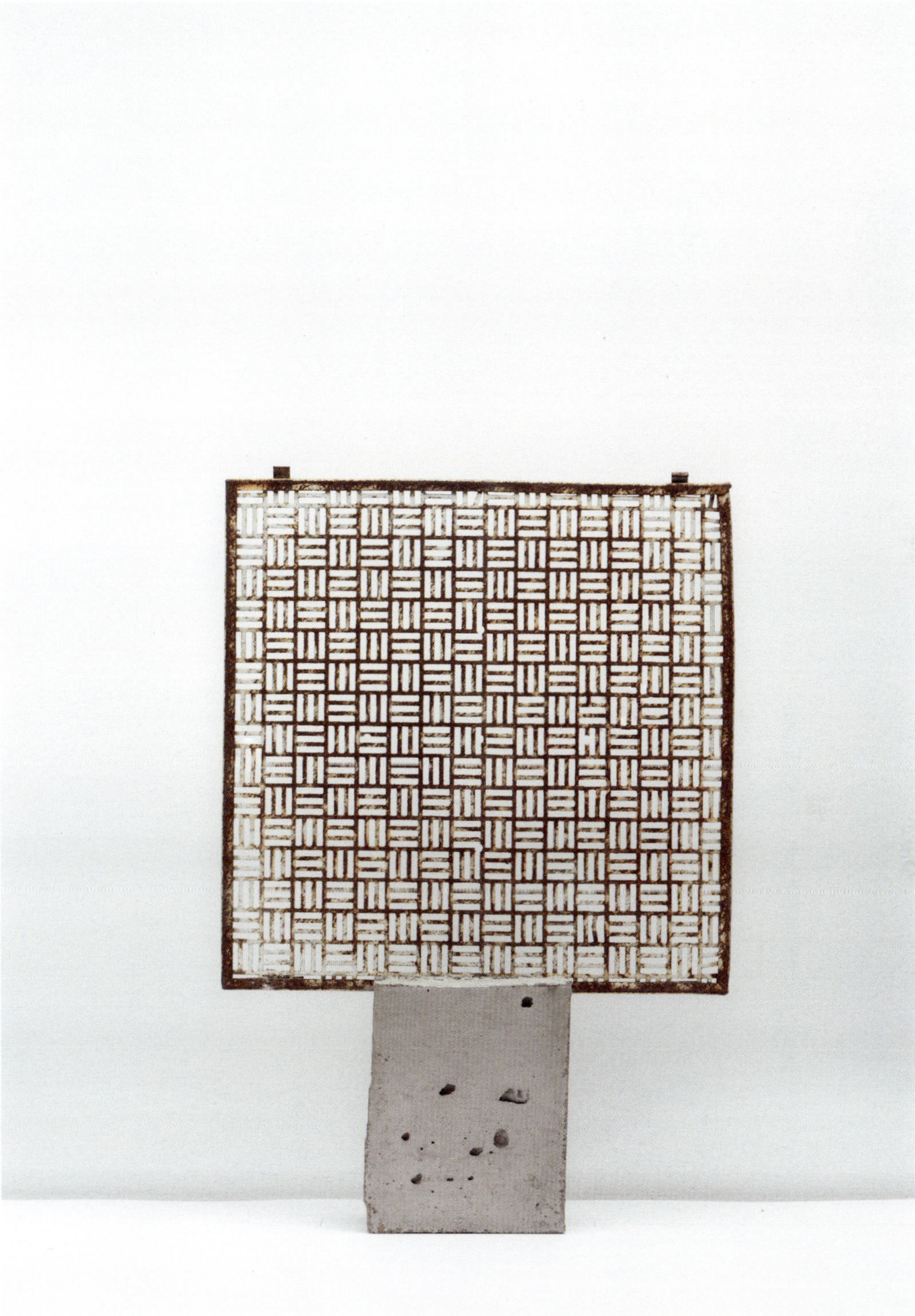

Alt-Concreto 05, 2018
Steel mesh, concrete
42 x 28.5 x 5 cm

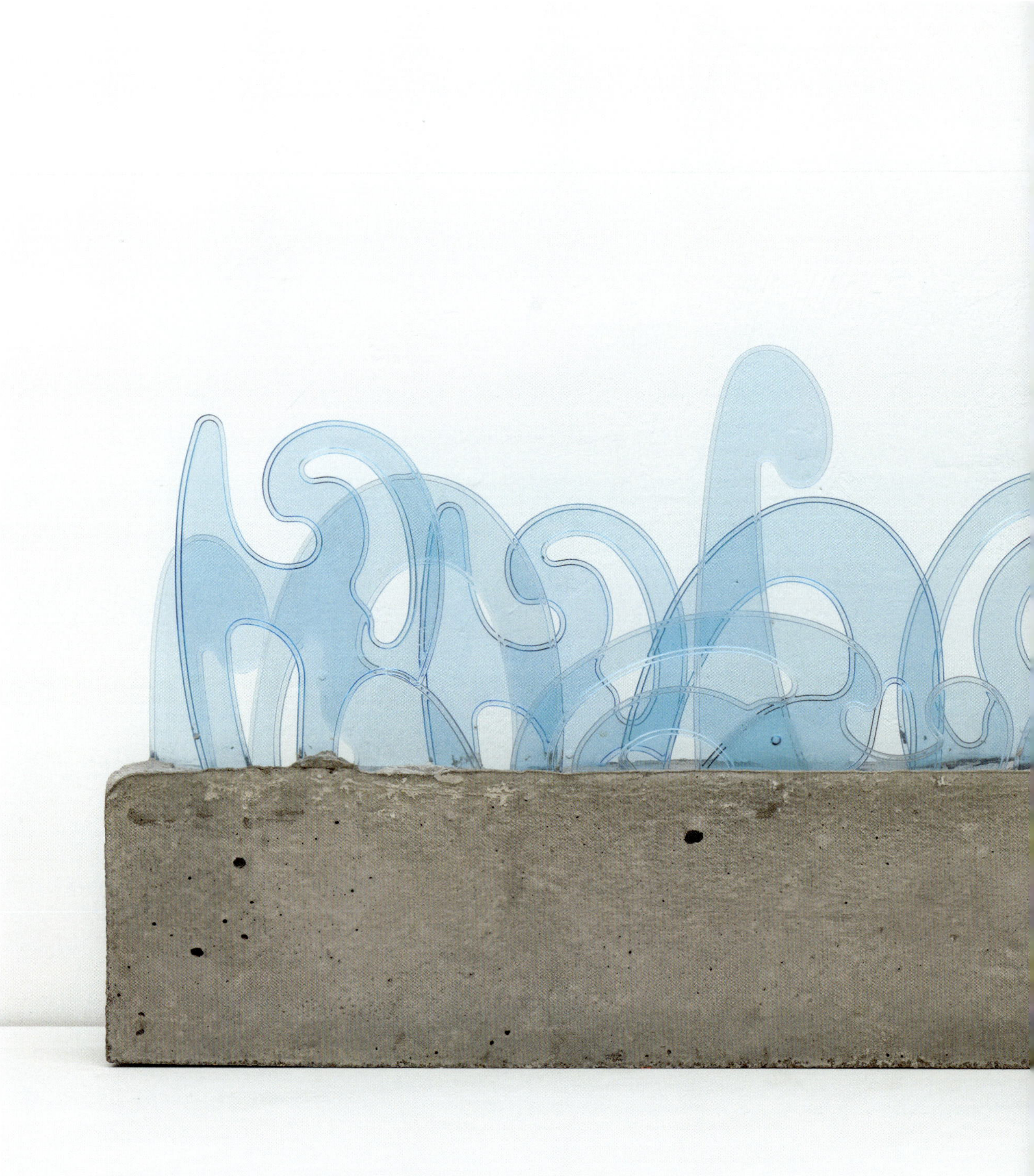

Alt-Concreto 10, 2018
Plastic French curves, concrete
20 x 51.5 x 6 cm

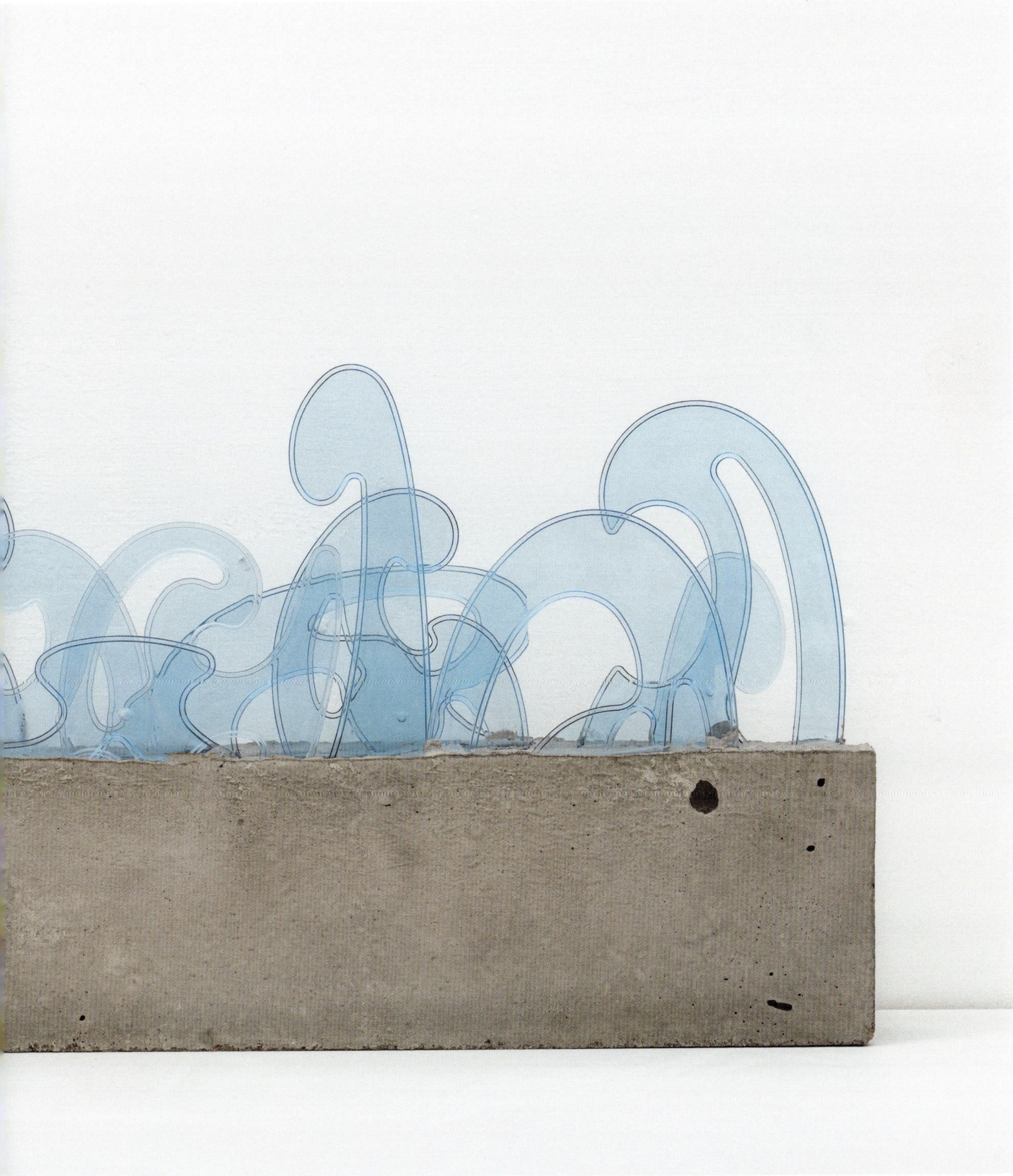

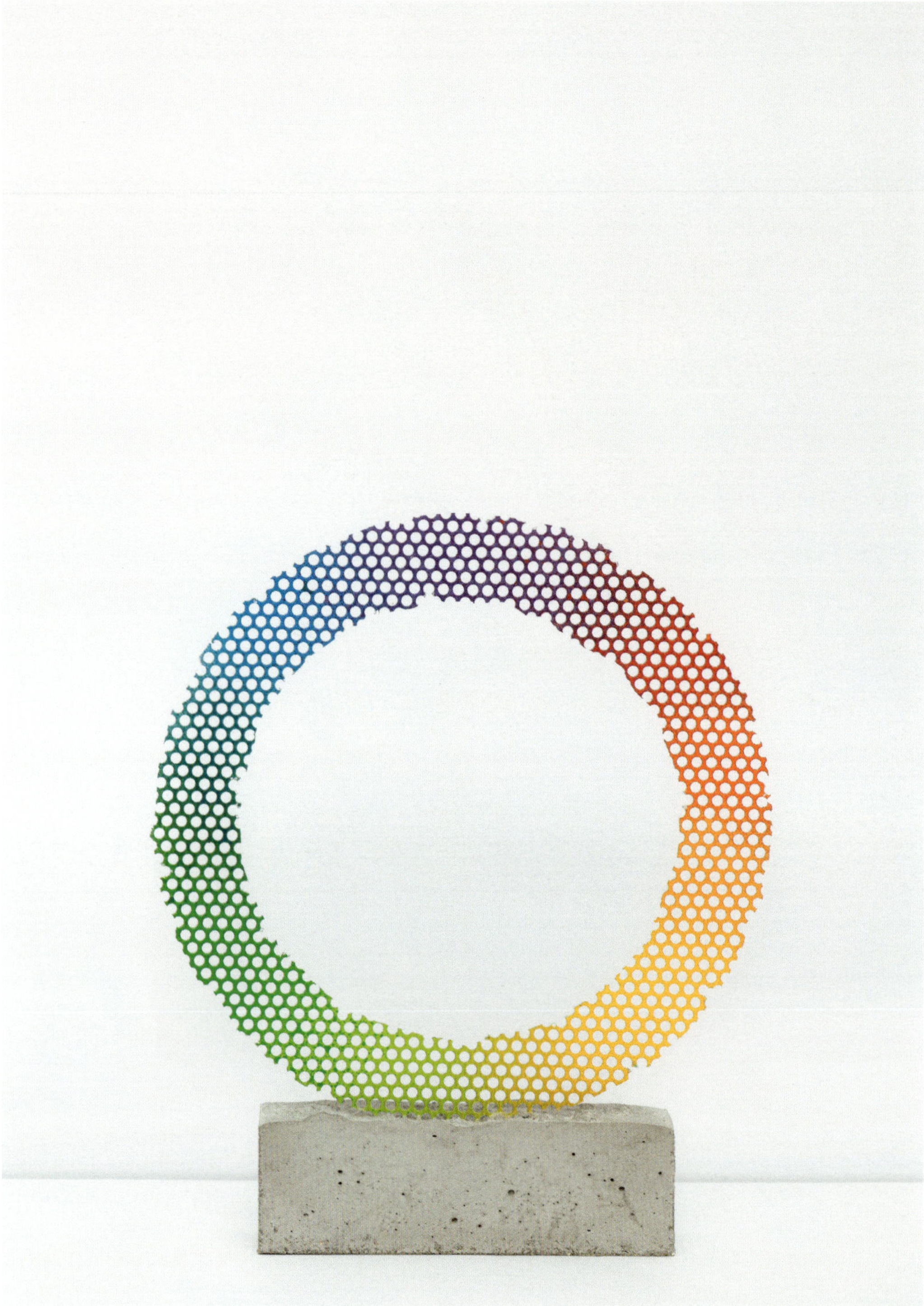

Alt-Concreto 13, 2017
Aluminium mesh, spray paint, concrete
38 x 27.5 x 5 cm

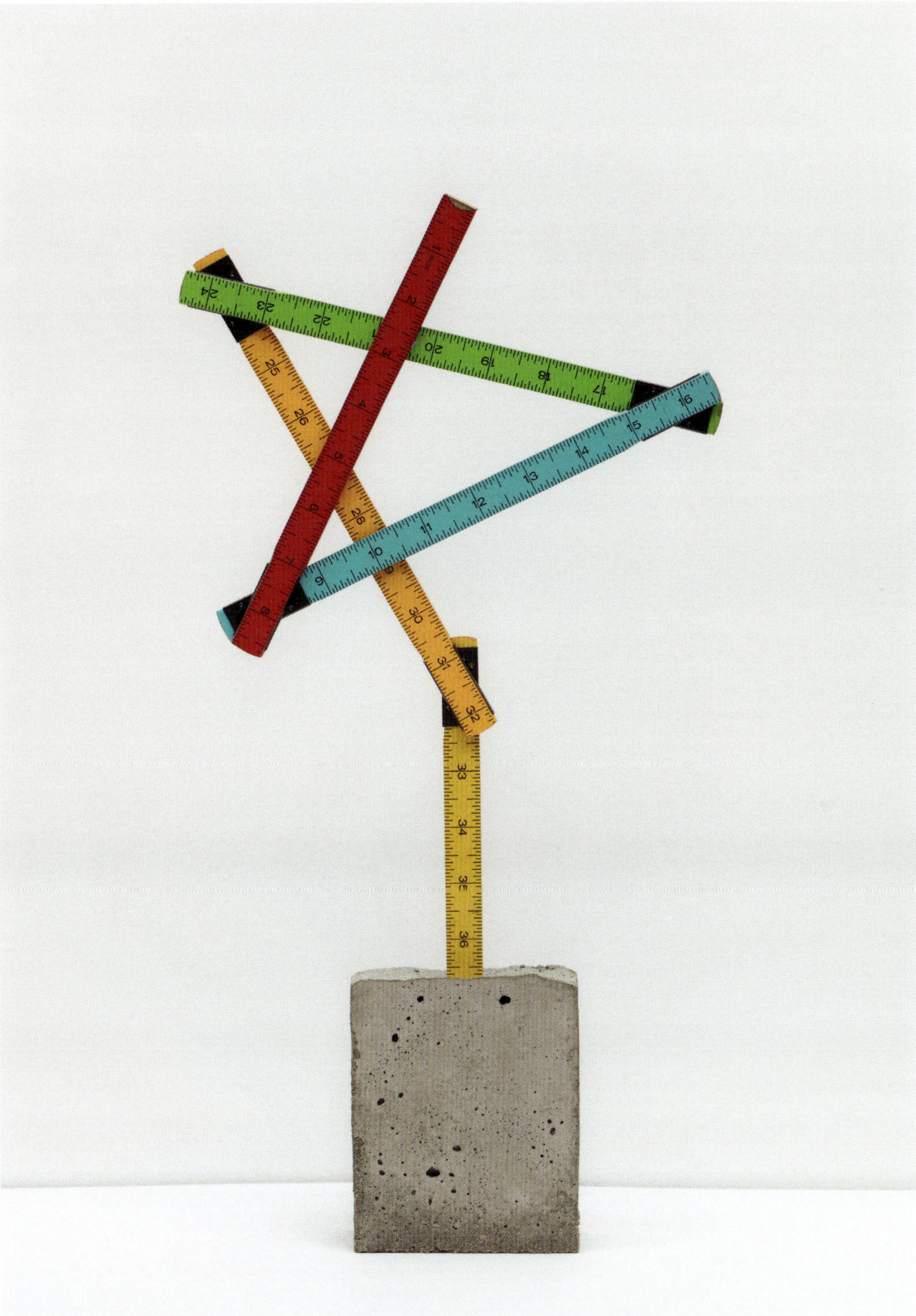

Alt-Concreto 18, 2017
Wooden ruler, concrete
47.5 x 24 x 5 cm

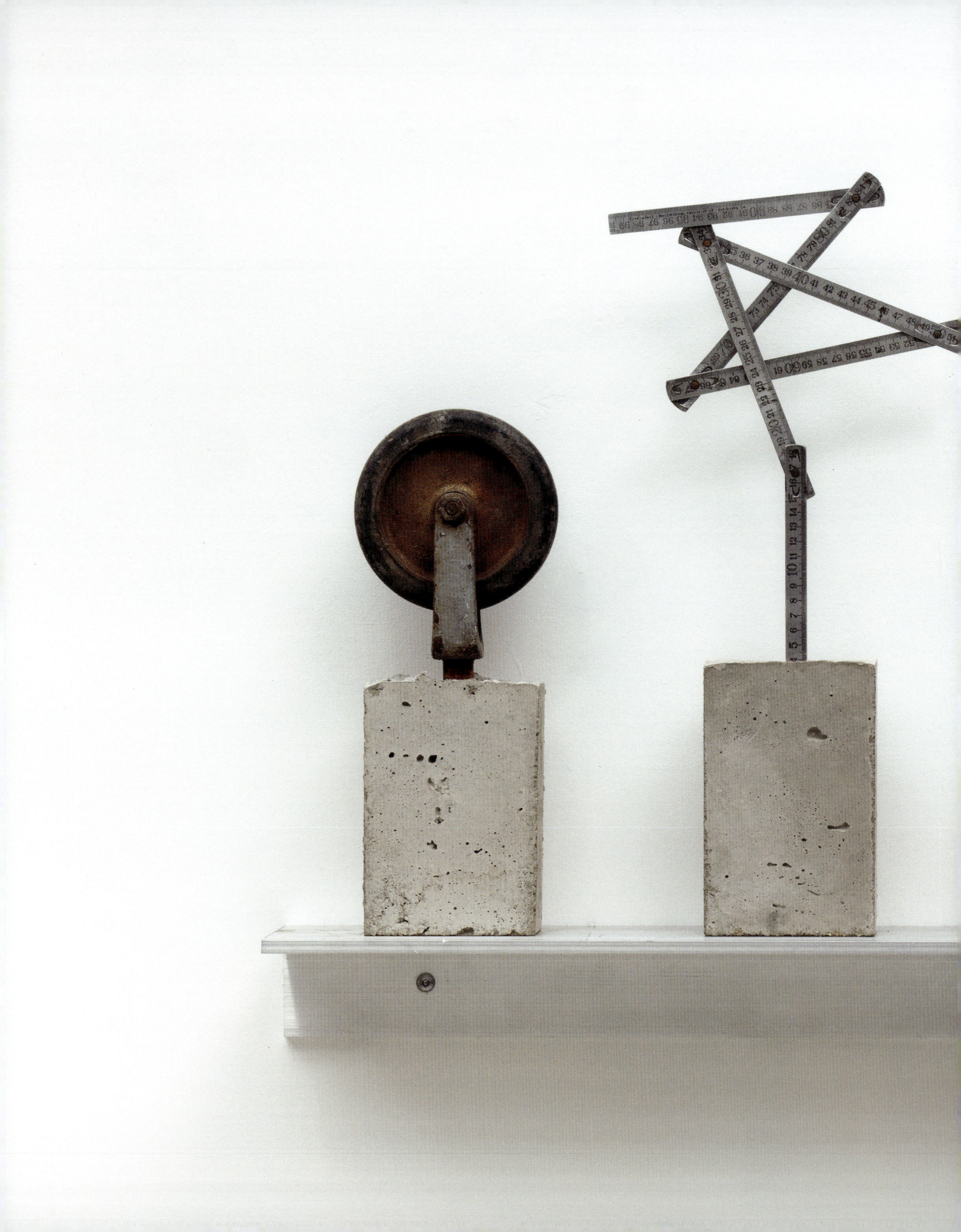

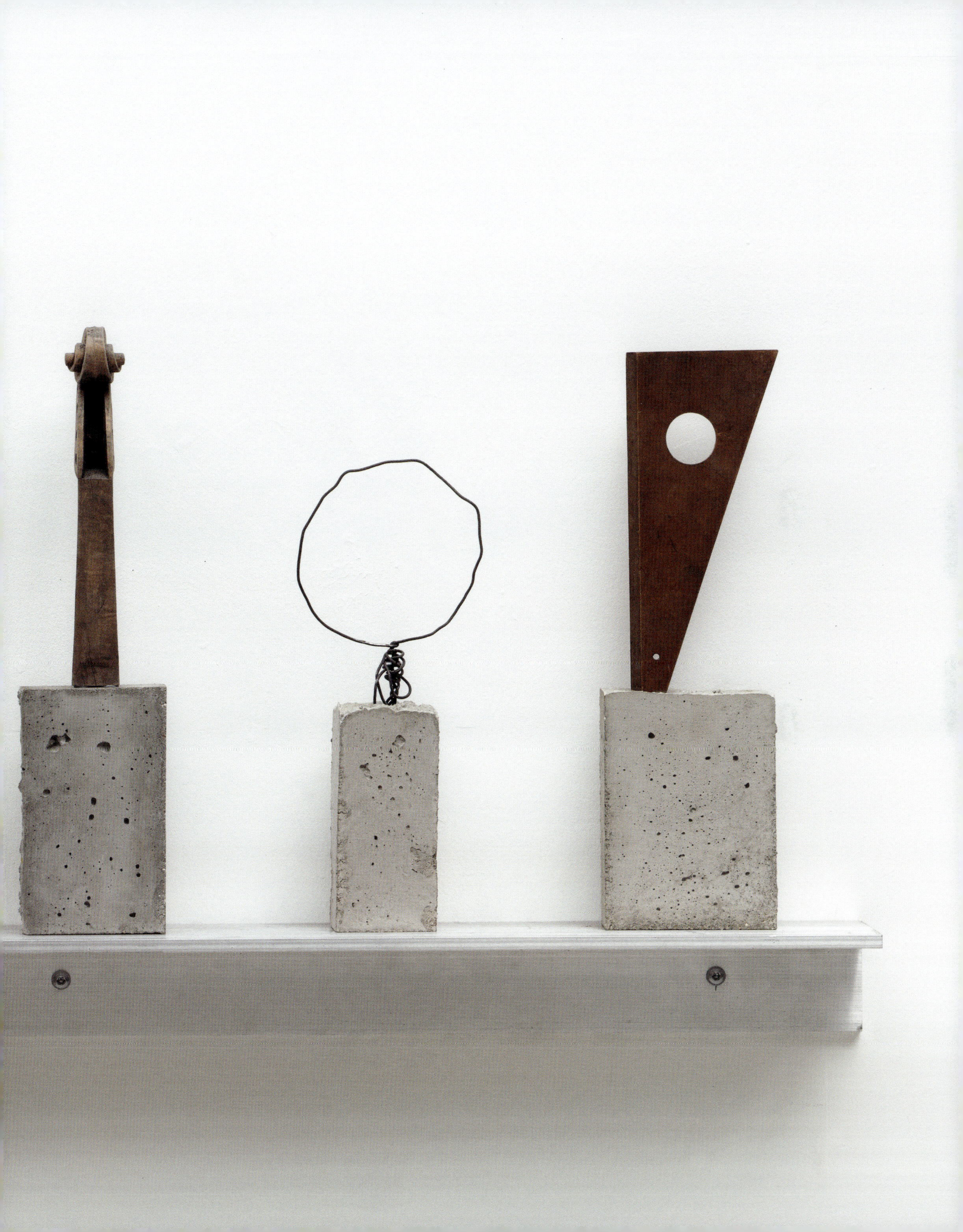

Previous pages:
Alt-Concreto 22, 2019
Steel and rubber wheel, steel ruler, violin neck, wire, wooden set square, concrete, aluminium
60 x 130 x 15 cm

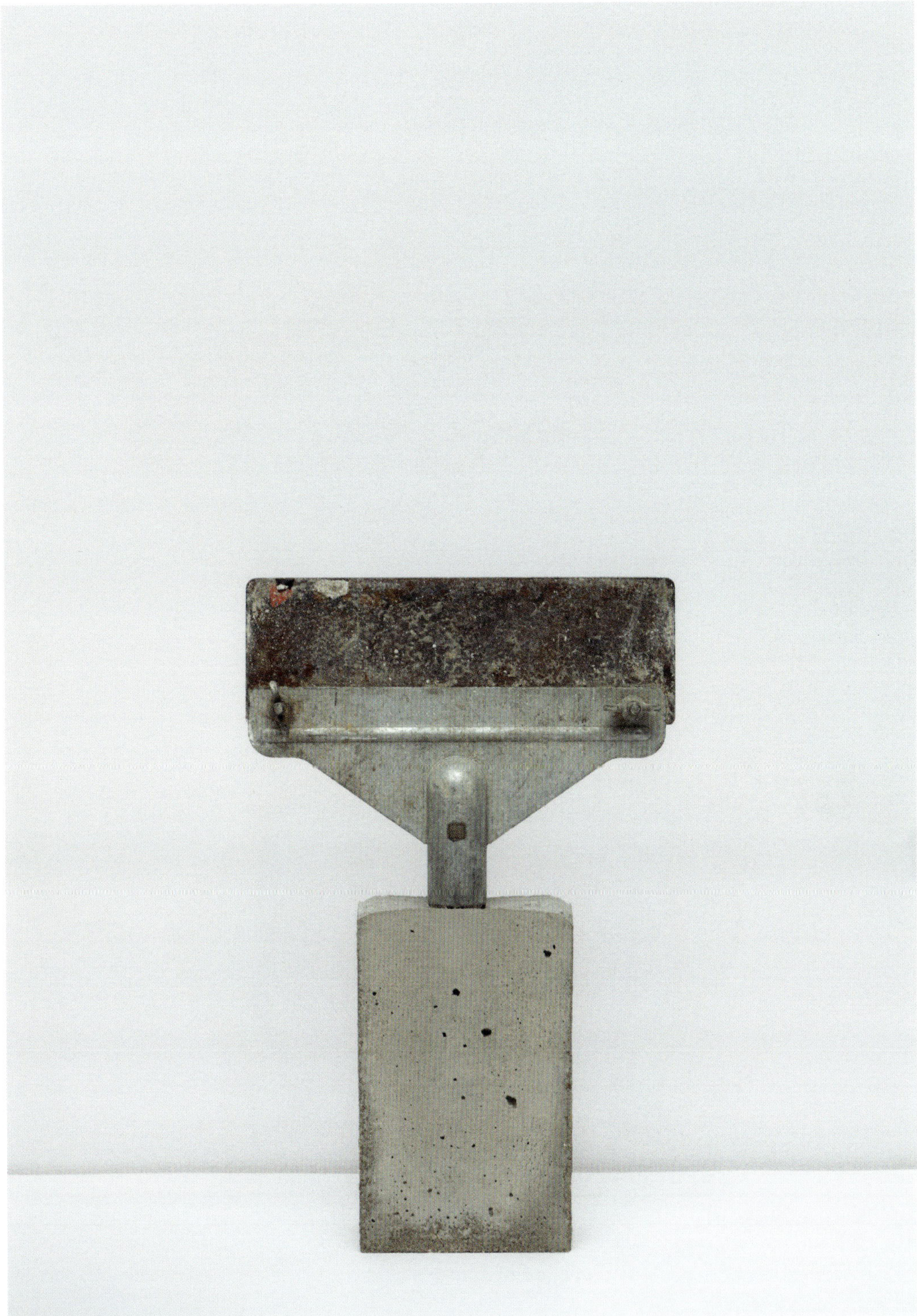

Alt-Concreto 23, 2019
Steel scraper, concrete
31.5 x 20.3 x 5 cm

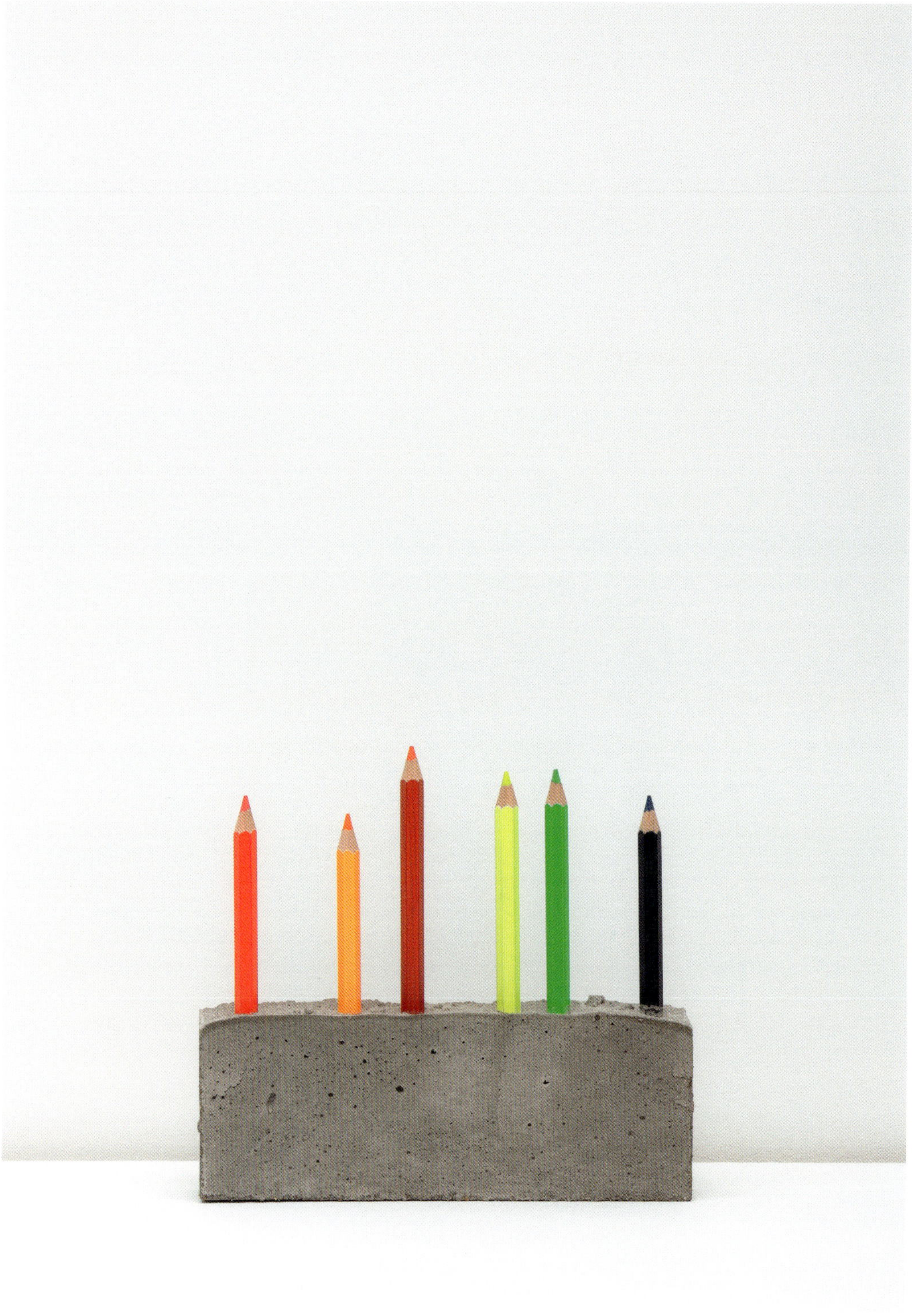

Alt-Concreto 29, 2019
Pencils, concrete
21 x 23.5 x 5 cm

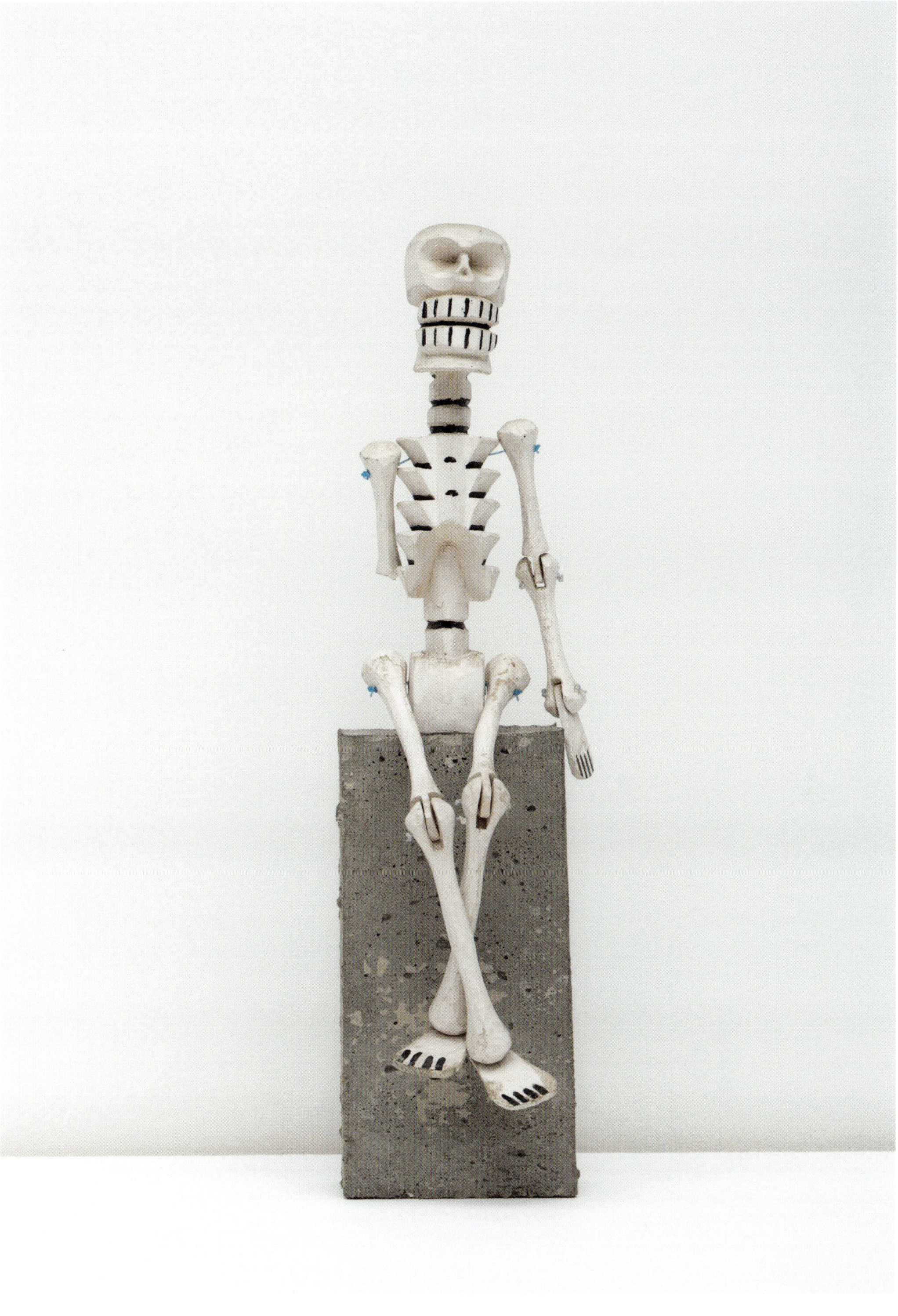

Alt-Concreto 31, 2020
Painted wooden skeleton, concrete
45 x 12 x 6 cm

Alt-Concretos, 2020
Wooden and plastic rulers, concrete
Dimensions variable

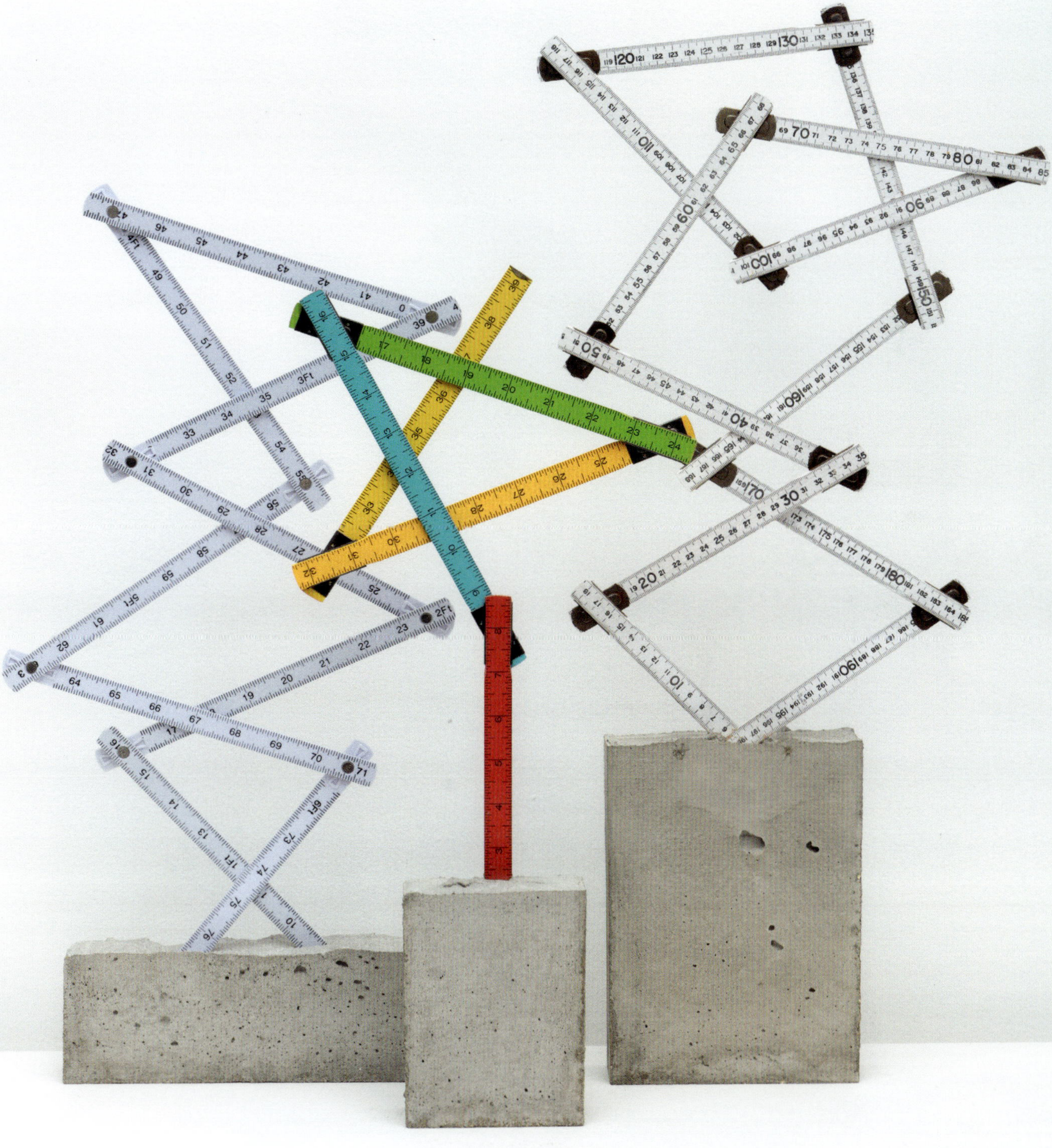

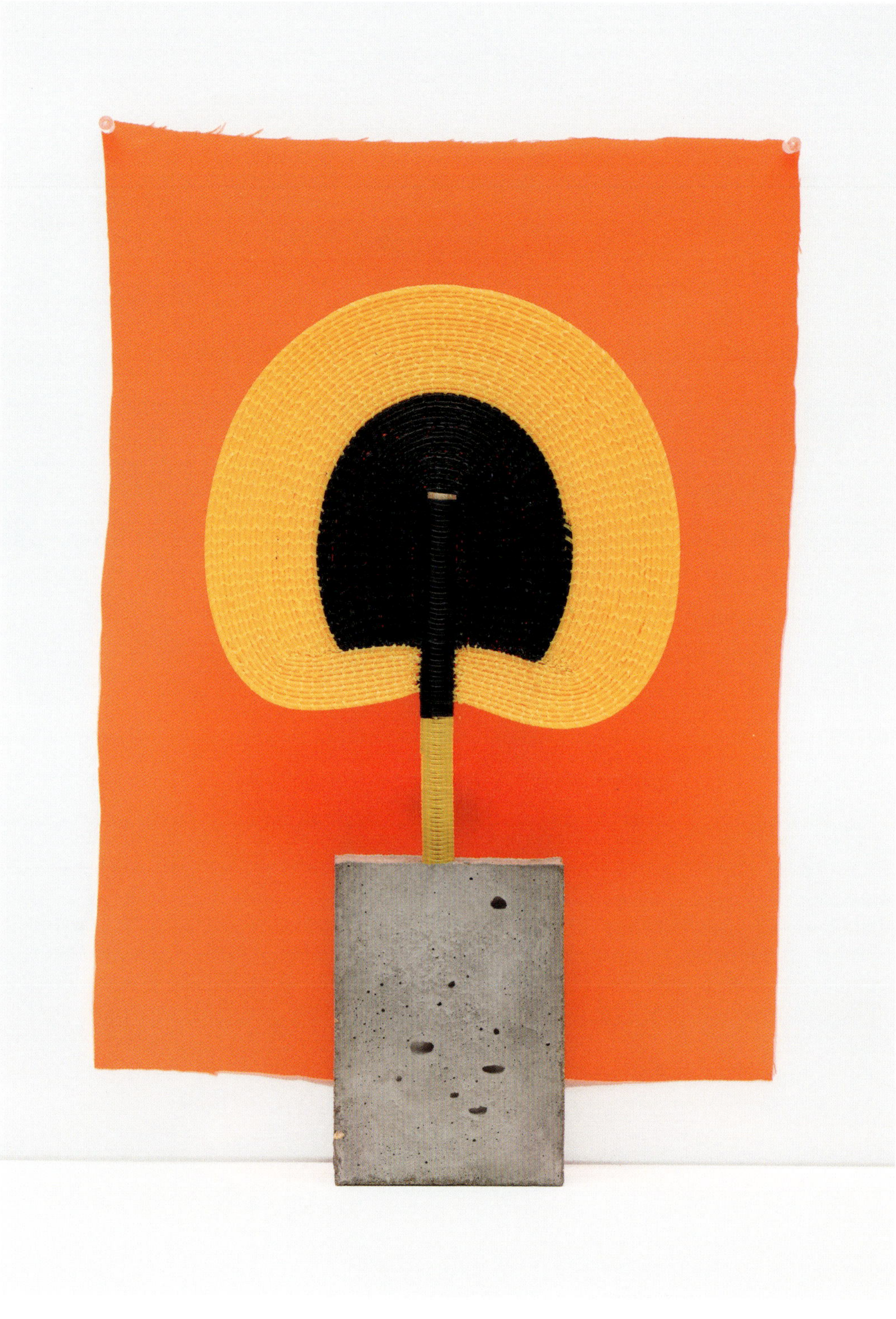

Alt-Concreto 32, 2022
Plastic fan, fabric, concrete
56 x 37 x 8.5 cm

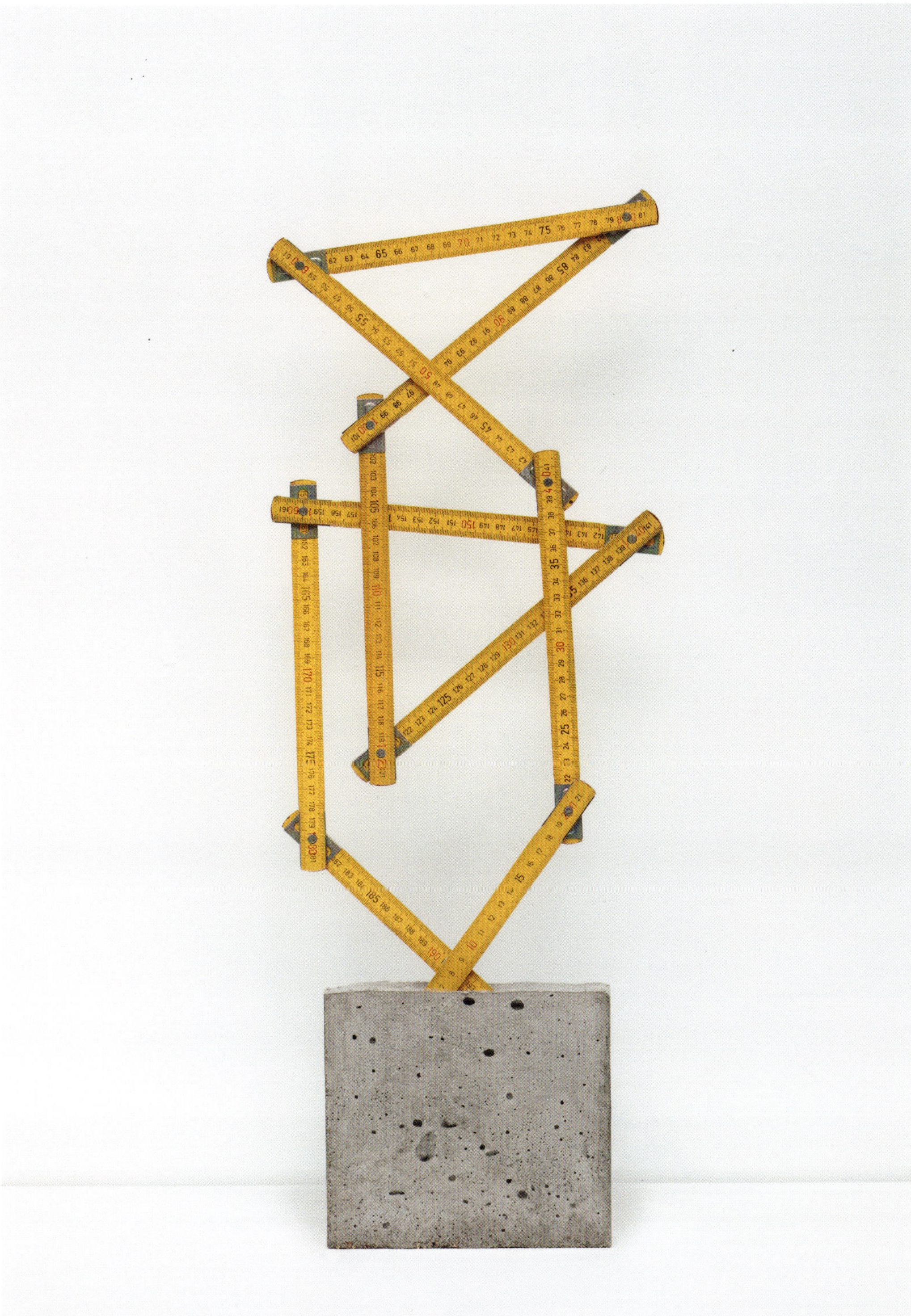

Alt-Concreto 33, 2022
Wooden ruler, concrete
64 x 24 x 5 cm

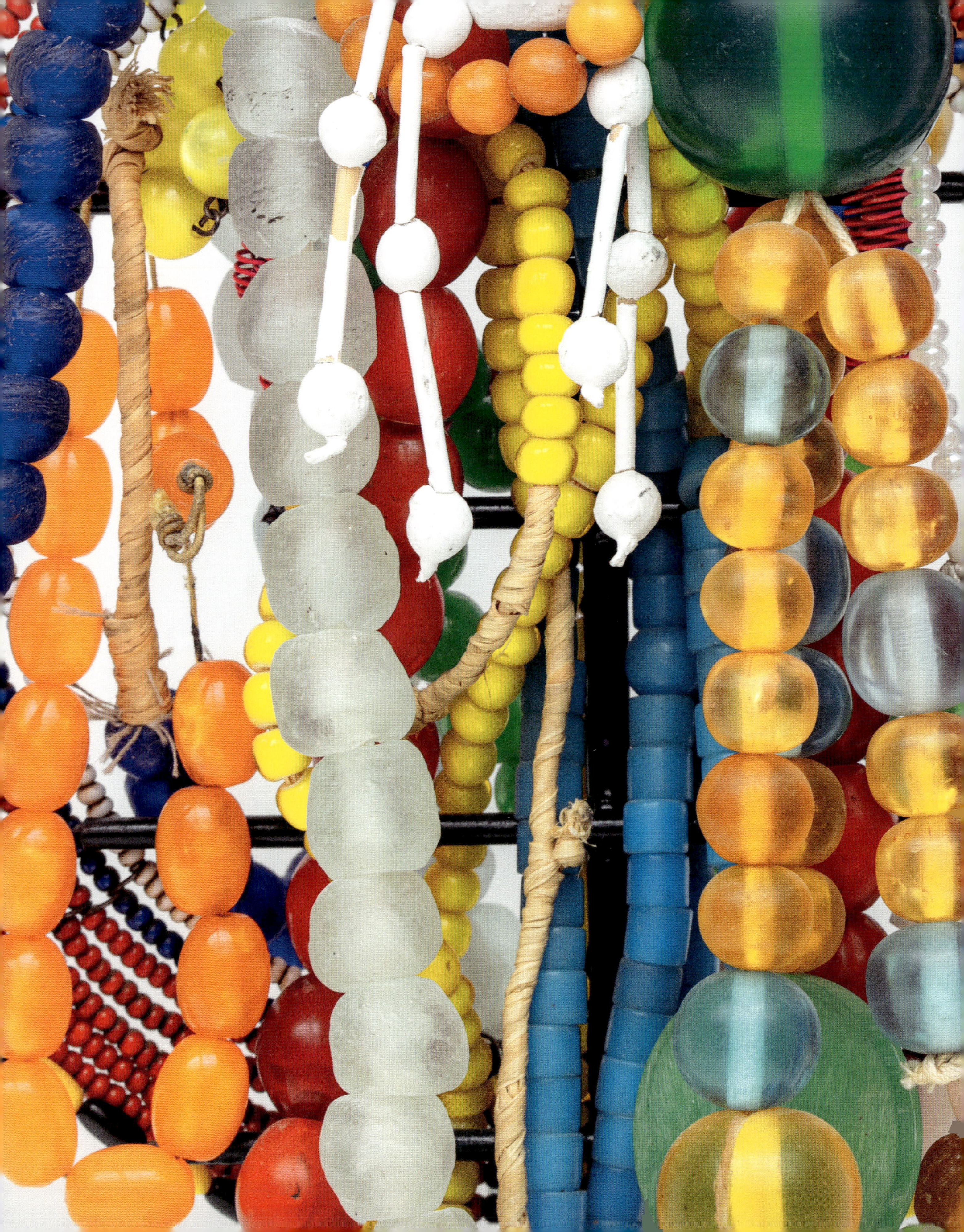

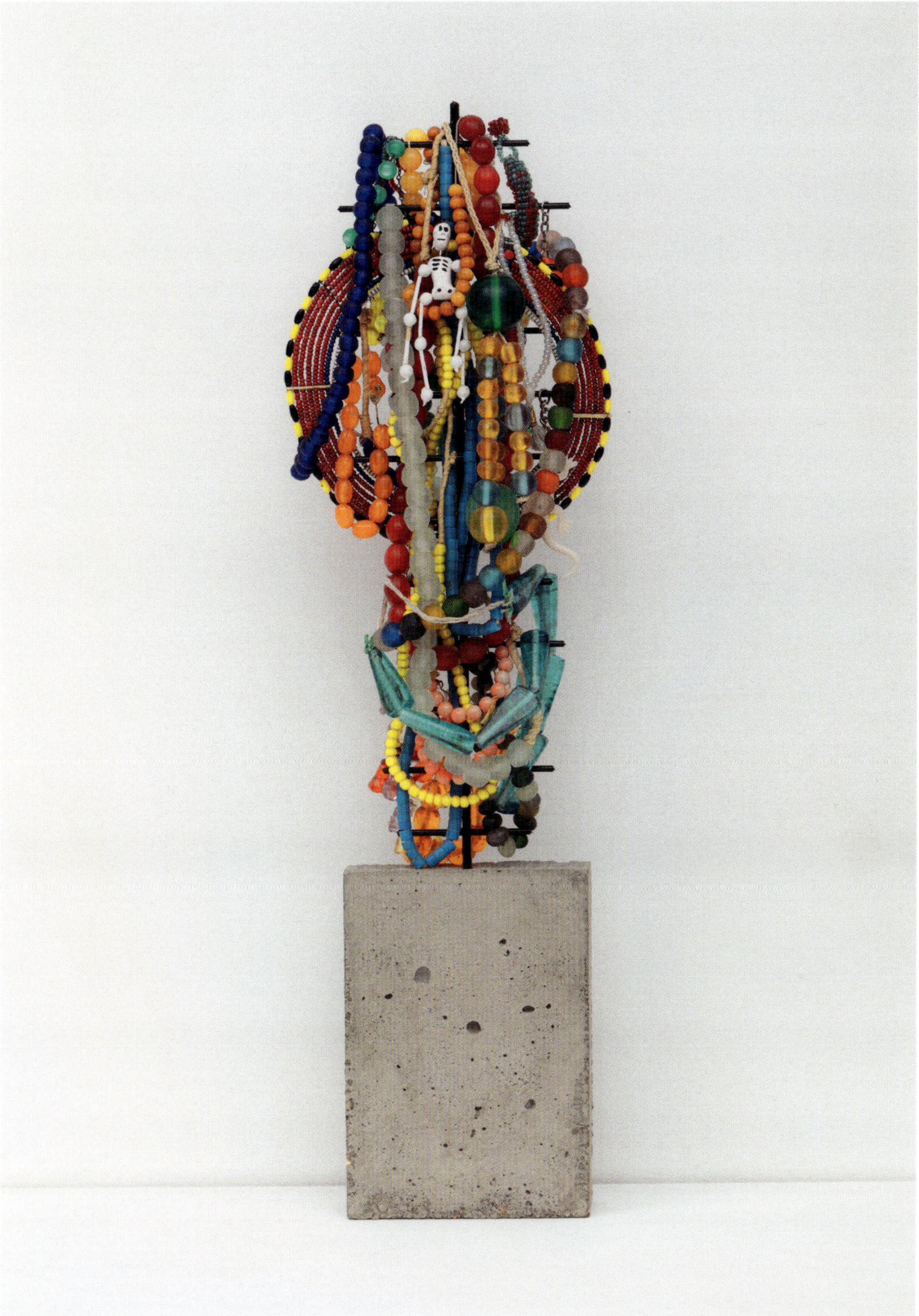

Alt-Concreto 34, 2022
Beads, plastic and wooden ornaments, steel, concrete
58.5 x 17 x 6 cm

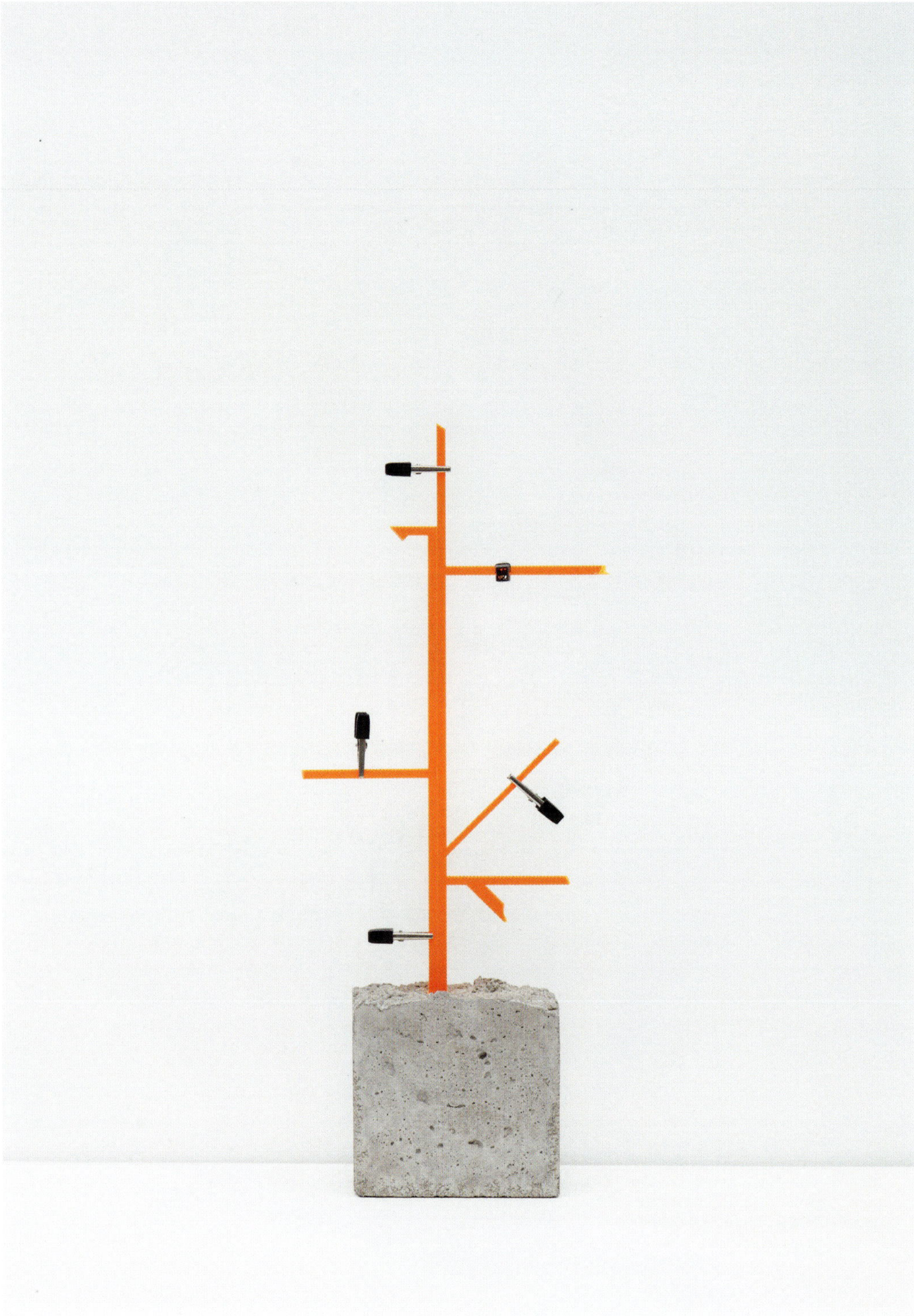

Alt-Concreto 35, 2022
Cast acrylic, electrical clips, concrete
39.5 x 16 x 6.5 cm

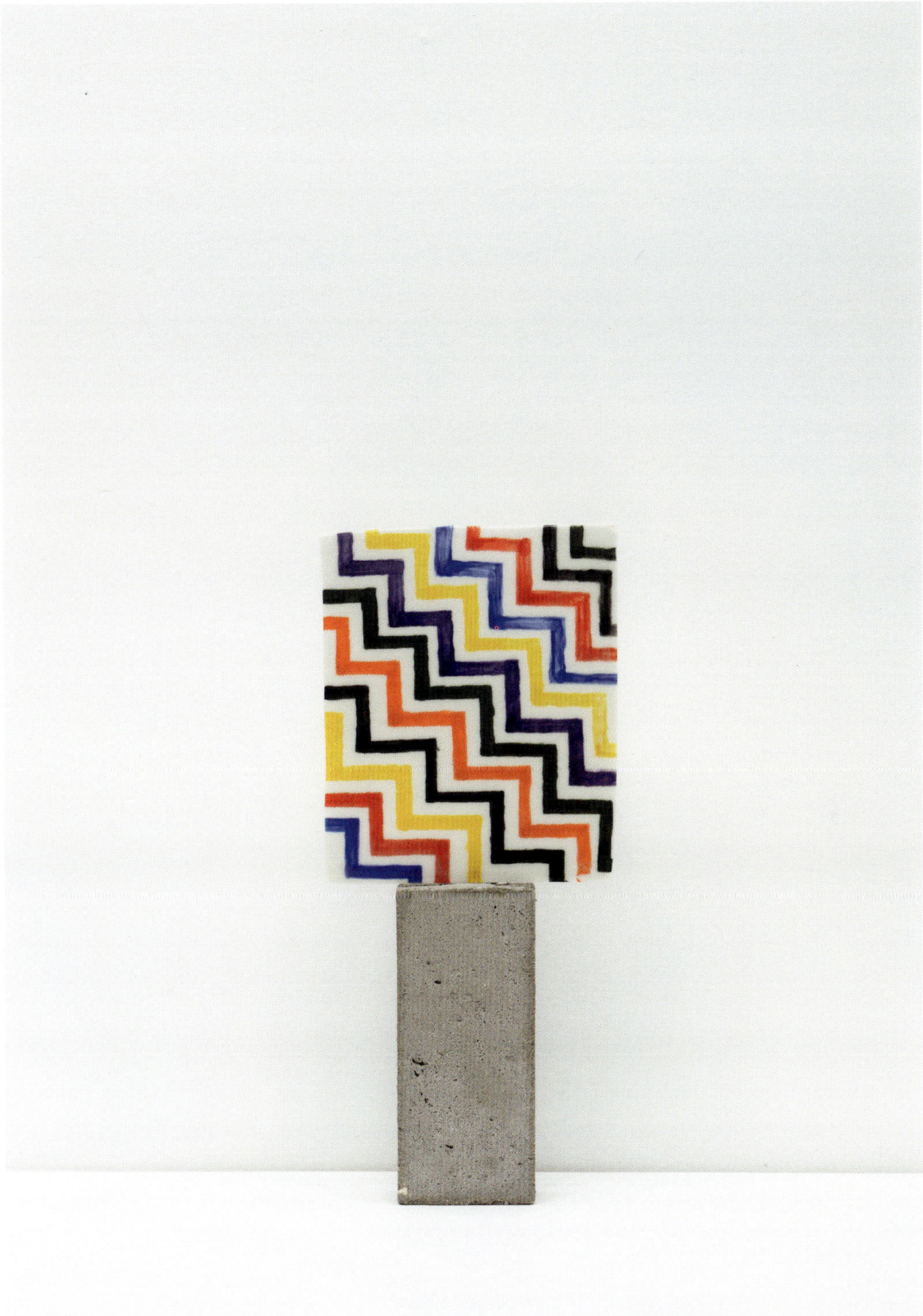

Alt-Concreto 36, 2022
Glazed ceramic, concrete
33.5 x 14.5 x 5 cm

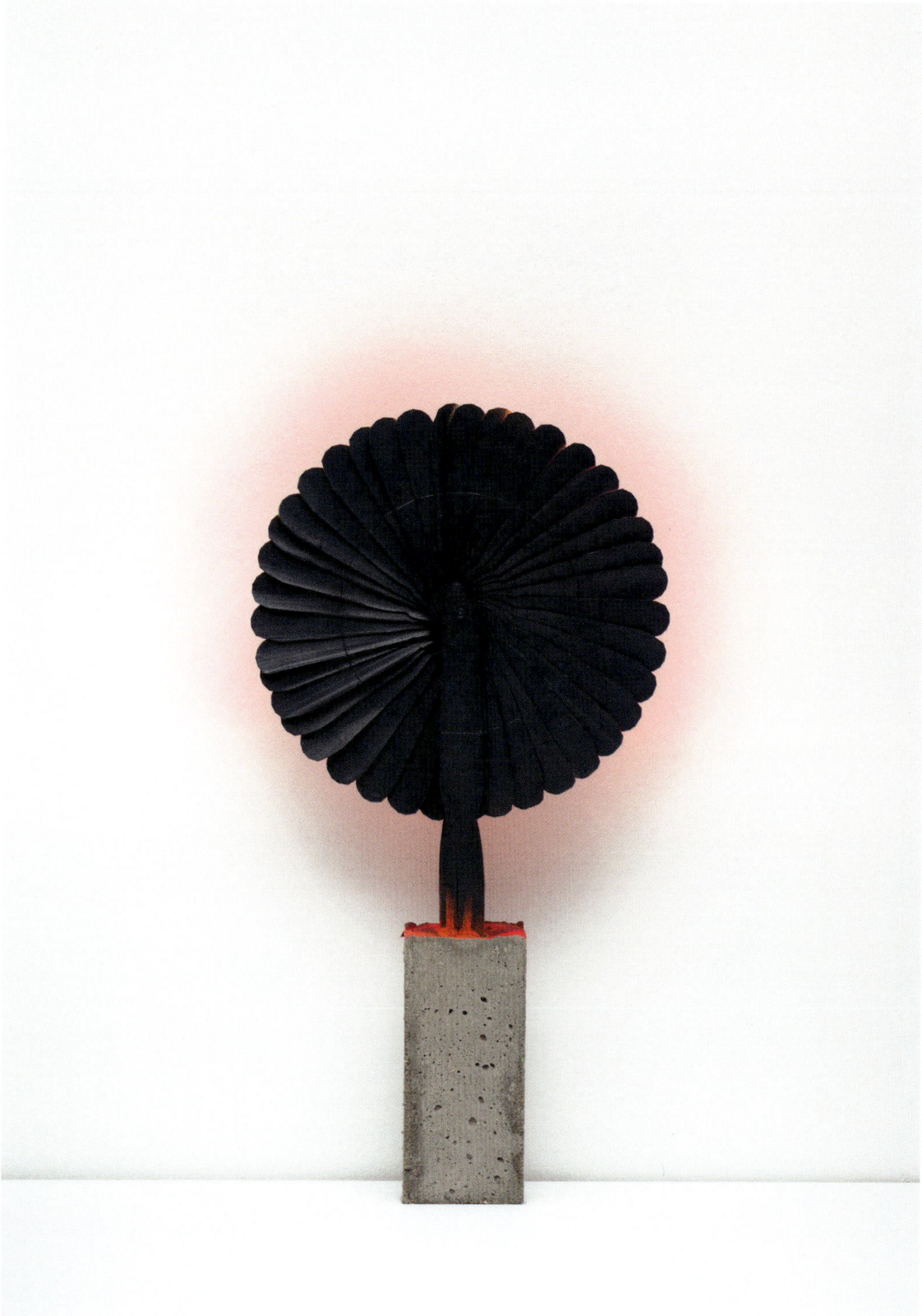

Alt-Concreto 37, 2022
Wooden fan, spray paint, concrete
44 x 23 x 5 cm

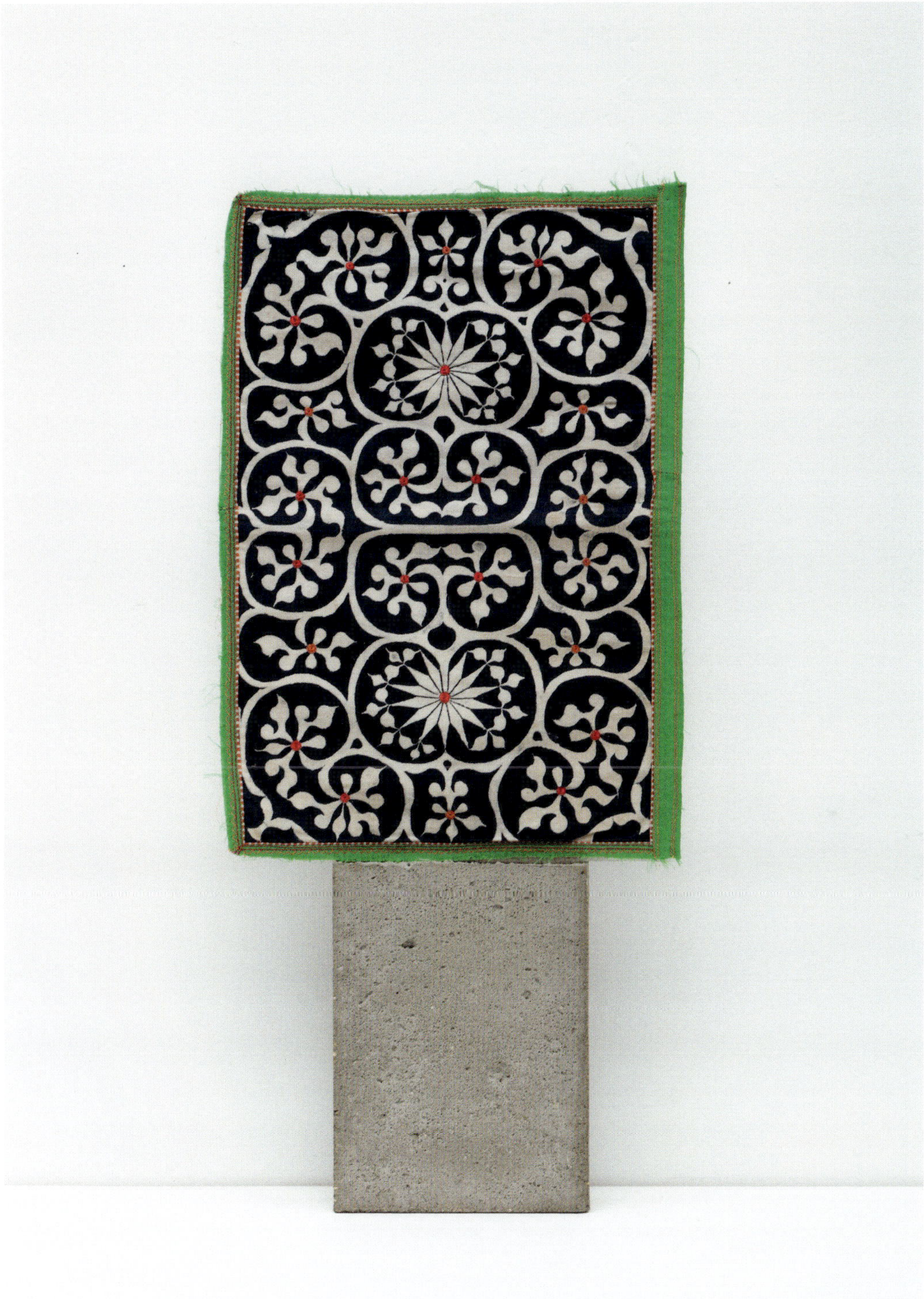

Alt-Concreto 38, 2022
Fabric, concrete
60 x 27 x 7 cm

Cons

Neo-Cons

Alt-Cons

Geo-Cons

Neo-Neo-Cons

I-Cons

Ex-Cons

2018 –

All the *Geo-Concretos* are made from left-over lids from tins of household and metallic paint I used for paintings. For several years I had failed to notice the poetic potential of these caked circles of saturated colour.

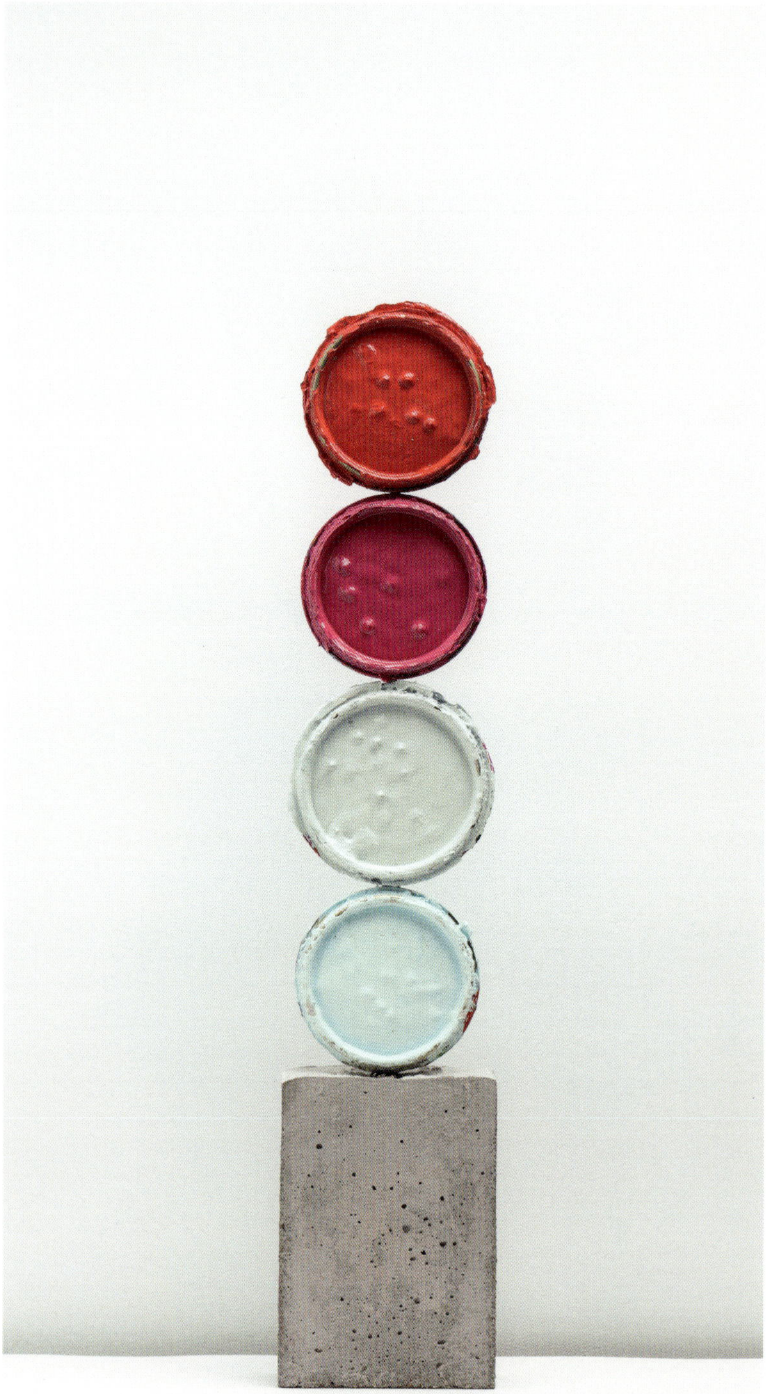

Geo-Concreto 03, 2018
Tin lids, gloss paint, concrete
59 x 11.5 x 5 cm

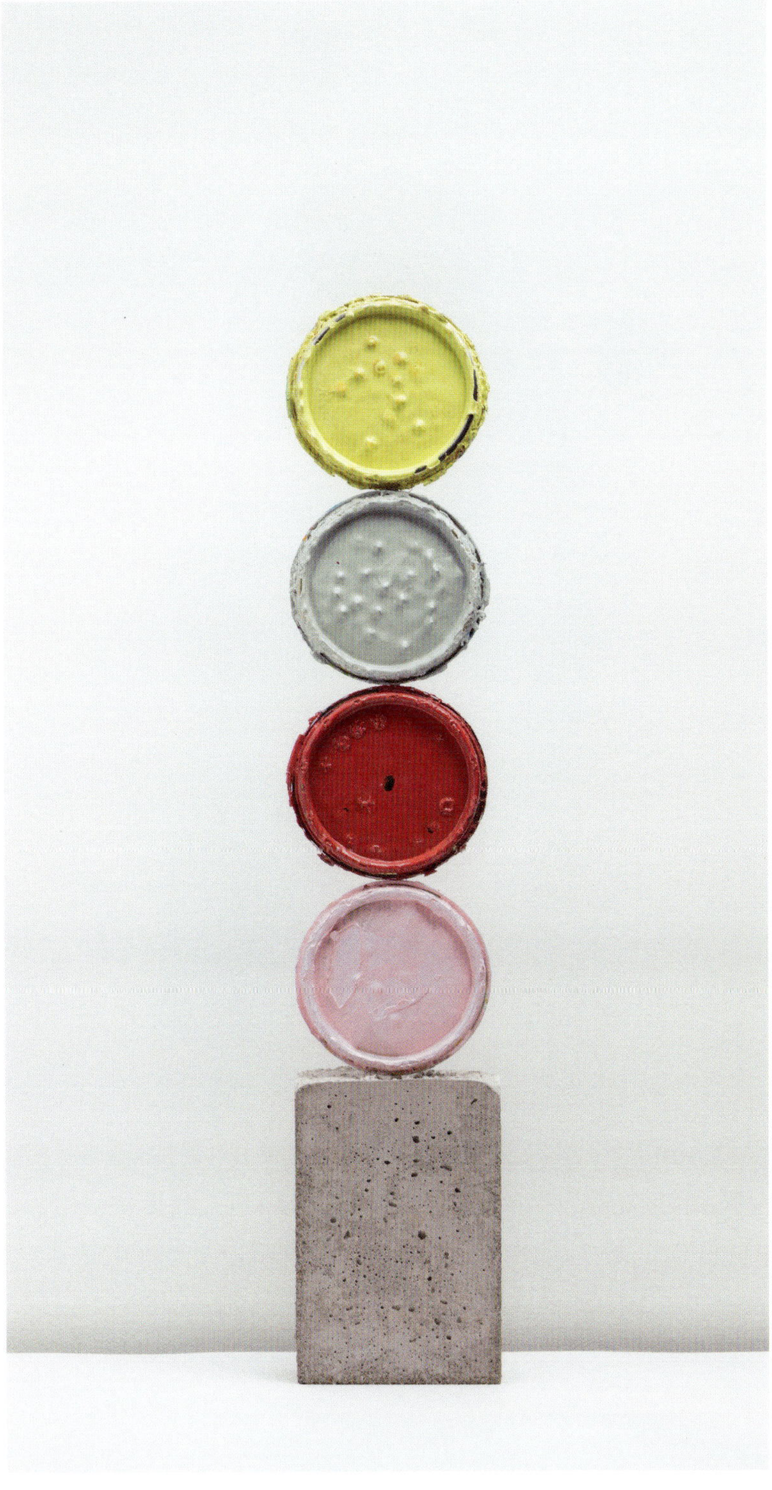

Geo-Concreto 05, 2018
Tin lids, gloss paint, concrete
60.5 x 11 x 5 cm

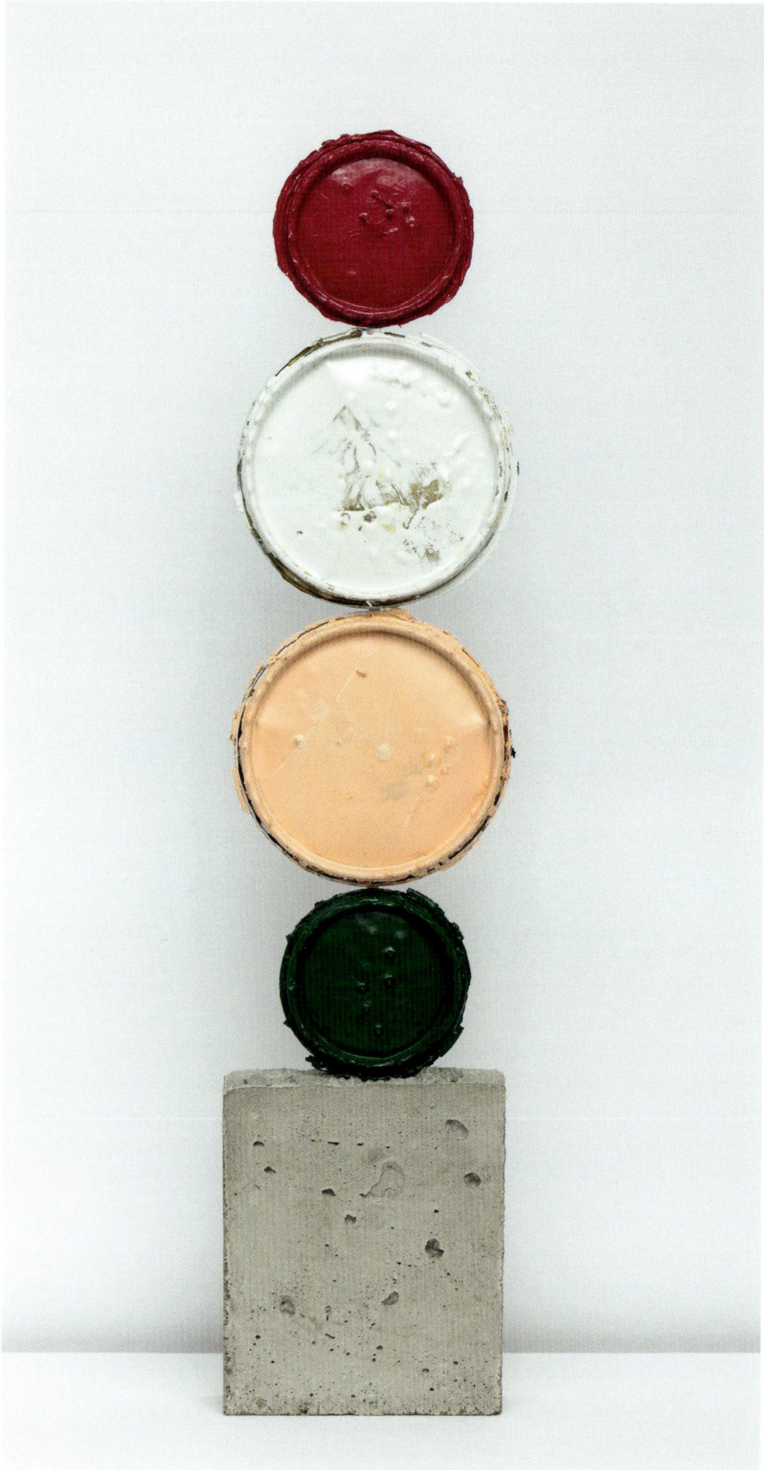

Geo-Concreto 07, 2018
Tin lids, gloss paint, concrete
68.5 x 15 x 5 cm

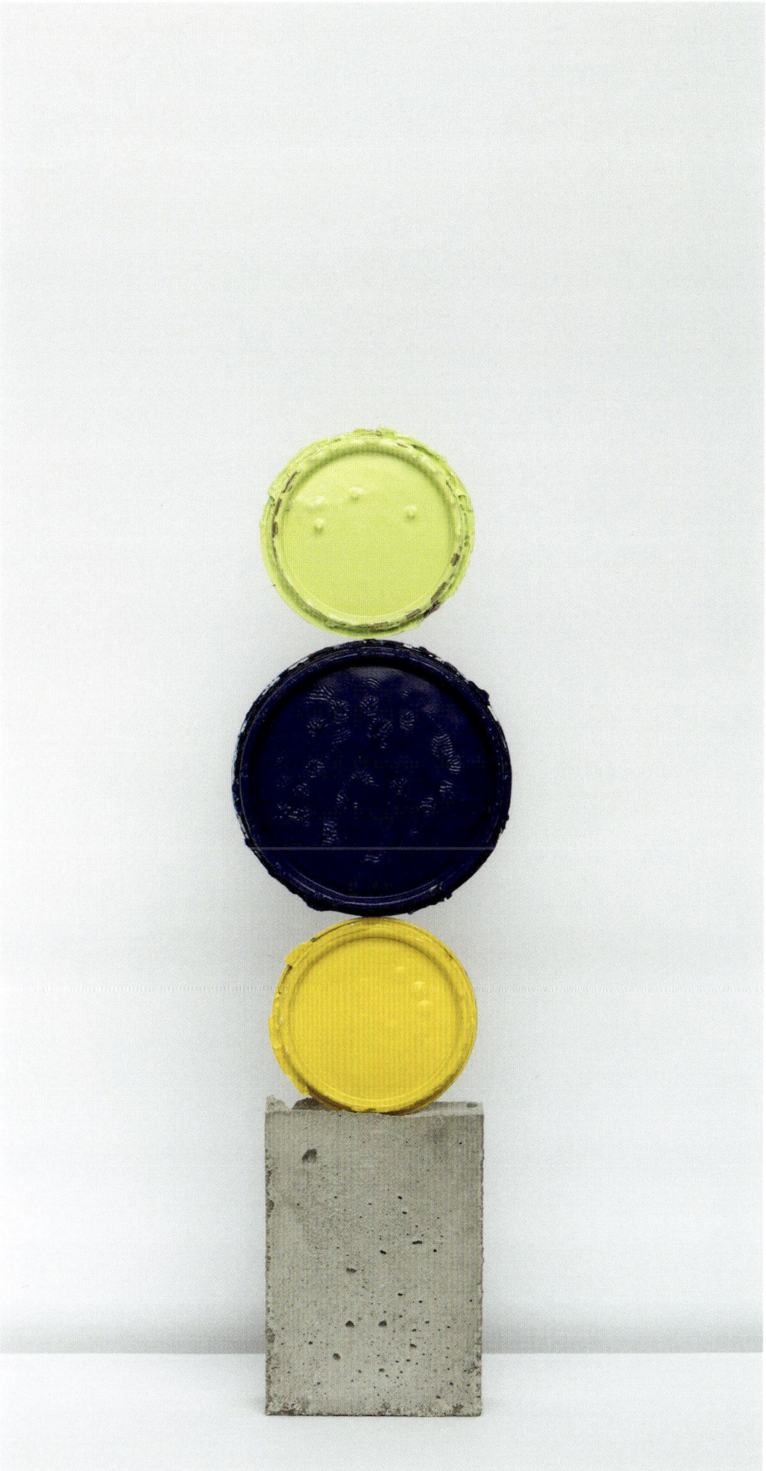

Geo-Concreto 14, 2018
Tin lids, gloss paint, concrete
53 x 11.5 x 5 cm

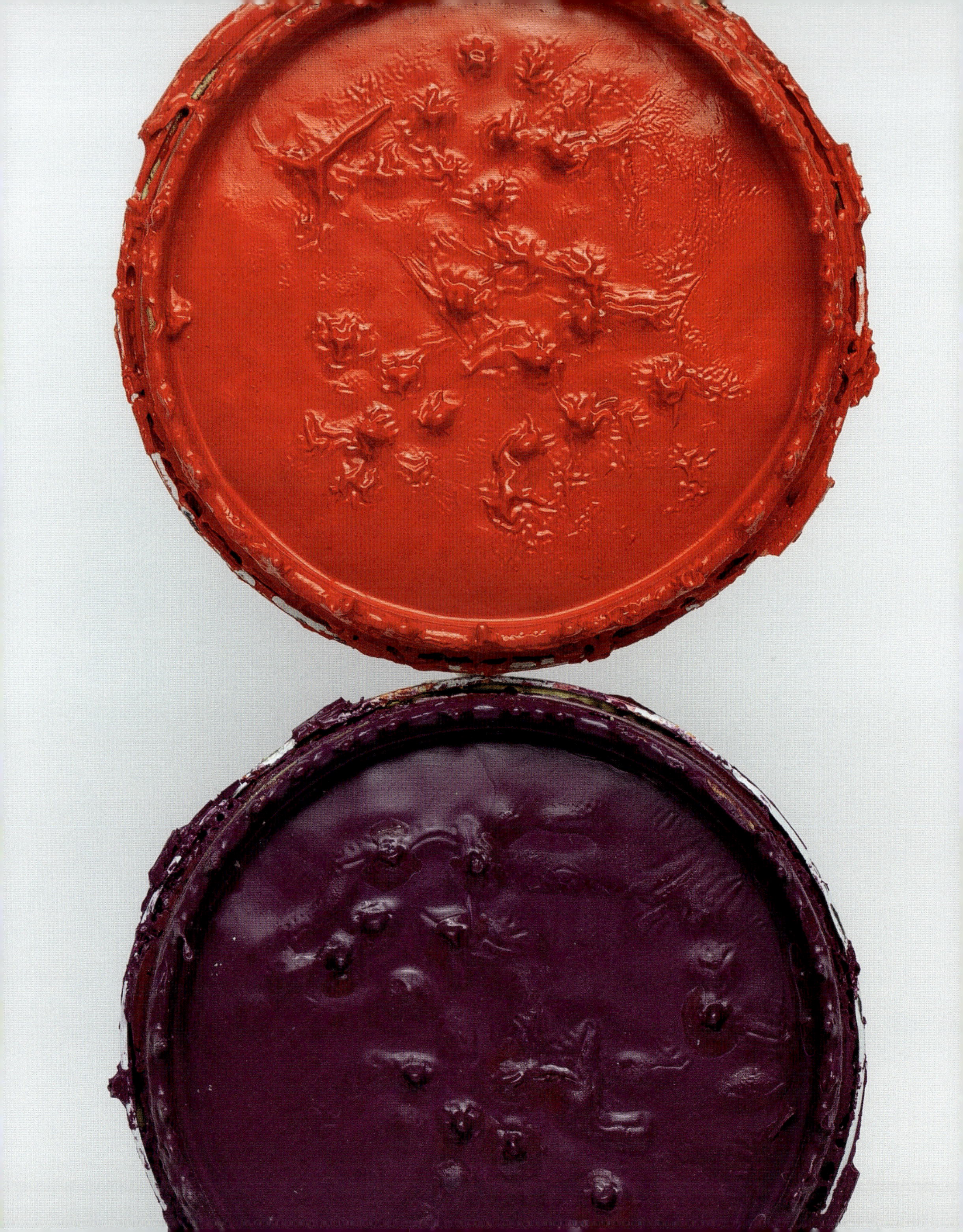

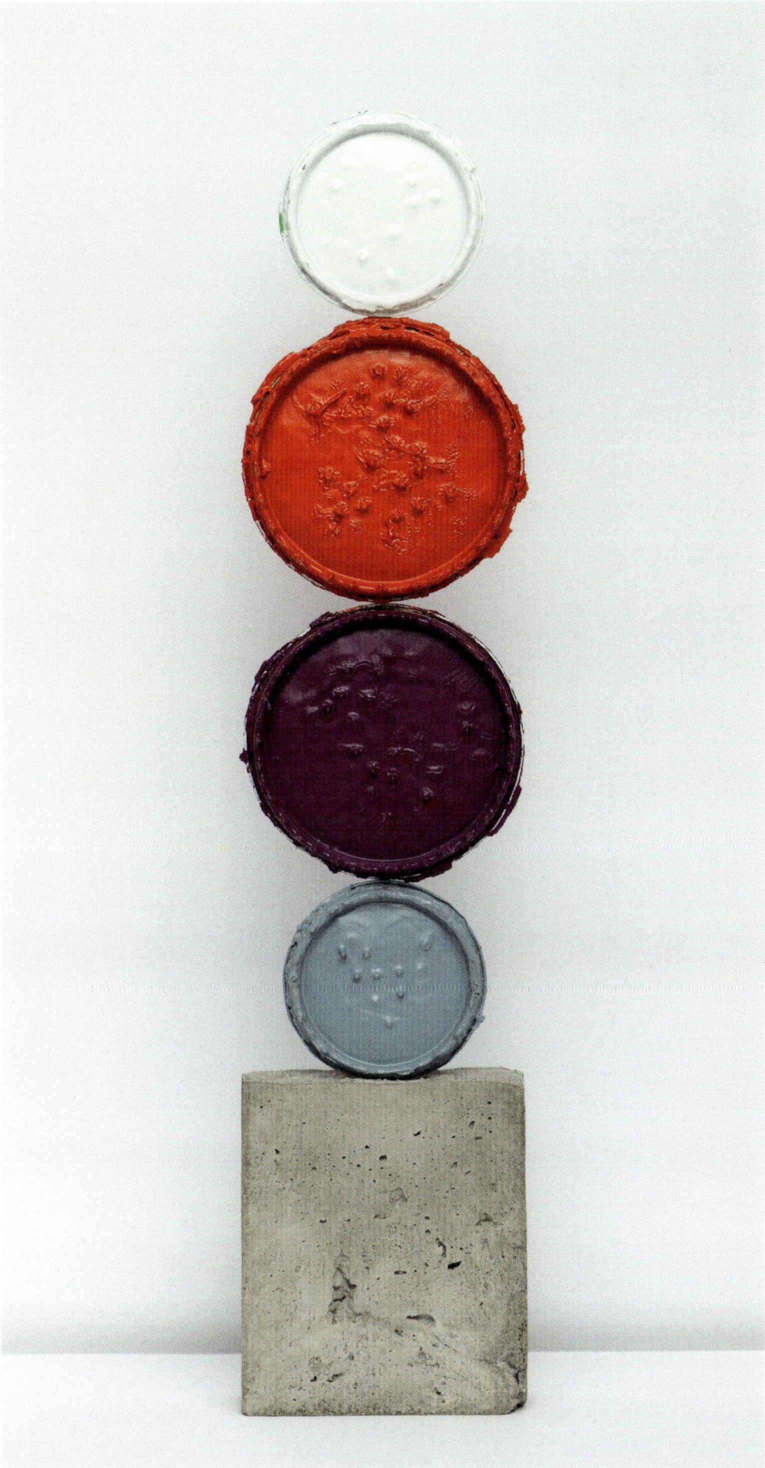

Geo-Concreto 12, 2018
Tin lids, gloss paint, concrete
70 x 15 x 5 cm

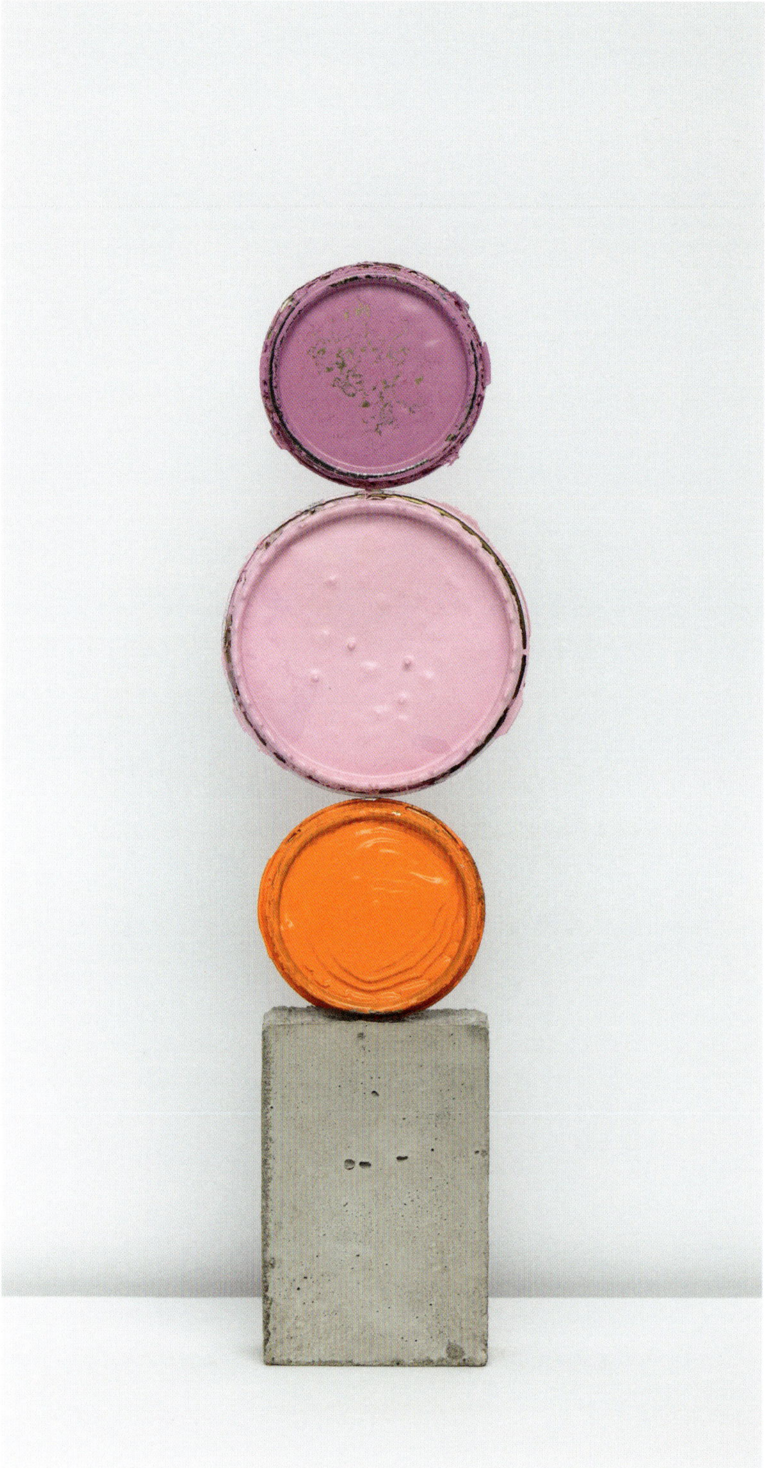

Geo-Concreto 09, 2018
Tin lids, gloss paint, concrete
53 x 11 x 5 cm

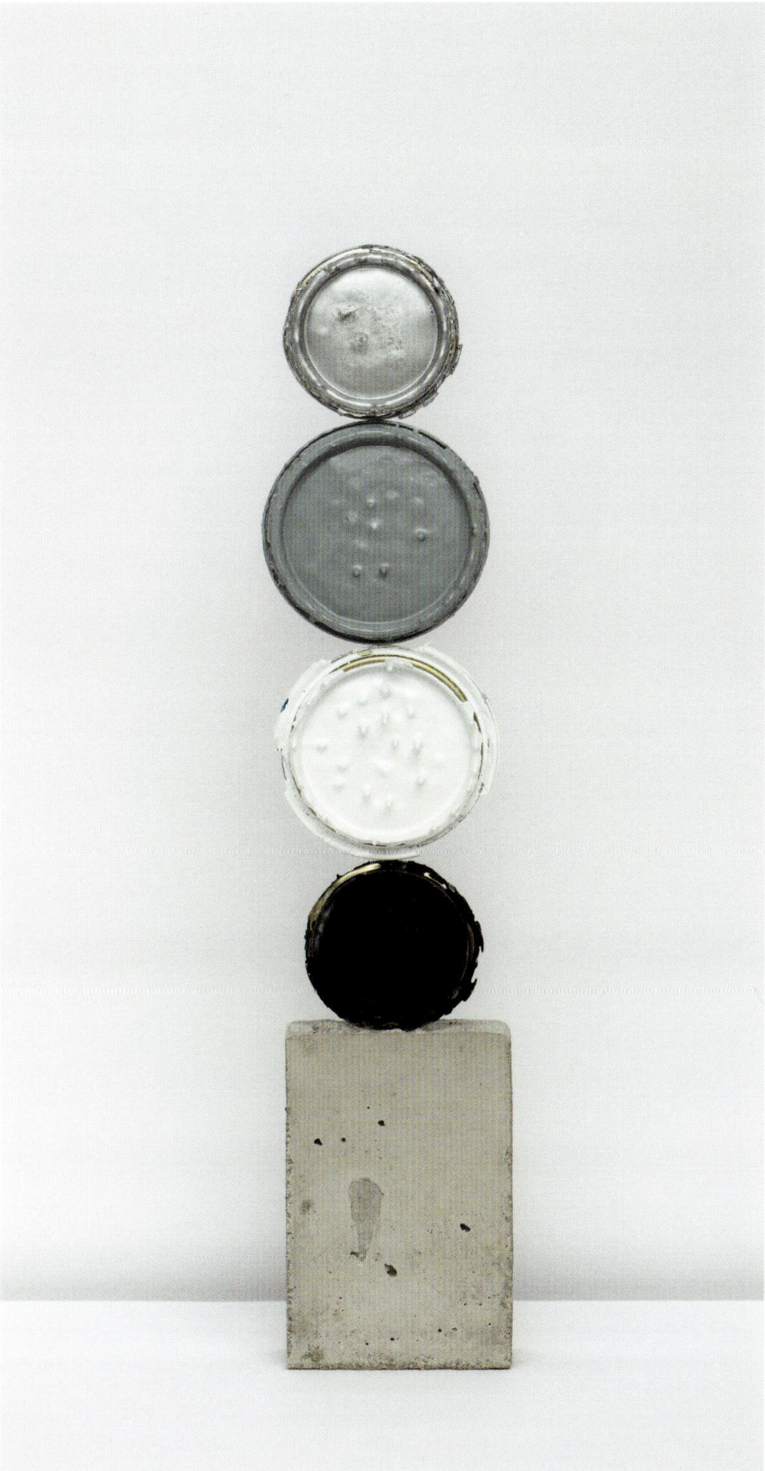

Geo-Concreto 10, 2018
Tin lids, gloss paint, concrete
55 x 11 x 5 cm

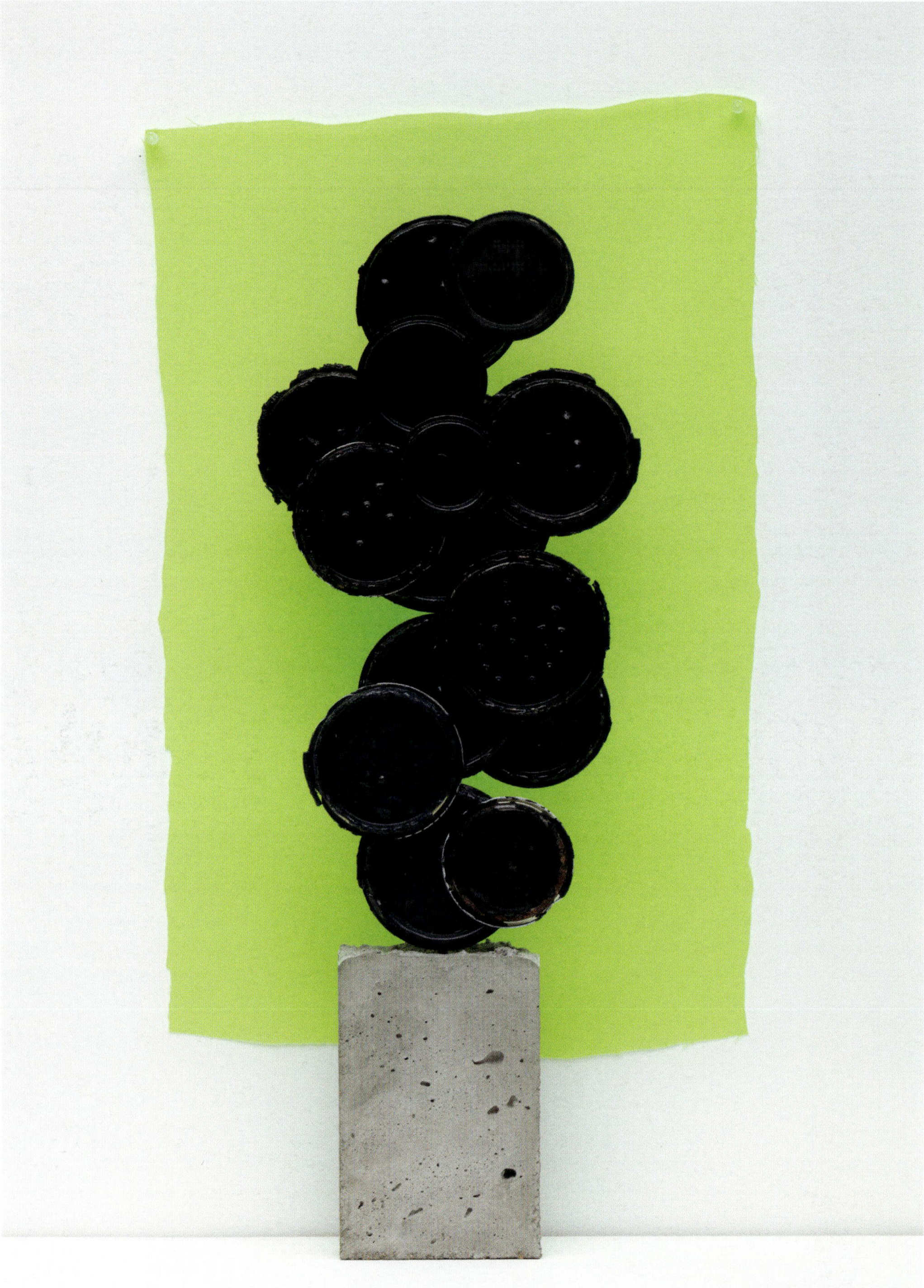

Geo-Concreto 20, 2022
Tin lids, gloss paint, concrete, fabric
71.5 x 32 x 8.5 cm

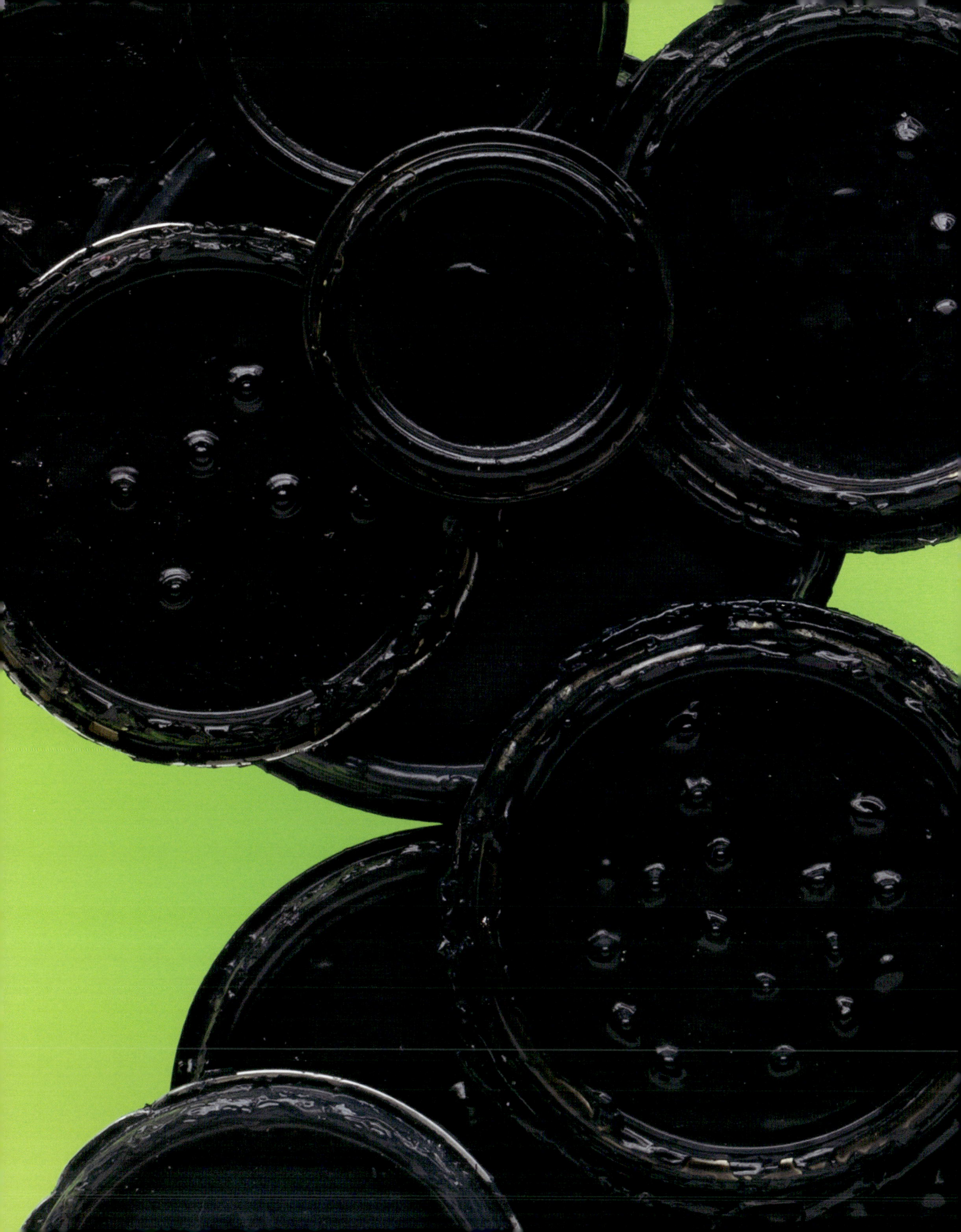

Cons
Neo-Cons
Alt-Cons
Geo-Cons
Neo-Neo-Cons
I-Cons
Ex-Cons

2019 –

Made with similar offcuts of transparent coloured acrylic sheet to the *Neo-Cons*, the *Neo-Neo-Concretos* all comprise several layers of acrylic in a single work.

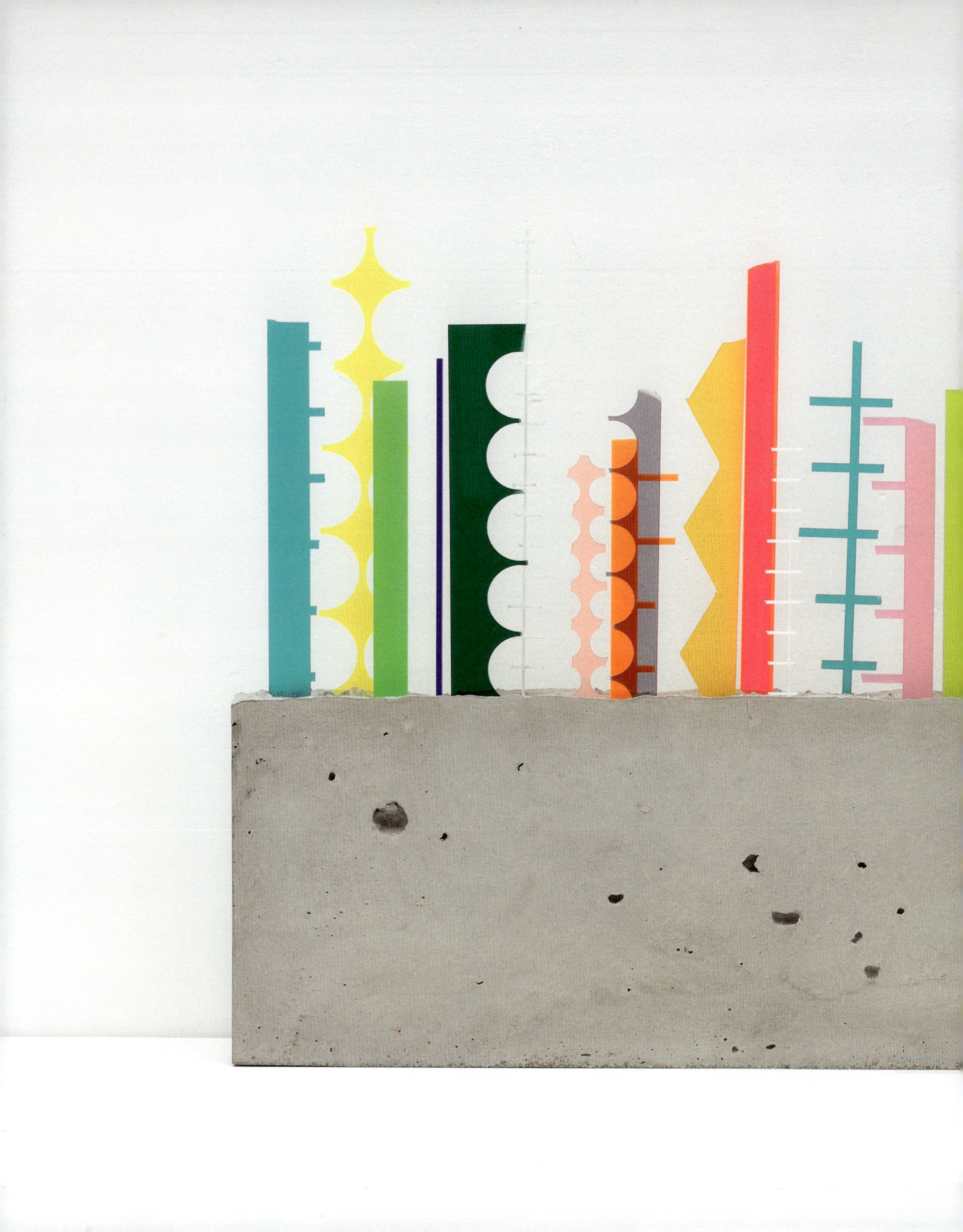

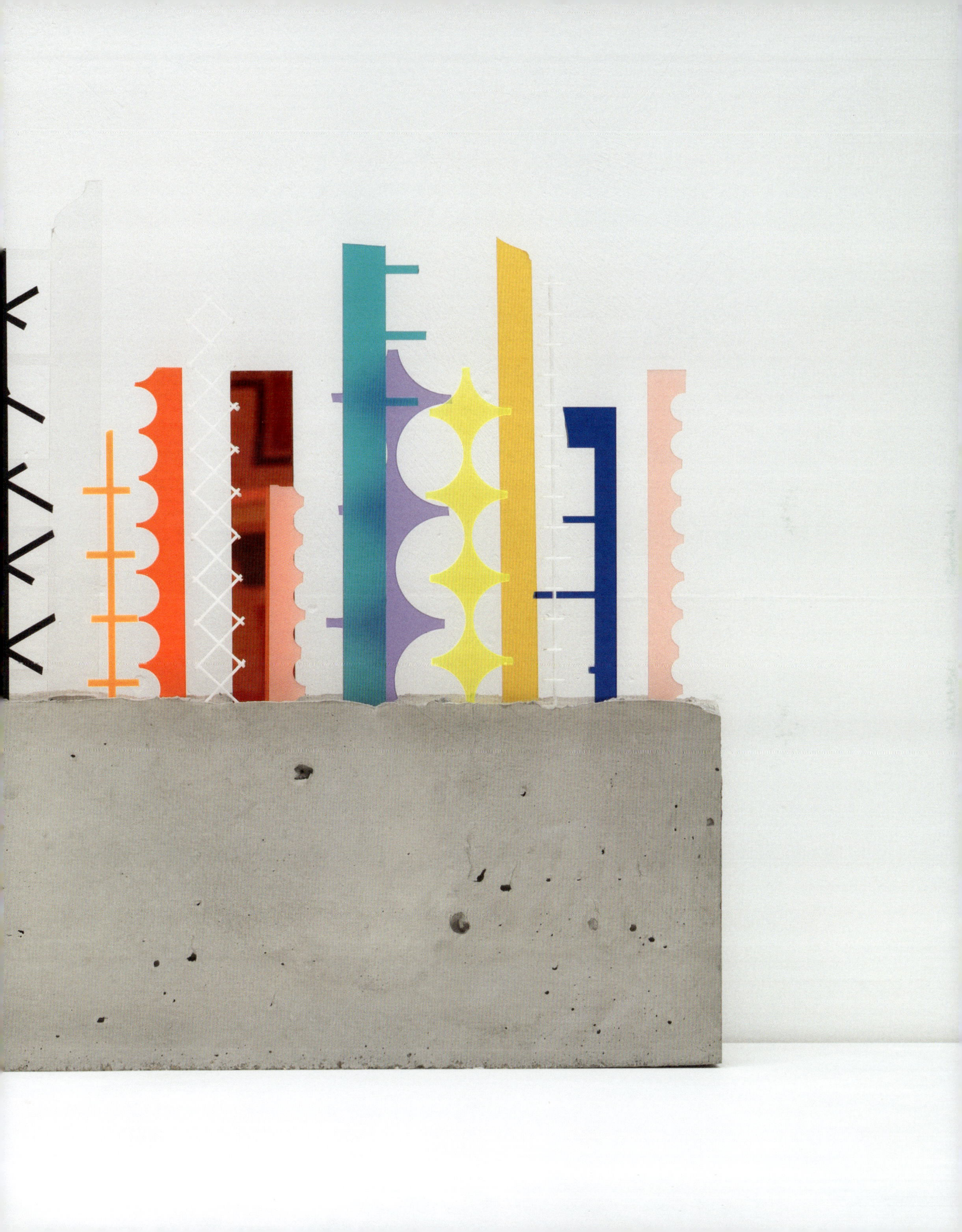

Previous pages:
Neo-Neo-Concreto 37, 2022
Cast acrylic, concrete
45 x 80 x 6 cm

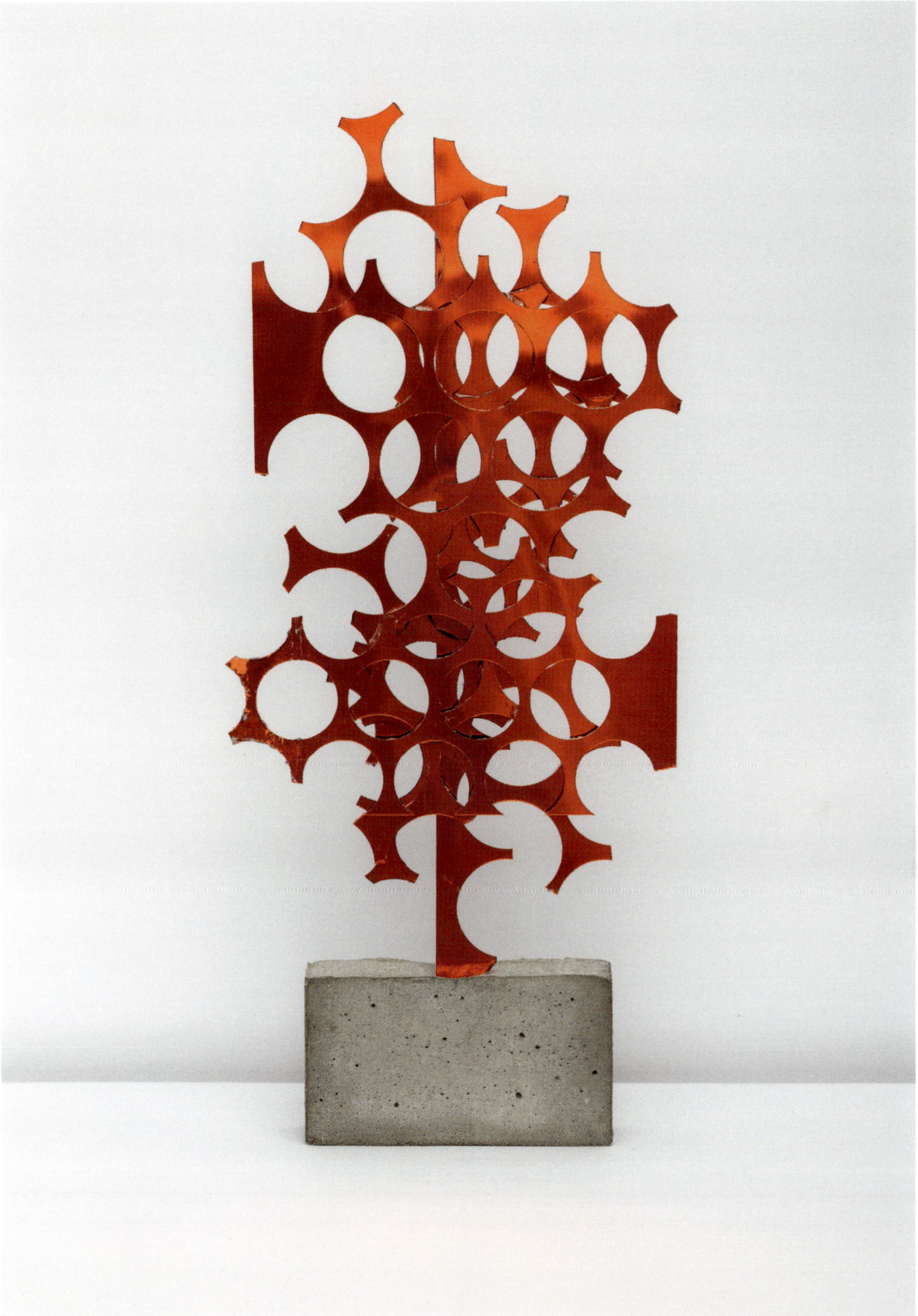

Neo-Neo-Concreto 07, 2019
Cast acrylic, concrete
52 x 25 x 5 cm

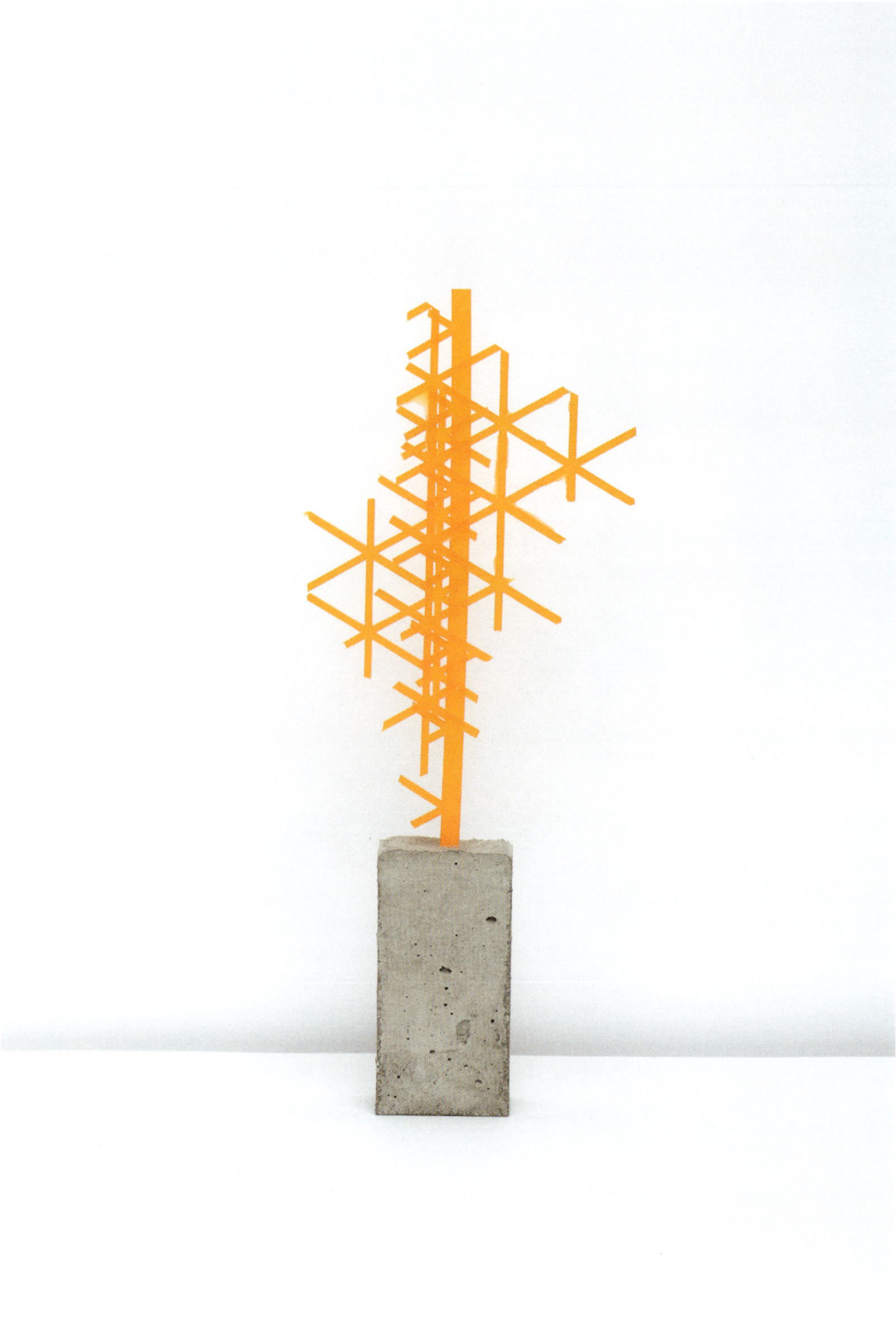

Neo-Neo-Concreto 16, 2019
Cast acrylic, concrete
41 x 16.5 x 5 cm

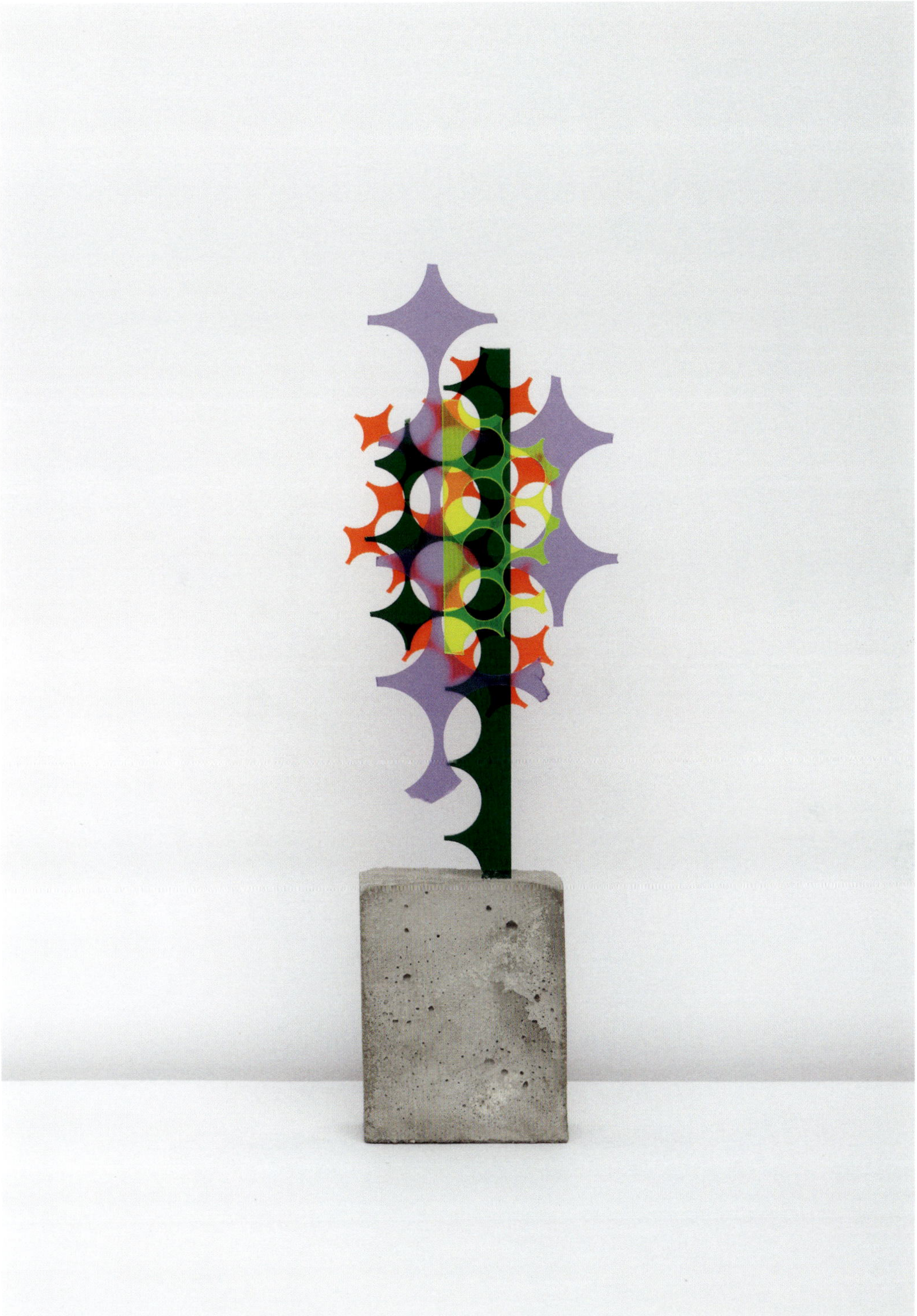

Neo-Neo-Concreto 06, 2019
Cast acrylic, concrete
43.5 x 14.5 x 5 cm

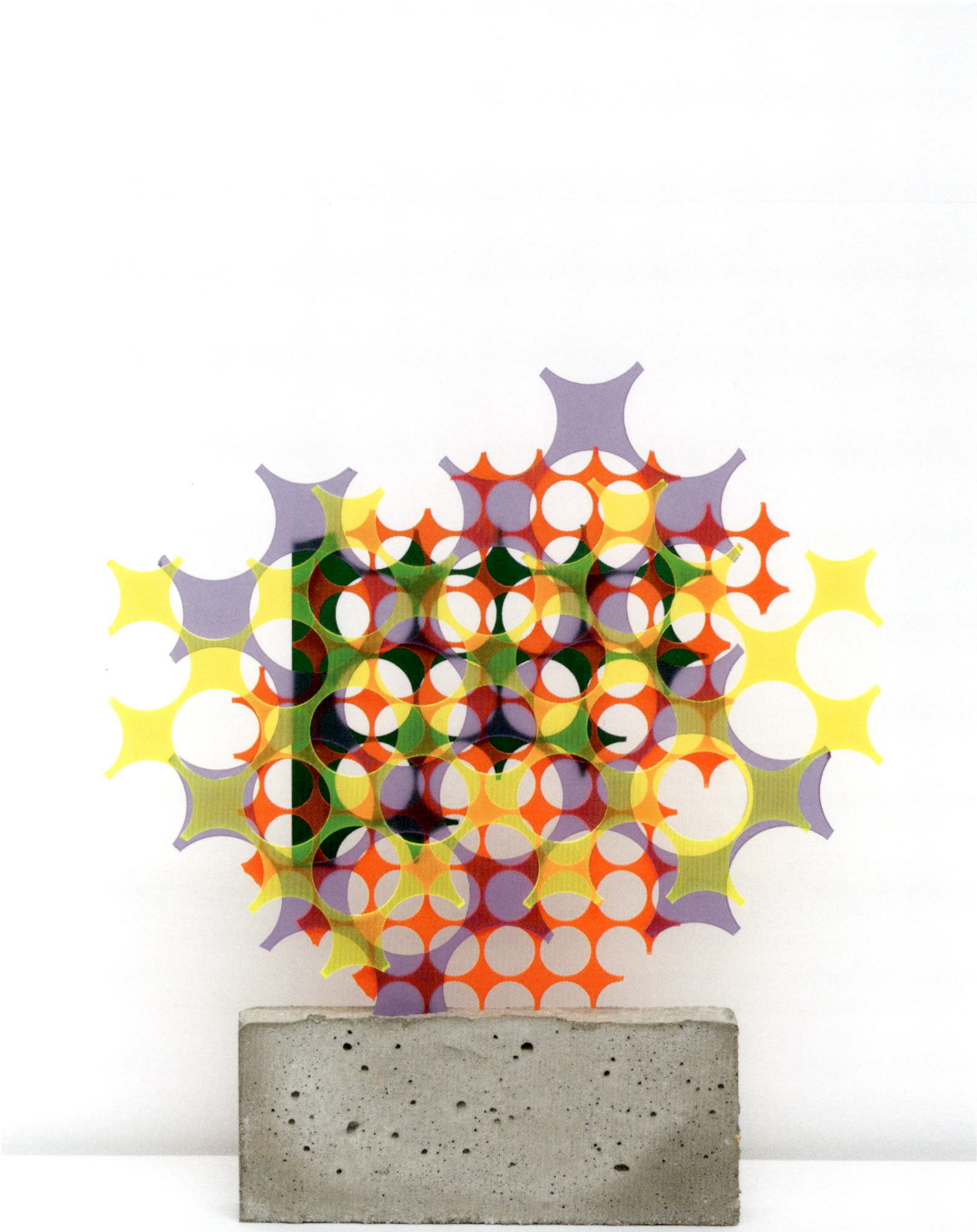

Neo-Neo-Concreto 09, 2019
Cast acrylic, concrete
38.5 x 36 x 5 cm

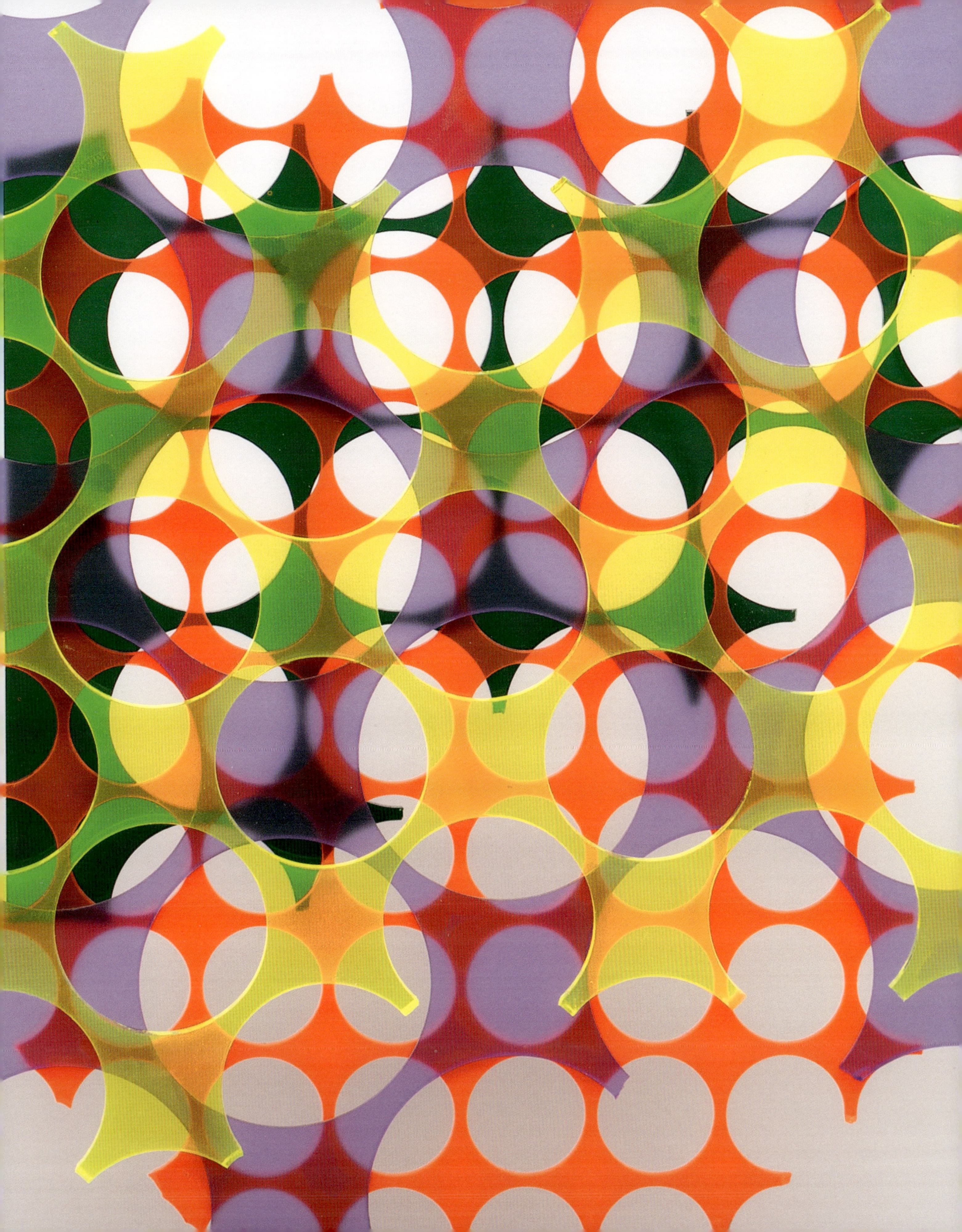

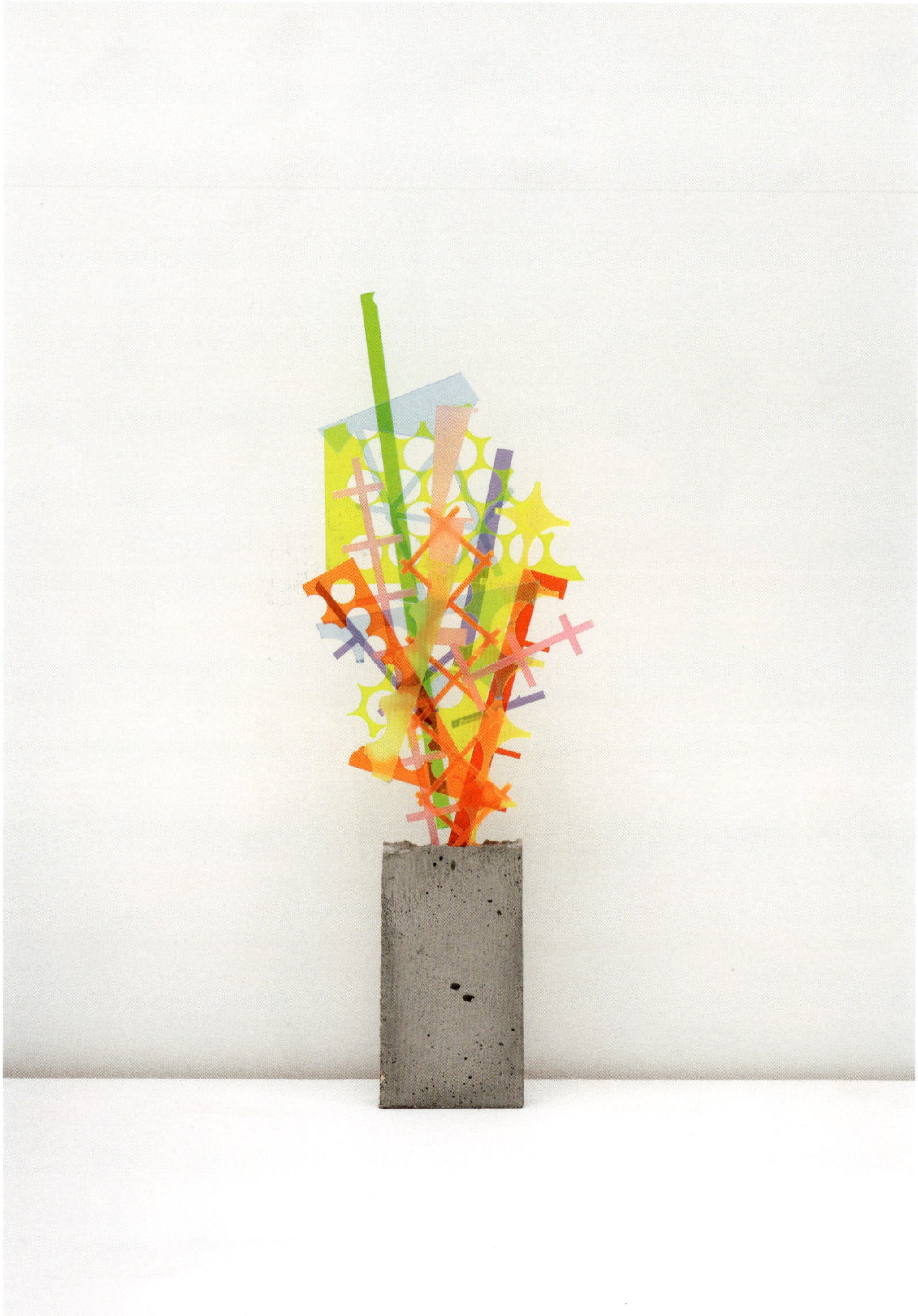

Neo-Neo-Concreto 33, 2020
Cast acrylic, concrete
50.5 x 18 x 5 cm

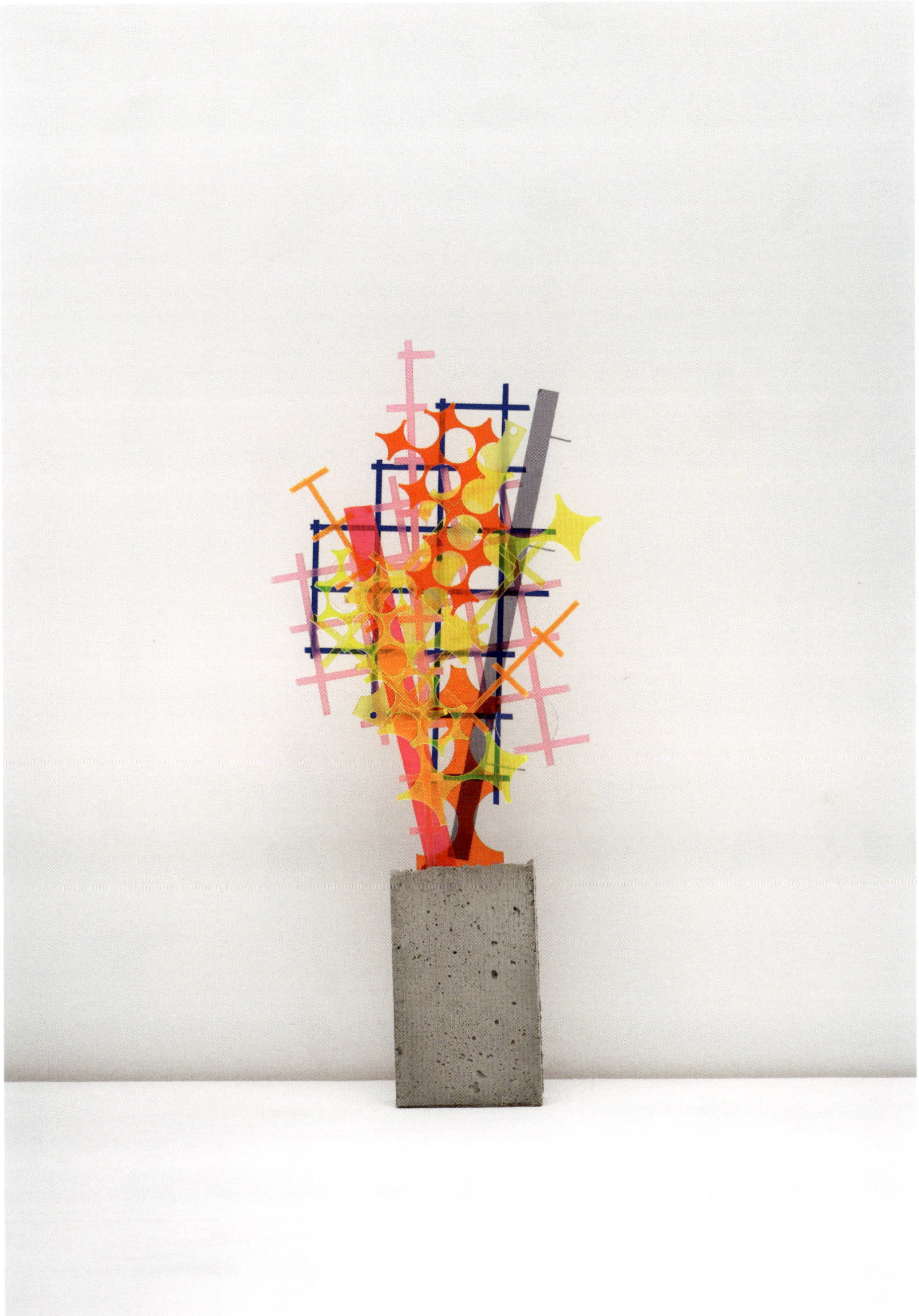

Neo-Neo-Concreto 34, 2020
Cast acrylic, concrete
49.5 x 21.5 x 5 cm

Cons
Neo-Cons
Alt-Cons
Geo-Cons
Neo-Neo-Cons
I-Cons
Ex-Cons

2019 —

The *Inter-Concretos* are defined more by their size than the materials or forms they use. Each is between around 80 and 150 cm tall, and while some are fabricated from layers of transparent acrylic, others are made from materials found in the street or the studio.

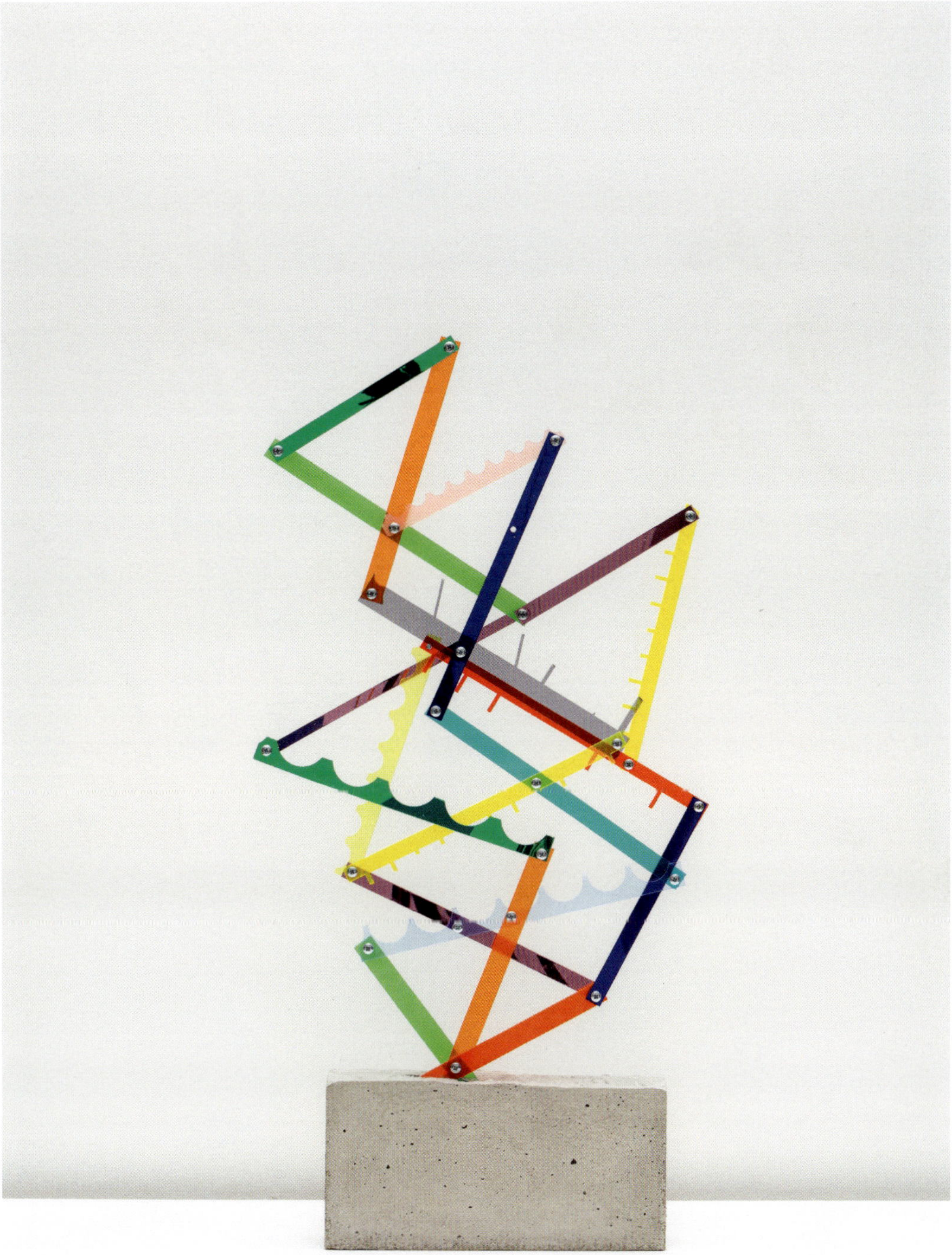

Inter-Concreto 02, 2019
Cast acrylic, concrete
81 x 41 x 6.5 cm

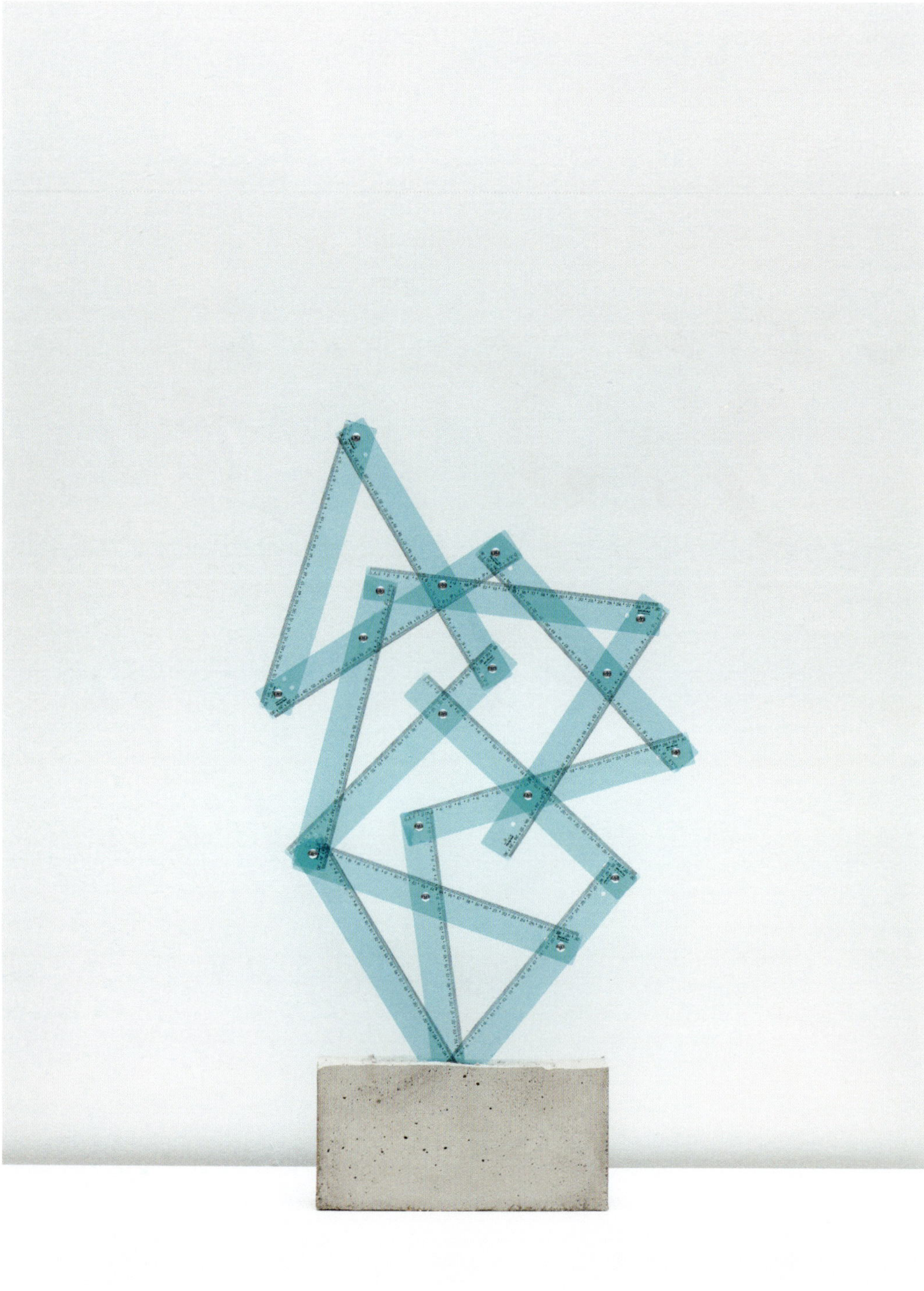

Inter-Concreto 01, 2019
Plastic rulers, concrete
81.5 x 46 x 6 cm

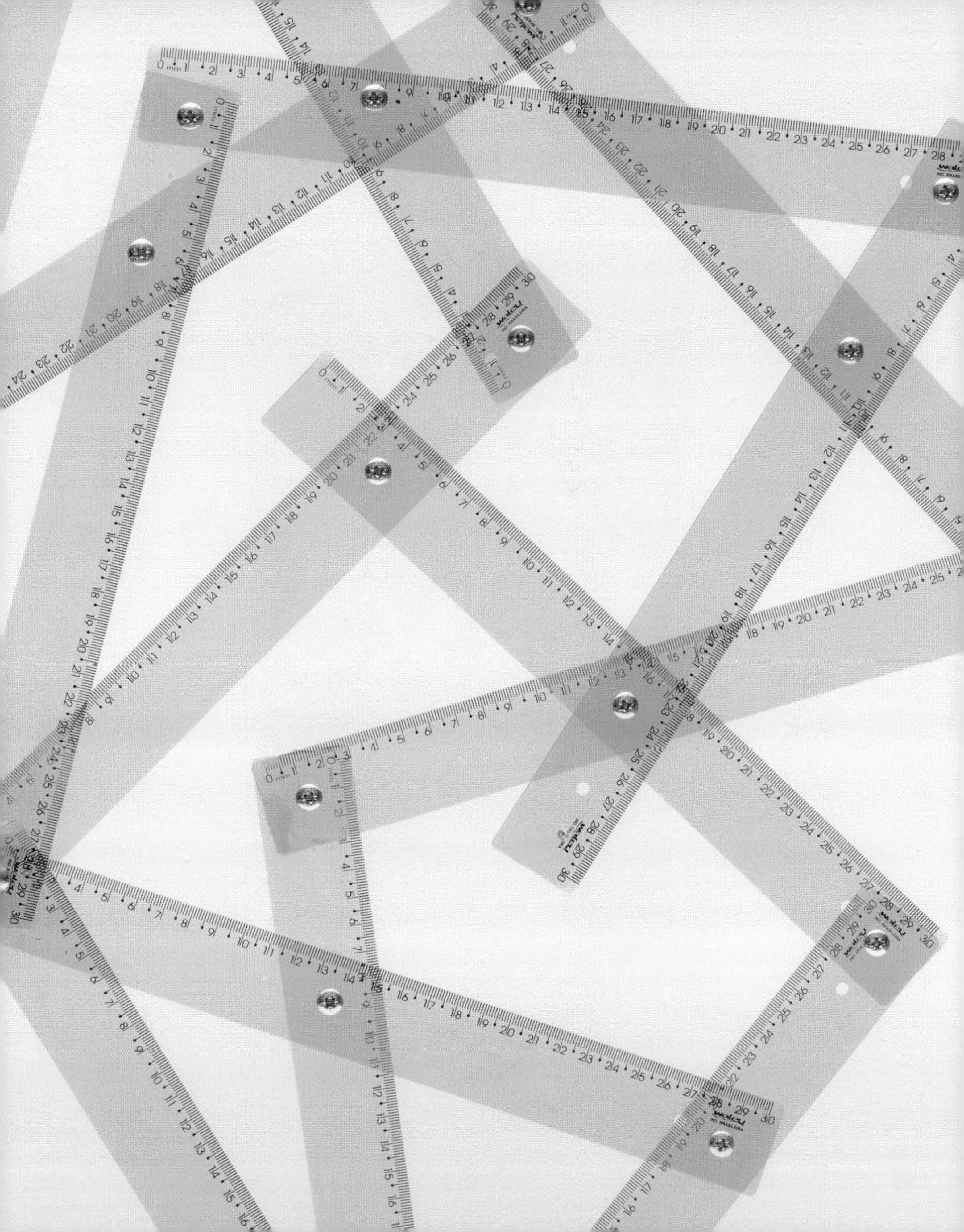

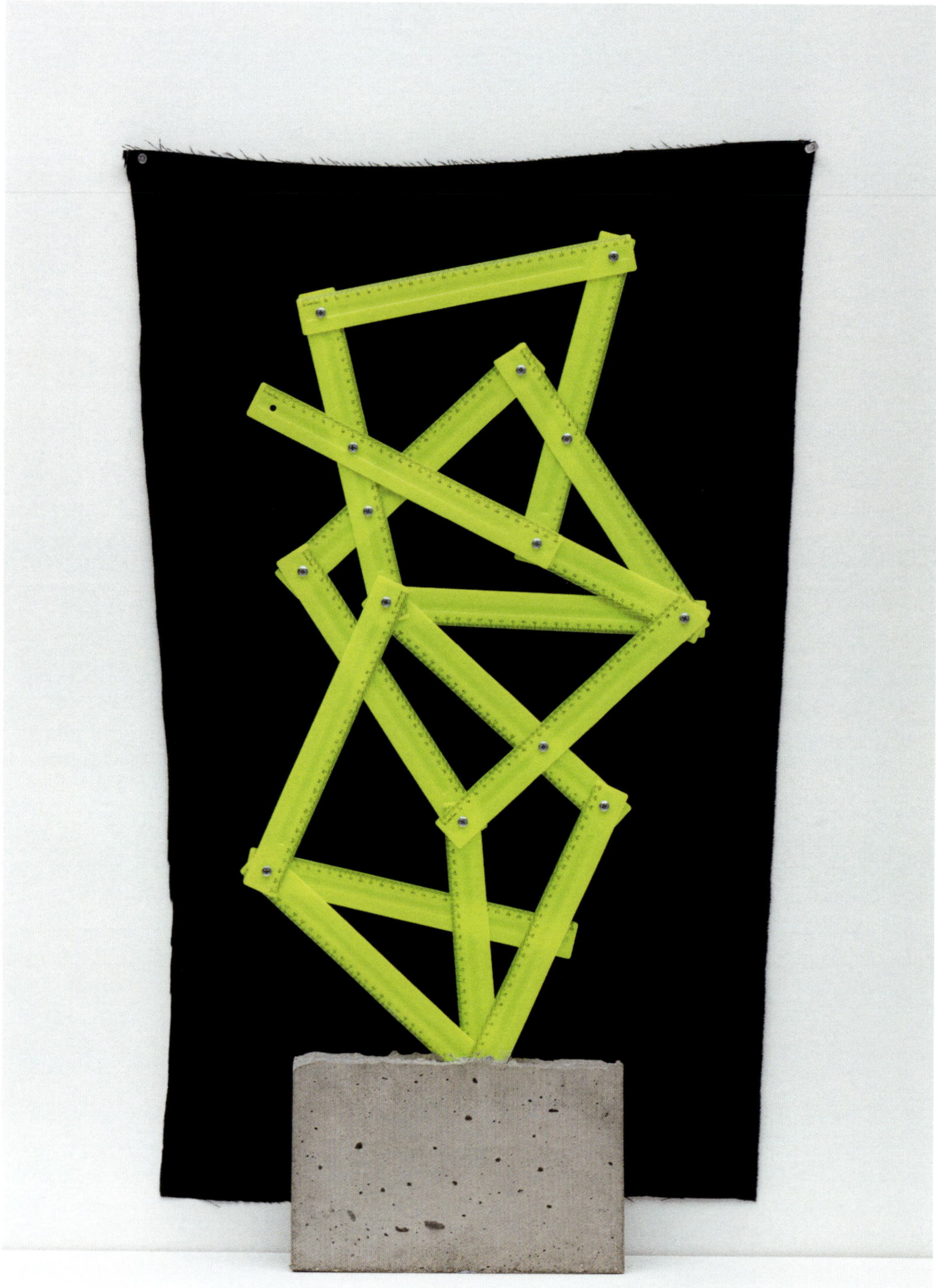

Inter-Concreto 03, 2022
Plastic rulers, fabric, concrete
107 x 58 x 11 cm

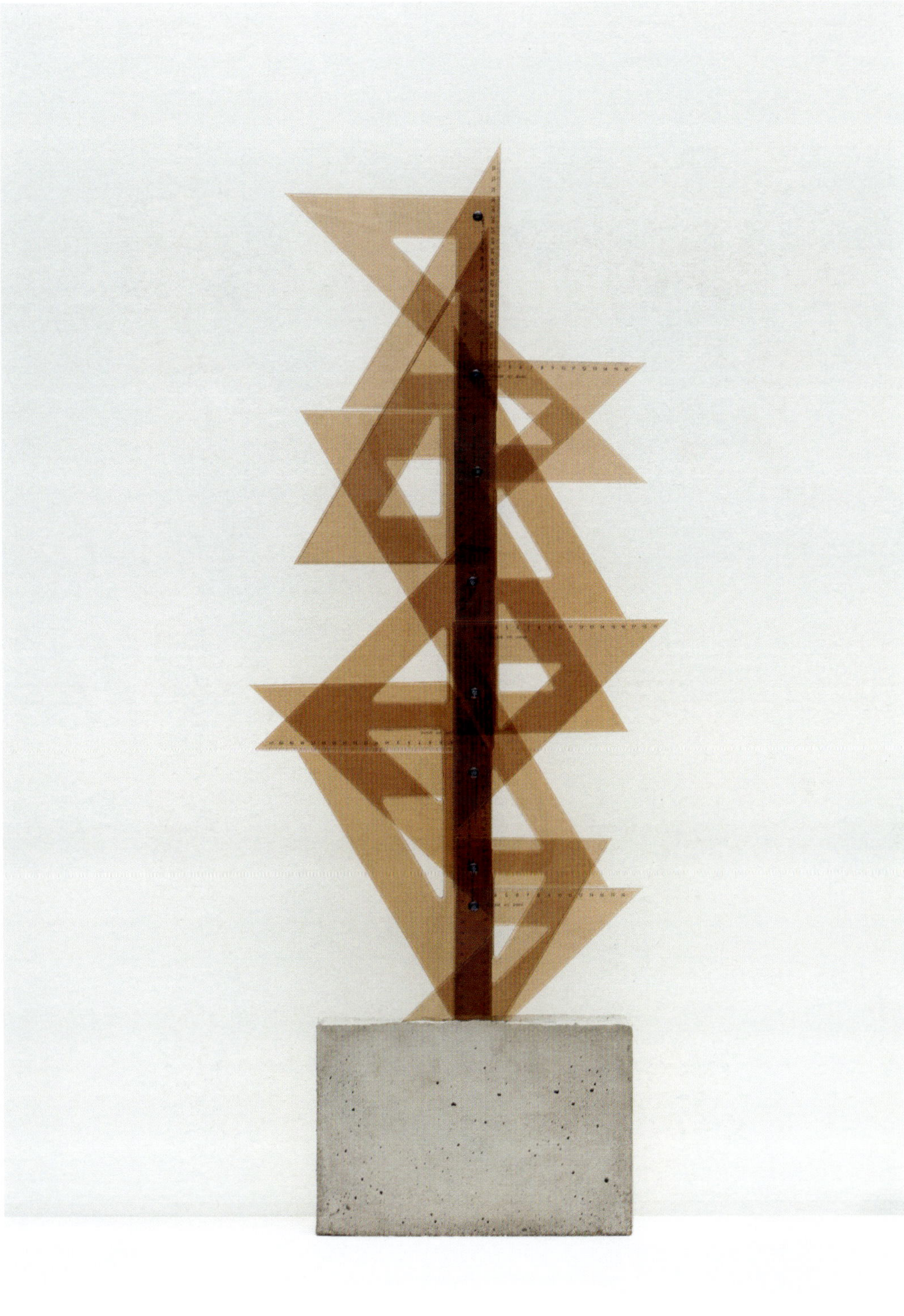

Inter-Concreto 05, 2019
Plastic set squares, concrete
103 x 39.5 x 6 cm

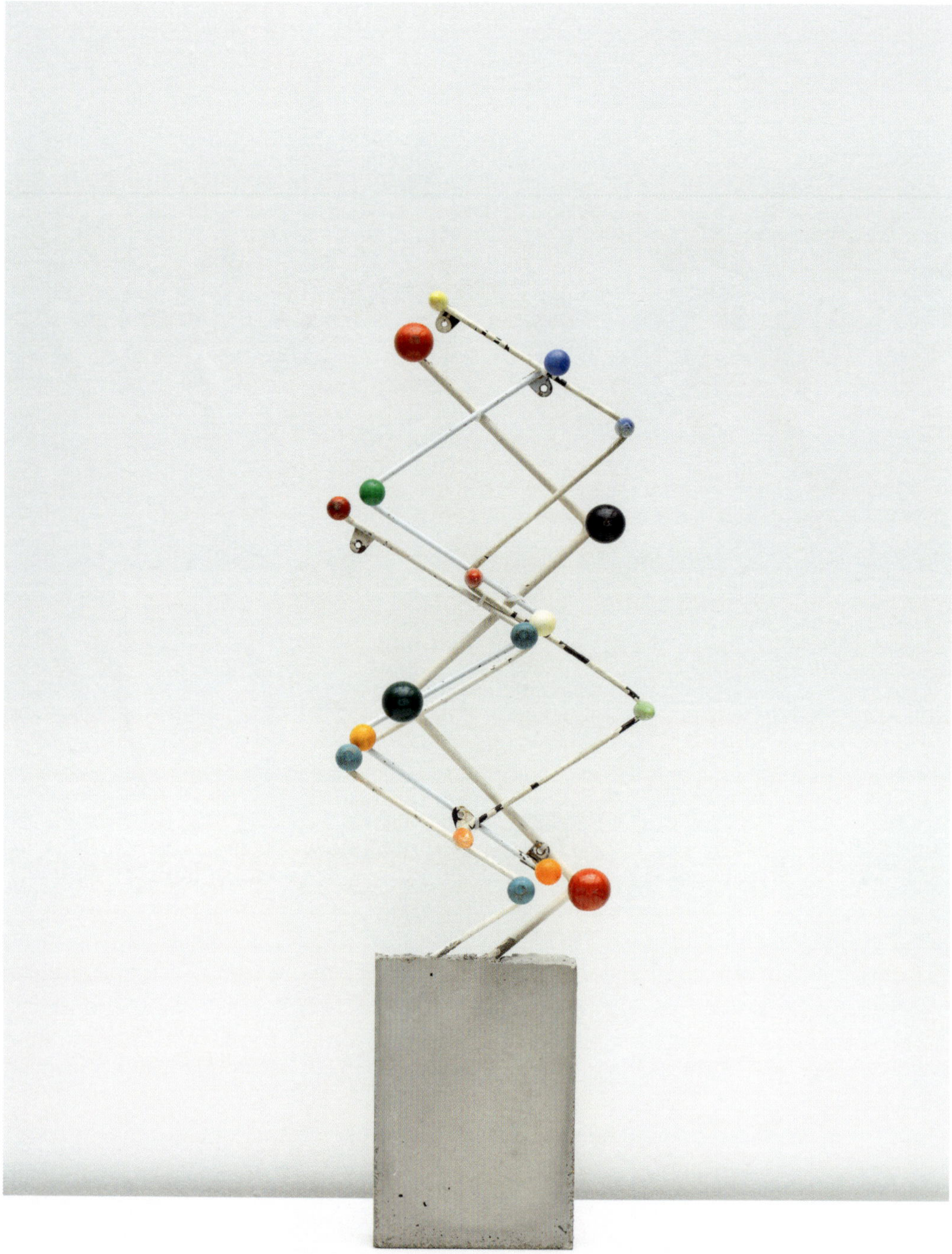

Inter-Concreto 06, 2019
Steel coat hangers, paint, wood, plastic, concrete
86 x 29 x 6 cm

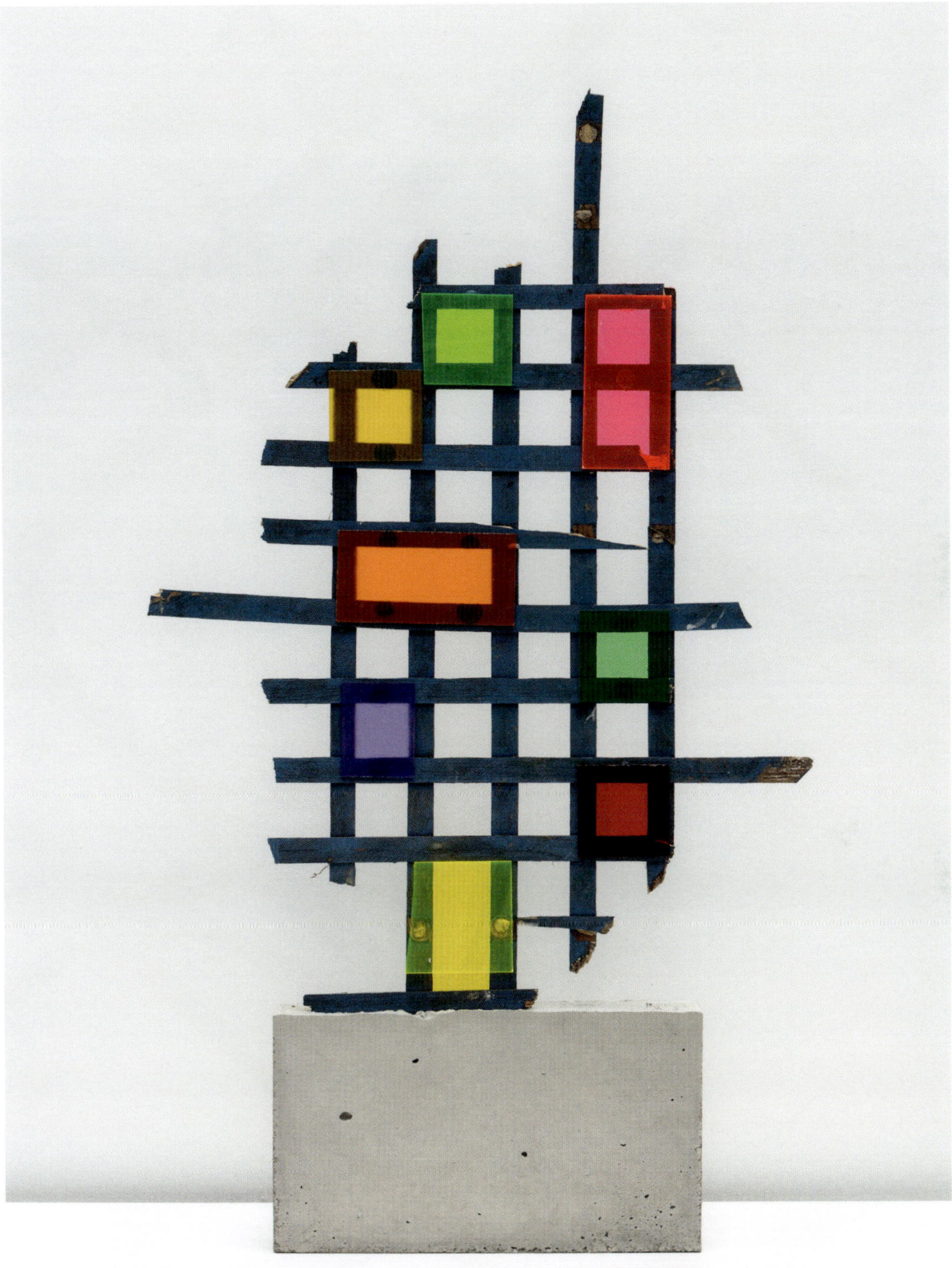

Inter-Concreto 08, 2019
Painted wooden trellis, cast acrylic, concrete
105 x 61 x 6 cm

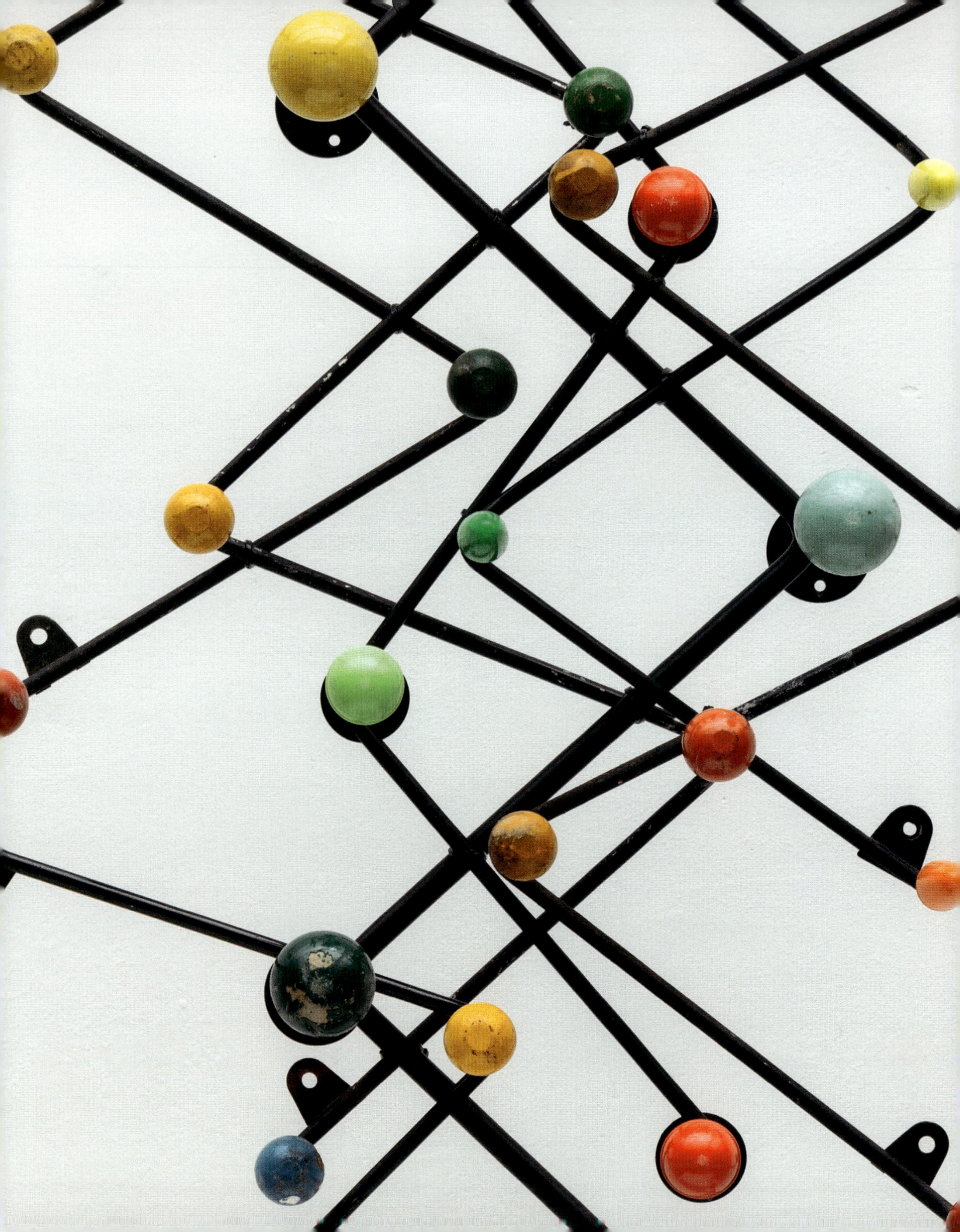

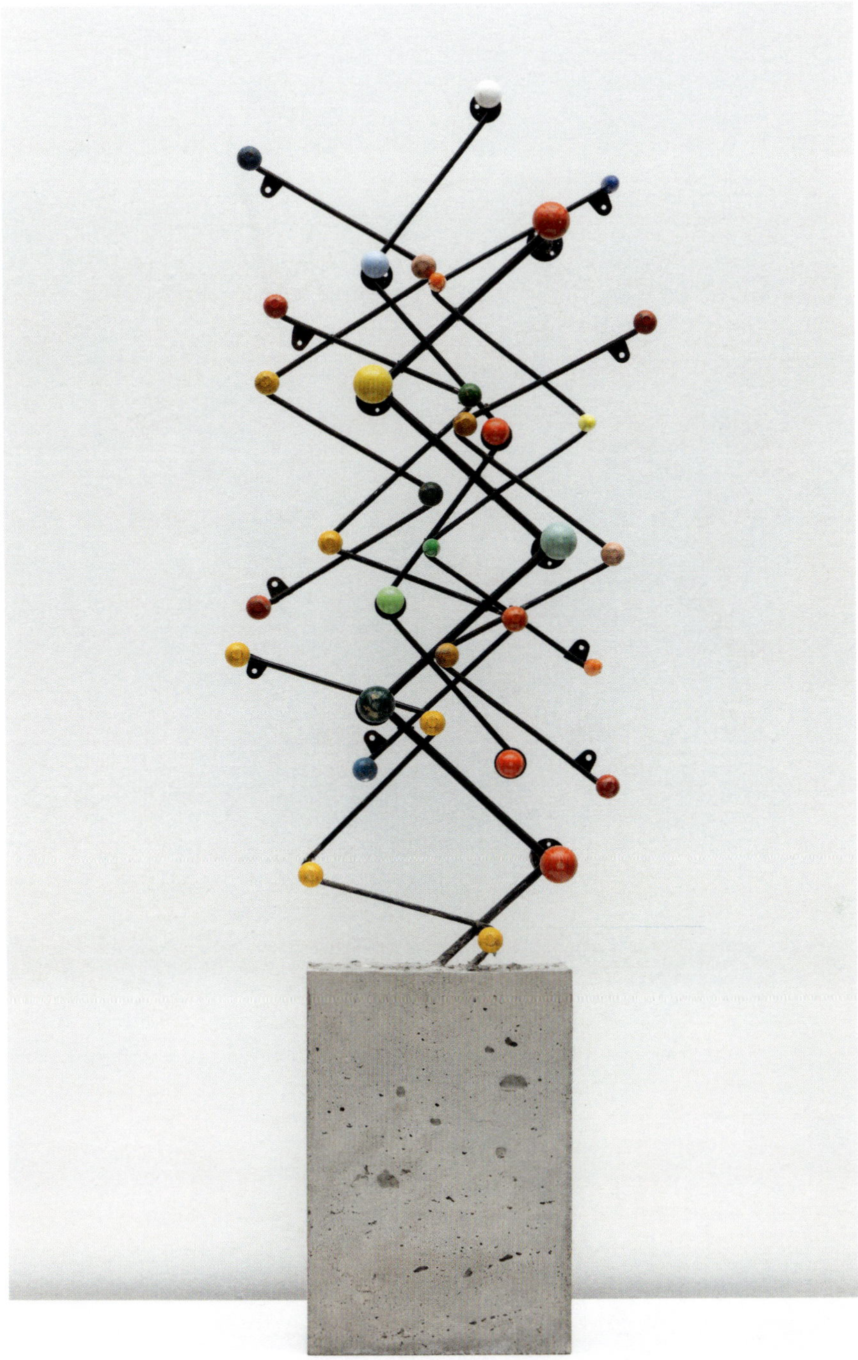

Inter-Concreto 10, 2019
Steel coat hangers, plastic, wood, concrete
125.5 x 43 x 11 cm

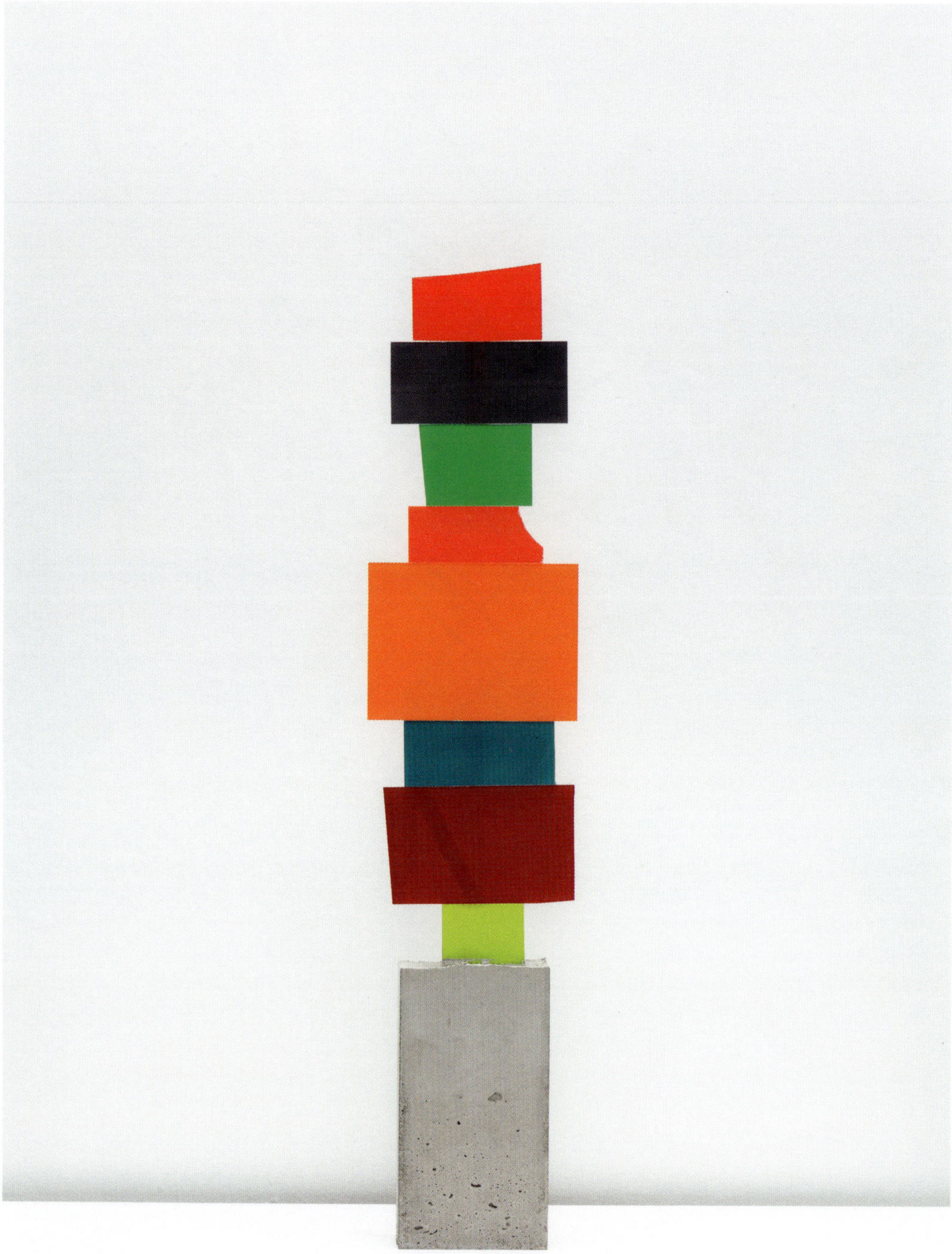

Inter-Concreto 14, 2019
Cast acrylic, concrete
99 x 21.3 x 6 cm

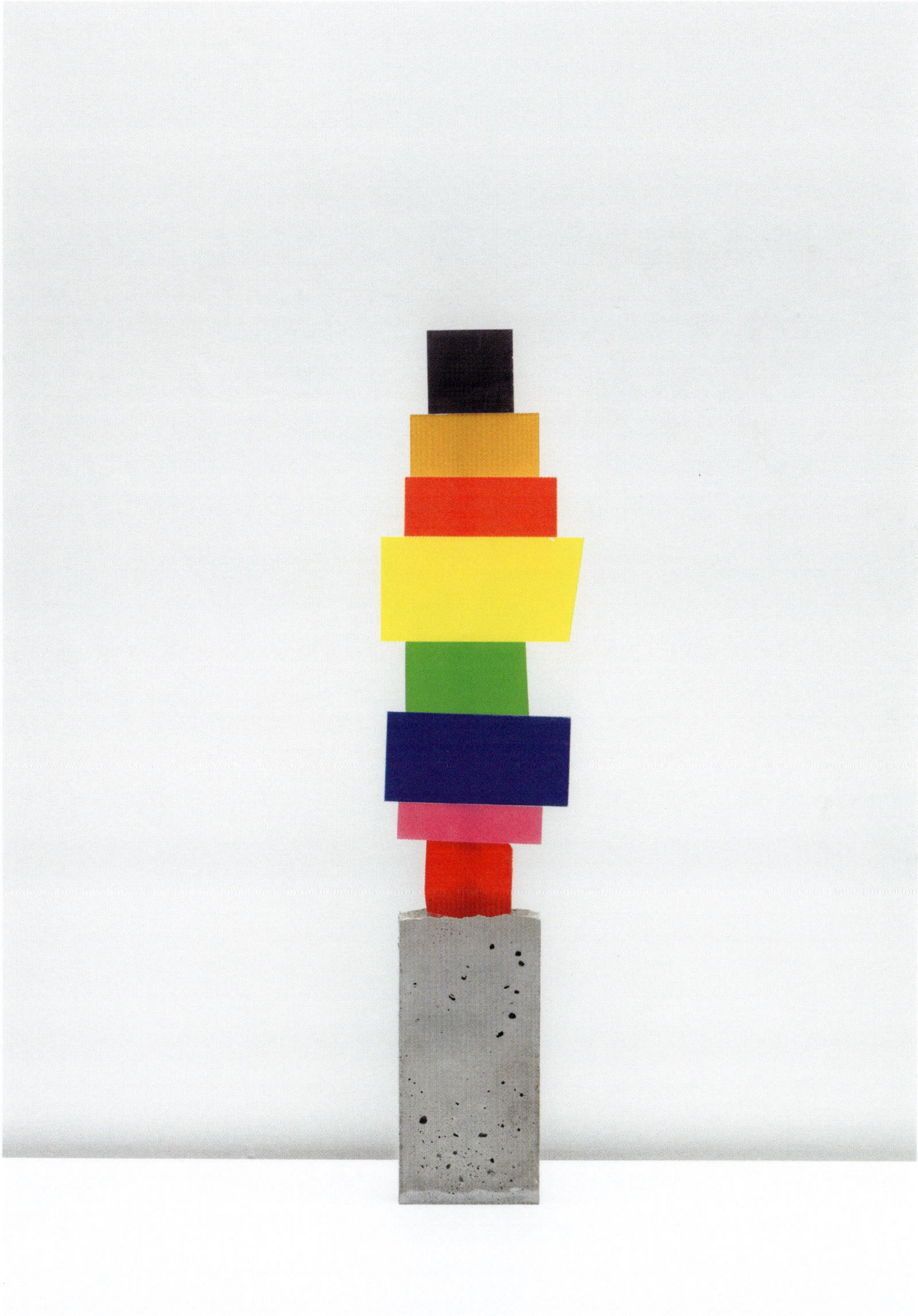

Inter-Concreto 15, 2019
Cast acrylic, concrete
84 x 19 x 6 cm

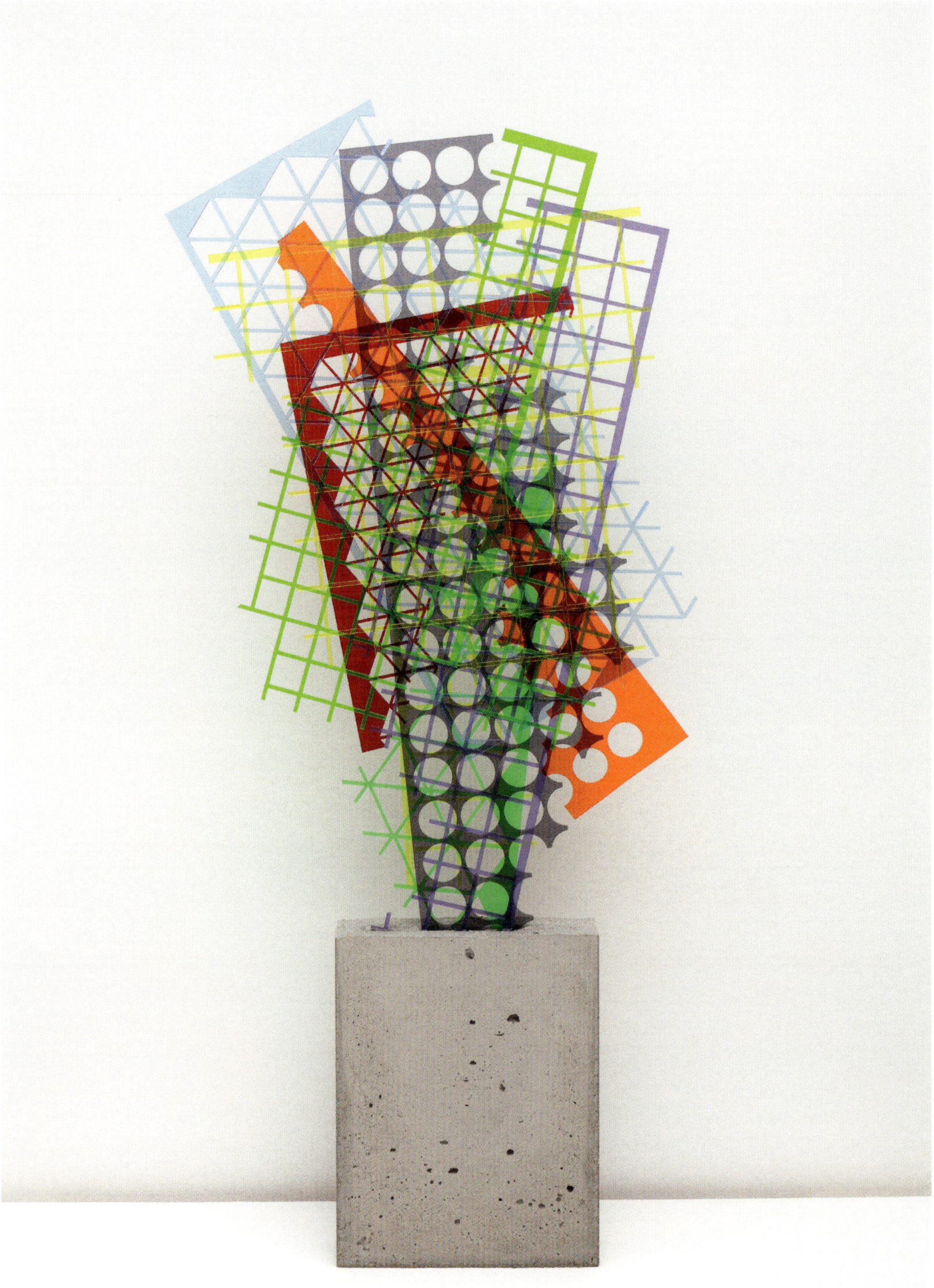

Inter-Concreto 16, 2020
Cast acrylic, concrete
135 x 57 x 10 cm

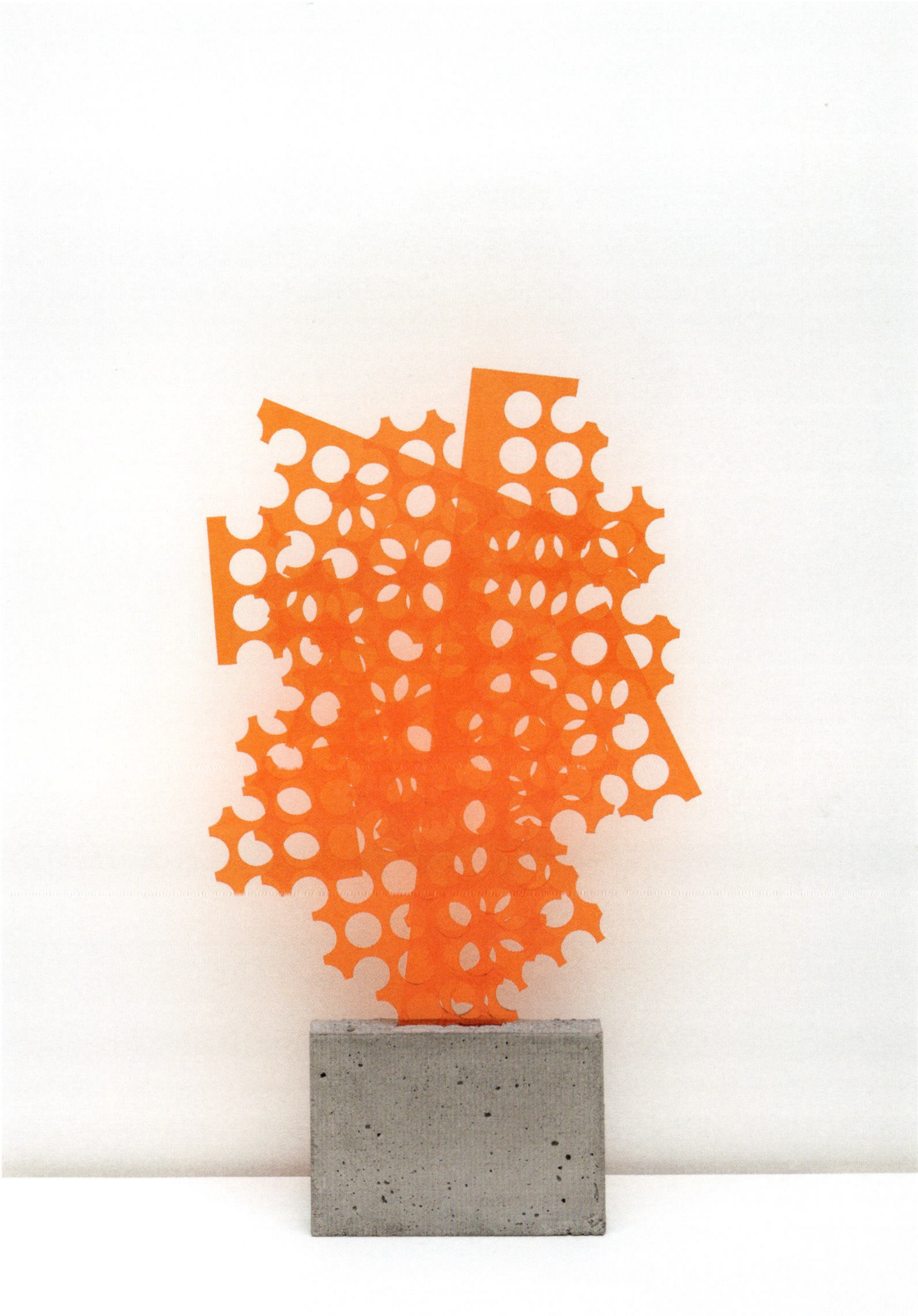

Inter-Concreto 18, 2020
Cast acrylic, concrete
90.5 x 50.5 x 9.5 cm

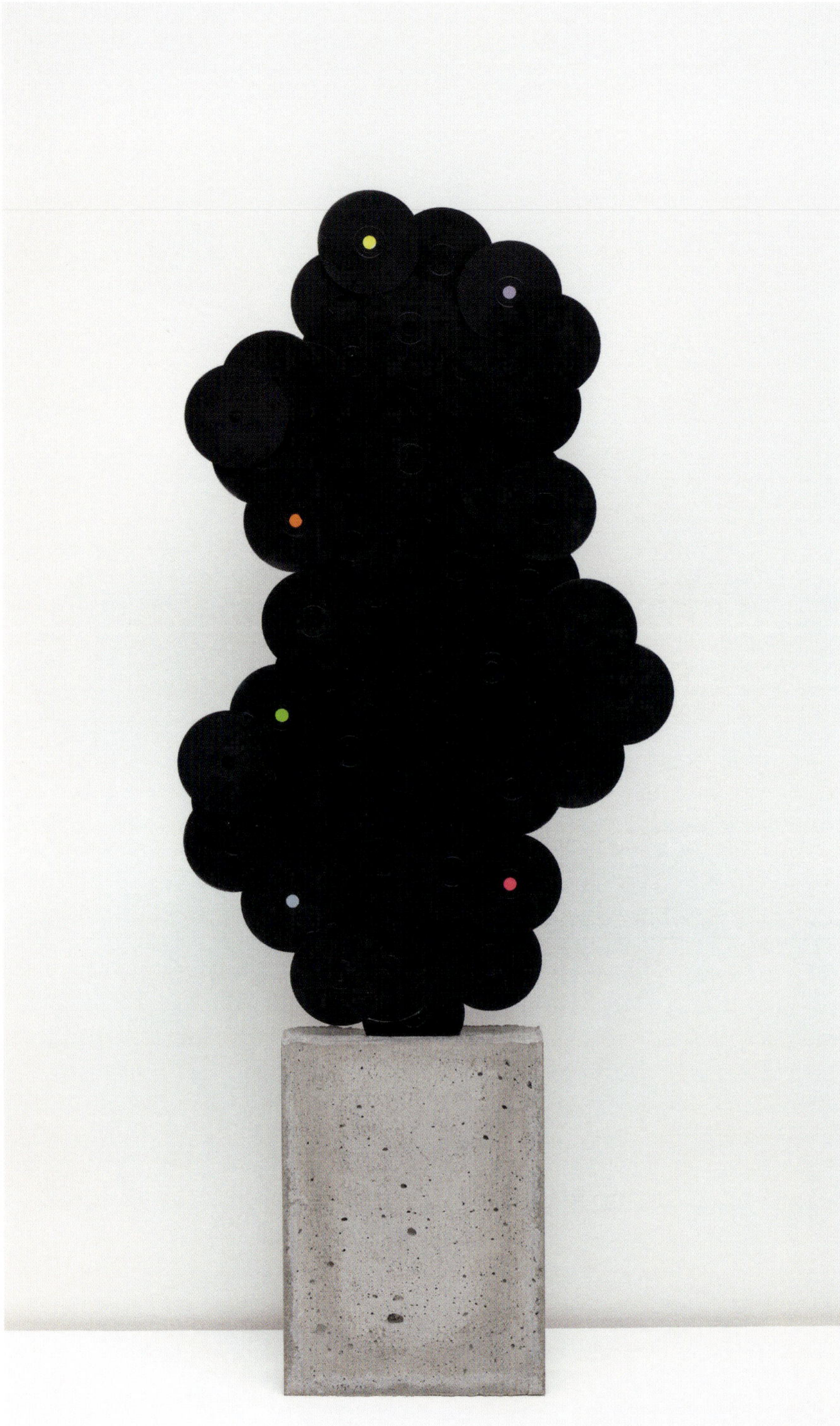

Inter-Concreto 19, 2020
CDs, spray paint, cast acrylic, concrete
139 x 58 x 9.5 cm

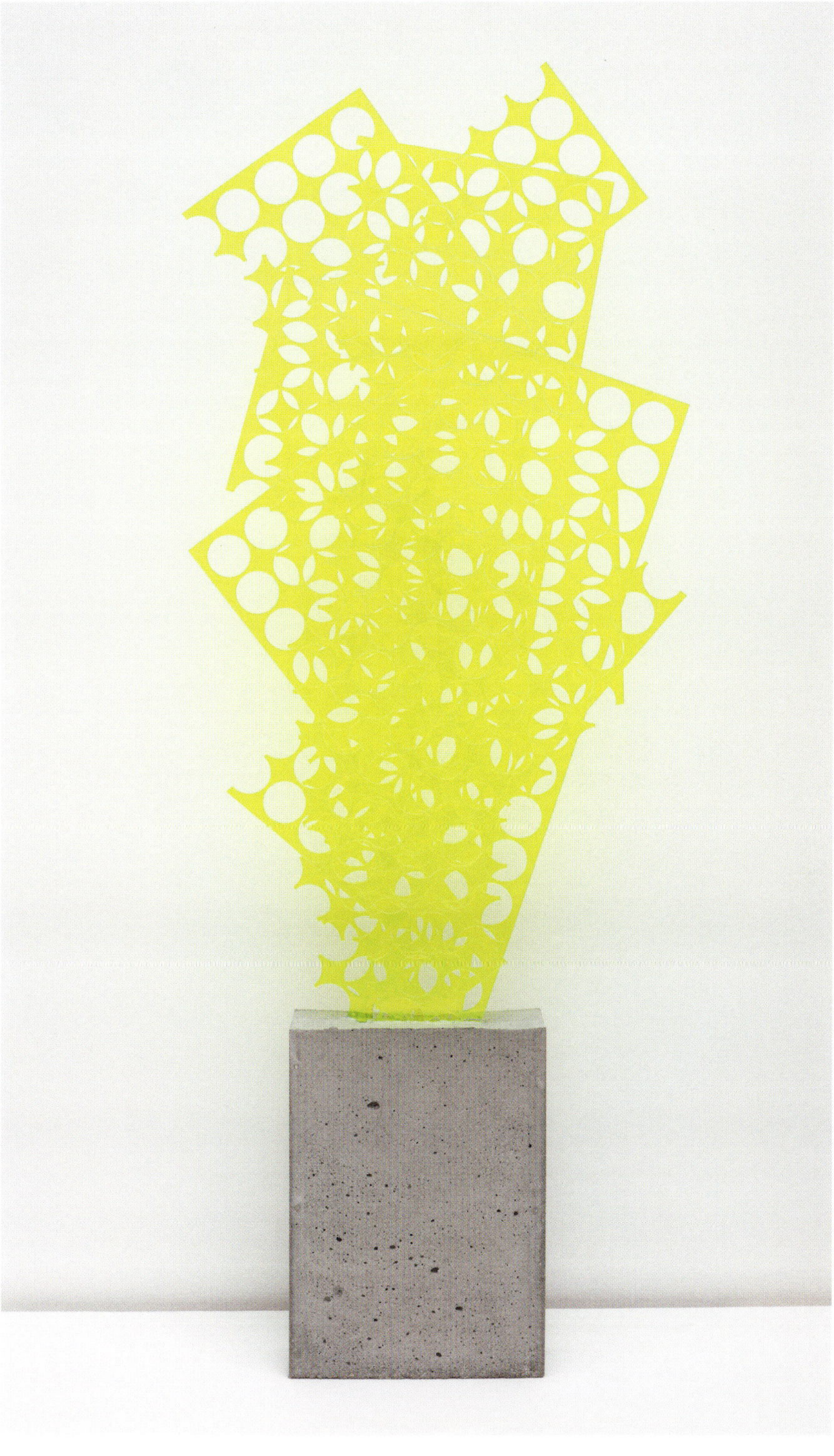

Inter-Concreto 20, 2020
Cast acrylic, concrete
157 x 60 x 10 cm

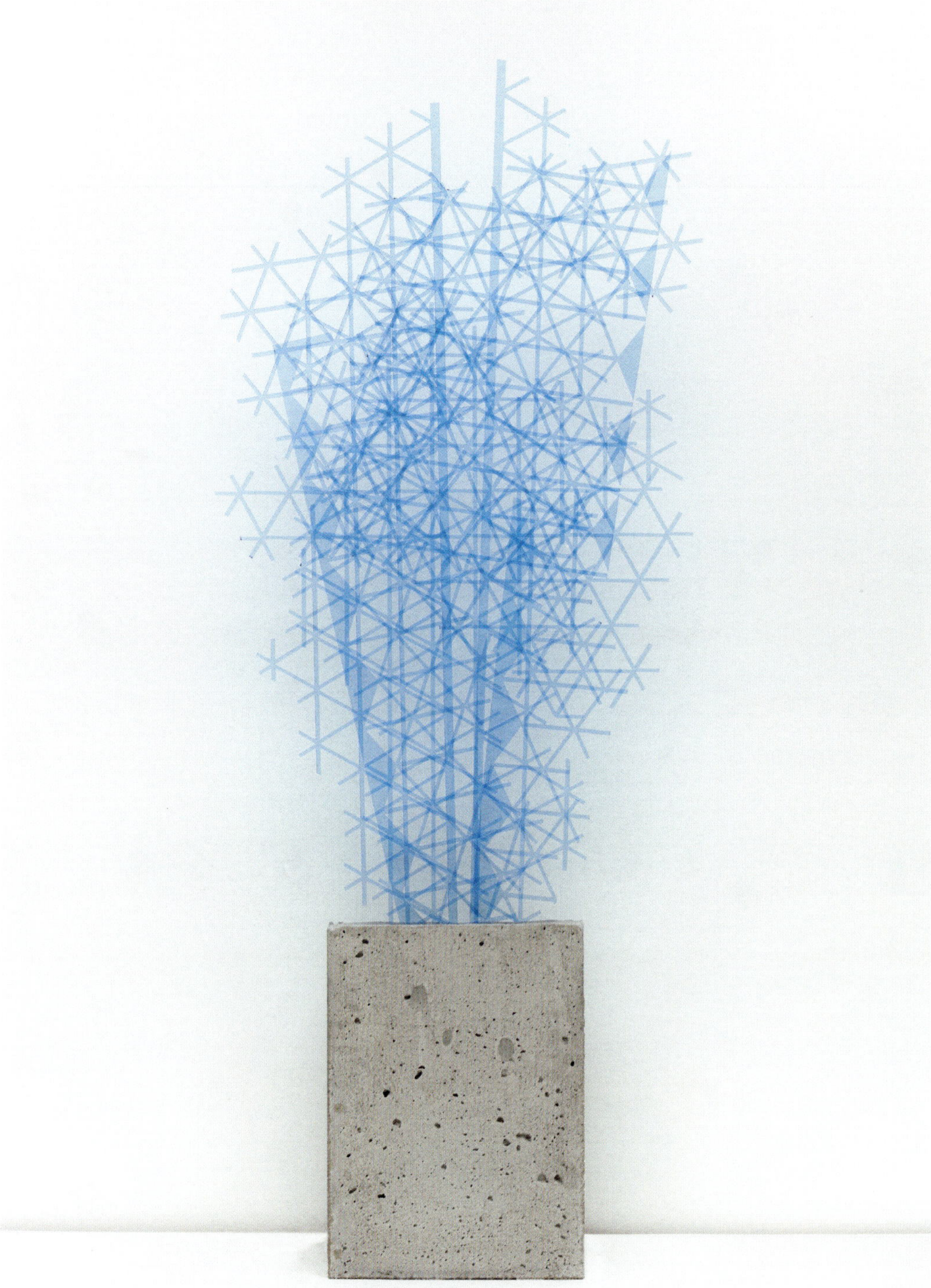

Inter-Concreto 26, 2020
Cast acrylic, concrete
136 x 56 x 10 cm

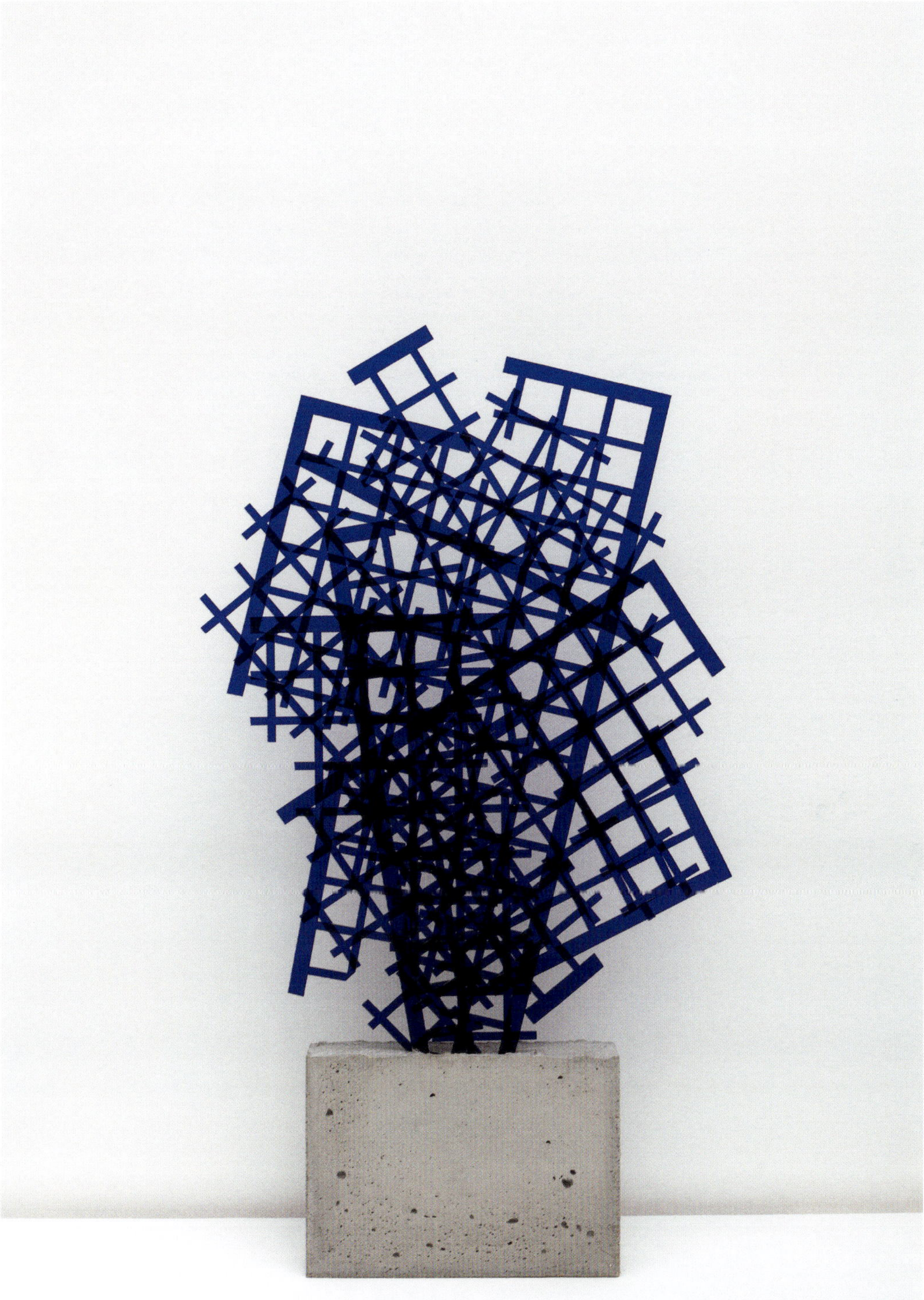

Inter-Concreto 23, 2020
Cast acrylic, concrete
114 x 65 x 8.5 cm

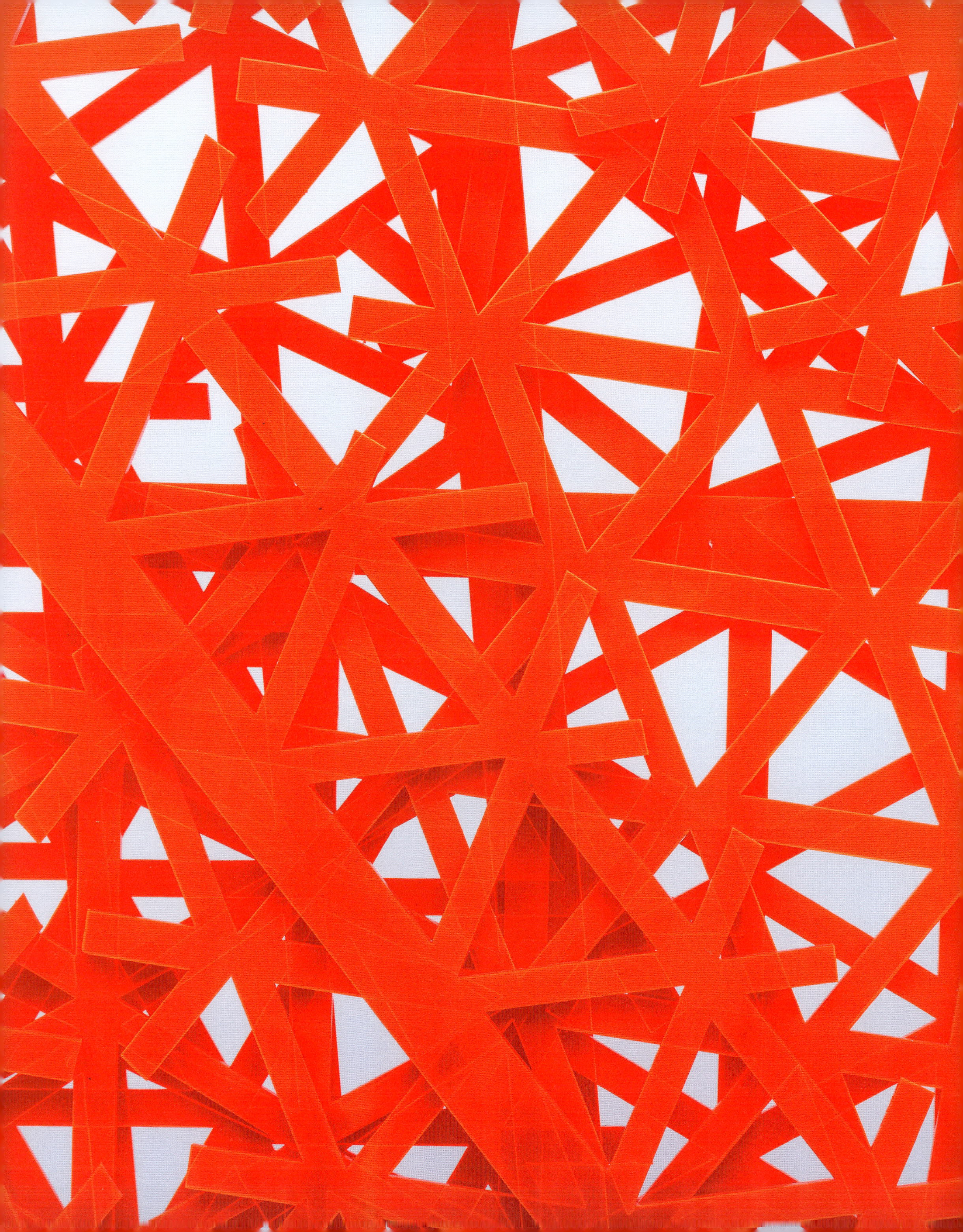

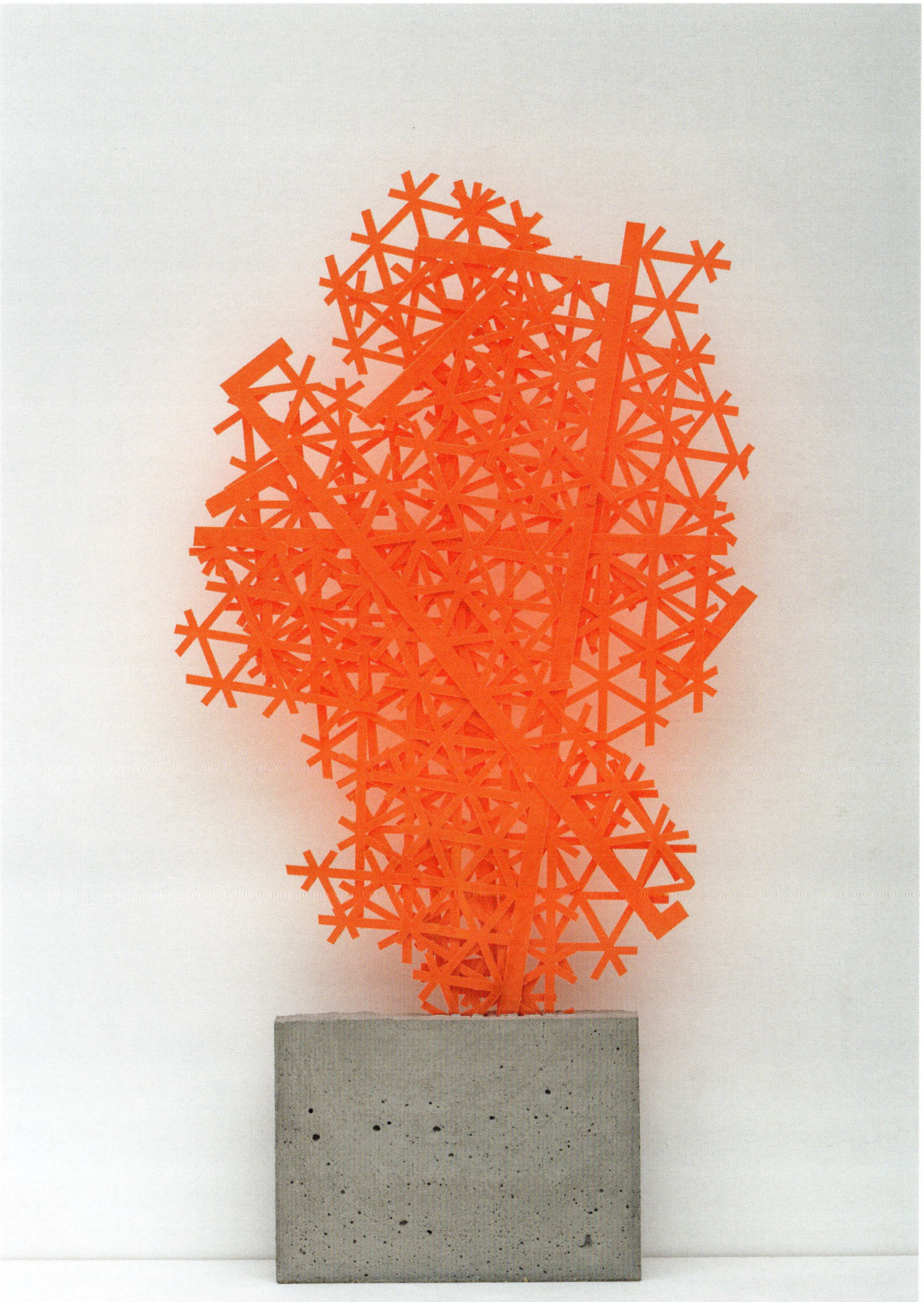

Inter-Concreto 24, 2020
Cast acrylic, concrete
114 x 60 x 10 cm

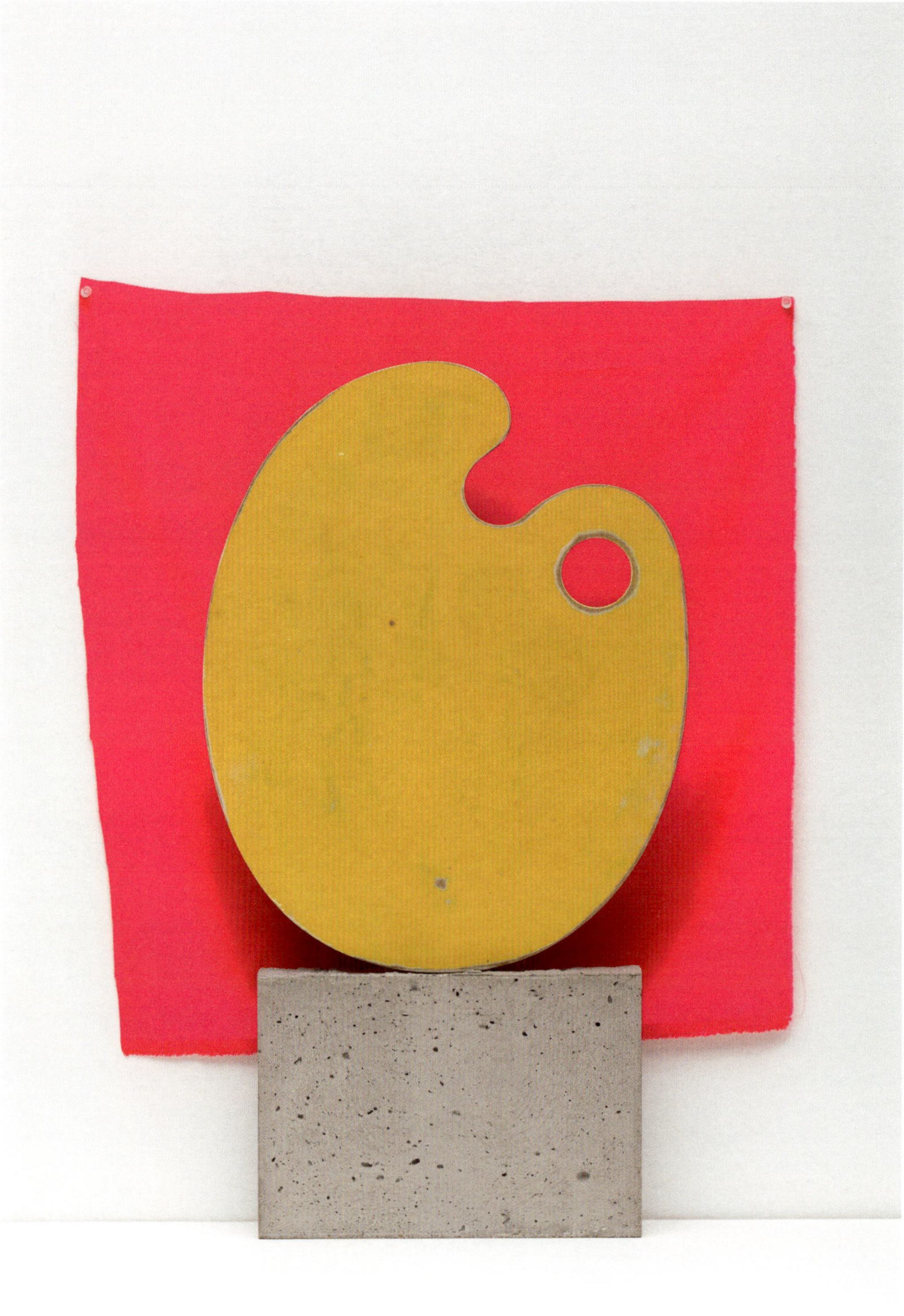

Inter-Concreto 28, 2020
Painted wooden palette, fabric, concrete
79 x 59 x 10 cm

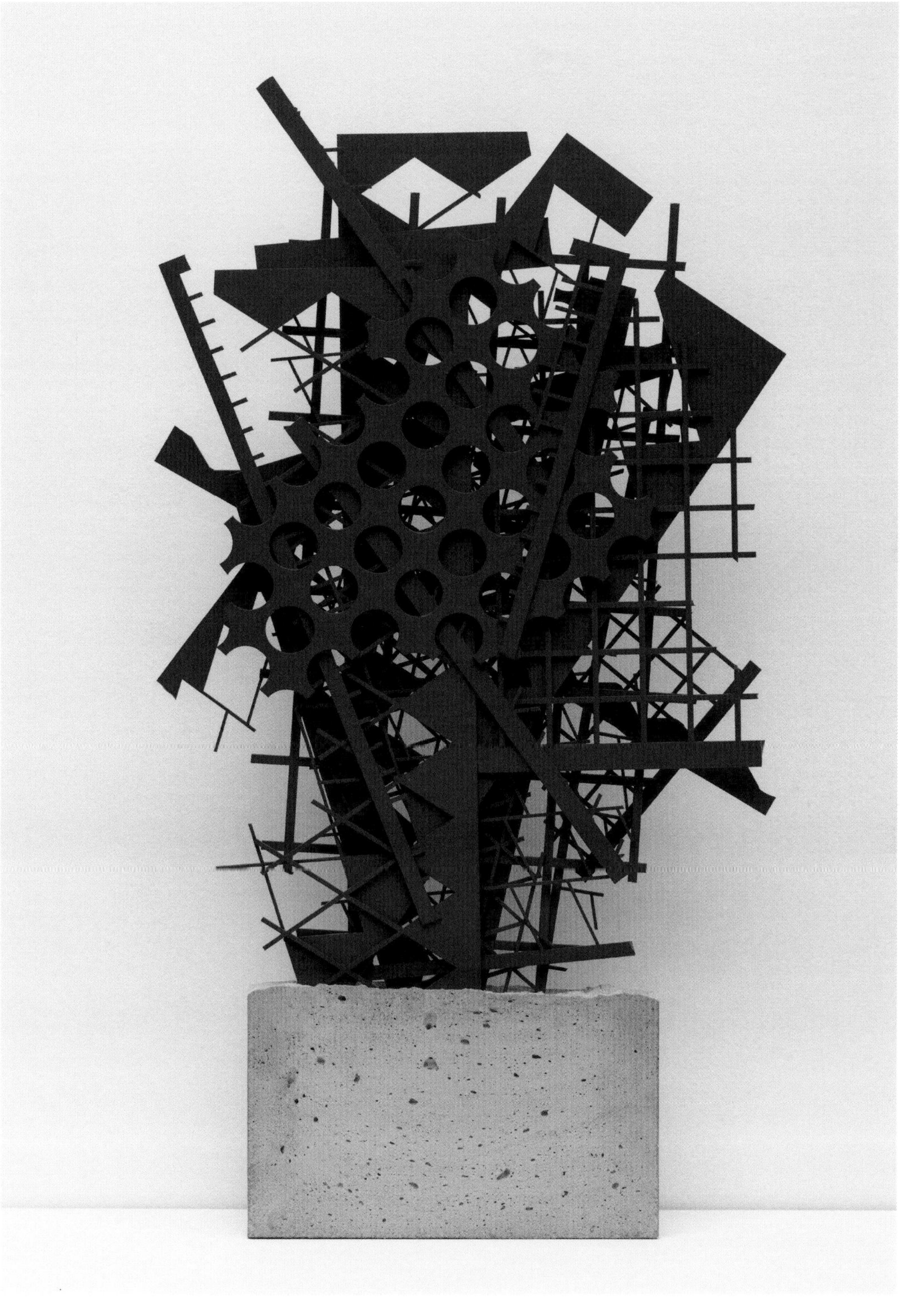

Inter-Concreto 30, 2022
Cast acrylic, spray paint, concrete
98 x 52 x 6.5 cm

Cons
Neo-Cons
Alt-Cons
Geo-Cons
Neo-Neo-Cons
I-Cons
Ex-Cons

2019 —

The *Extra-Concretos* are the largest and most recent of this series of works. They are all free-standing, floor-based works that range from about 150 to 300 cm tall.

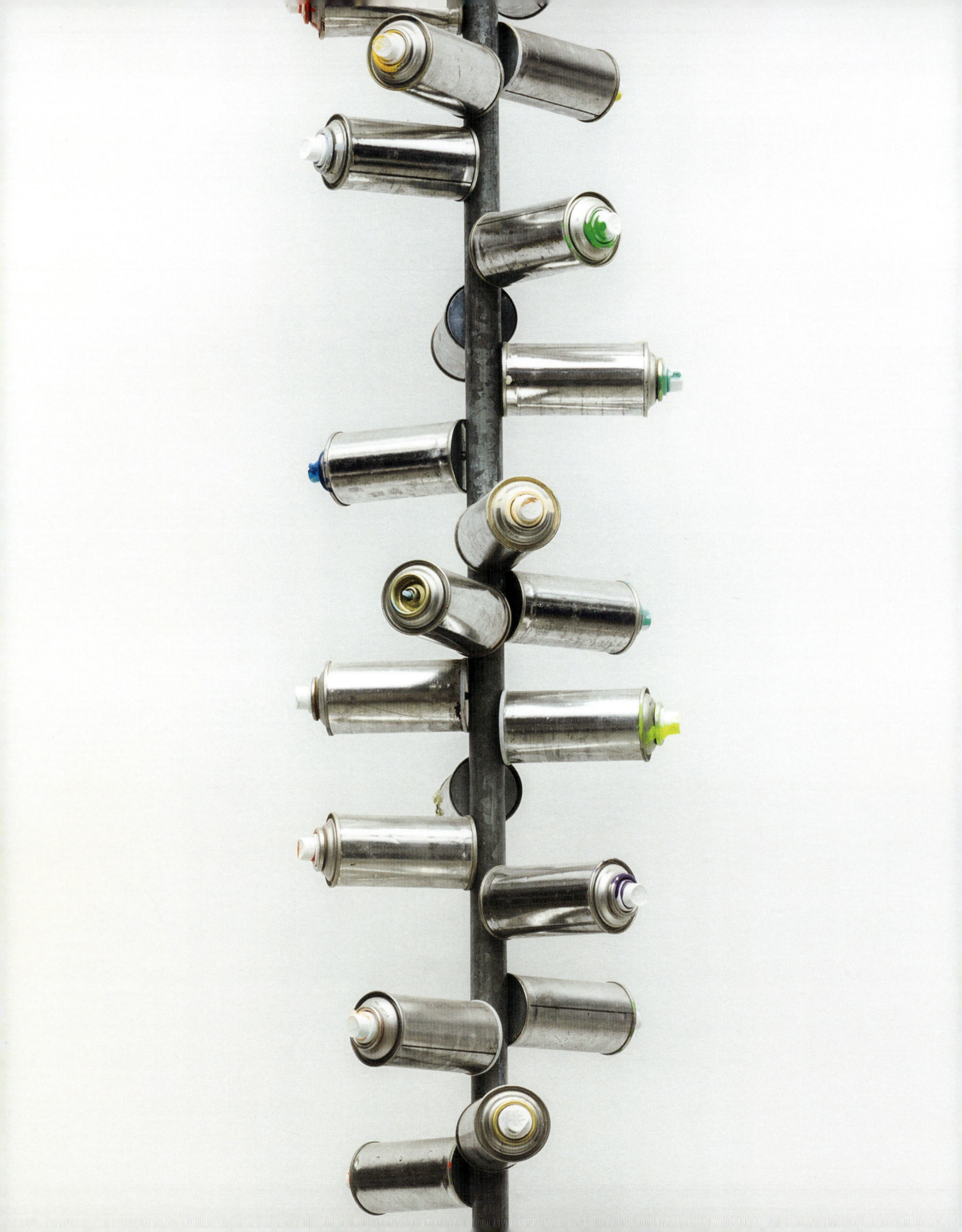

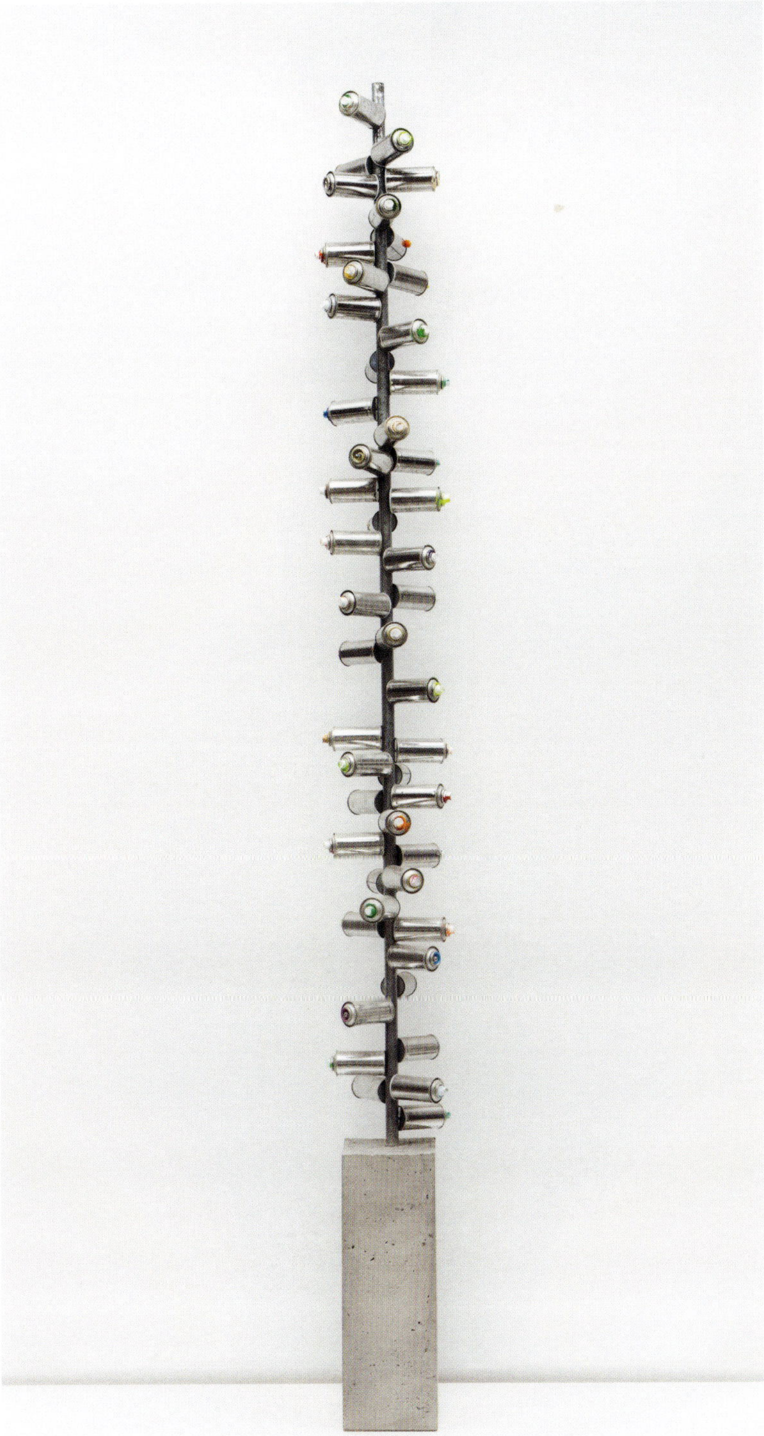

Extra-Concreto 01, 2019
Spray paint cans, spray paint, steel, concrete
290 x 19 x 19 cm

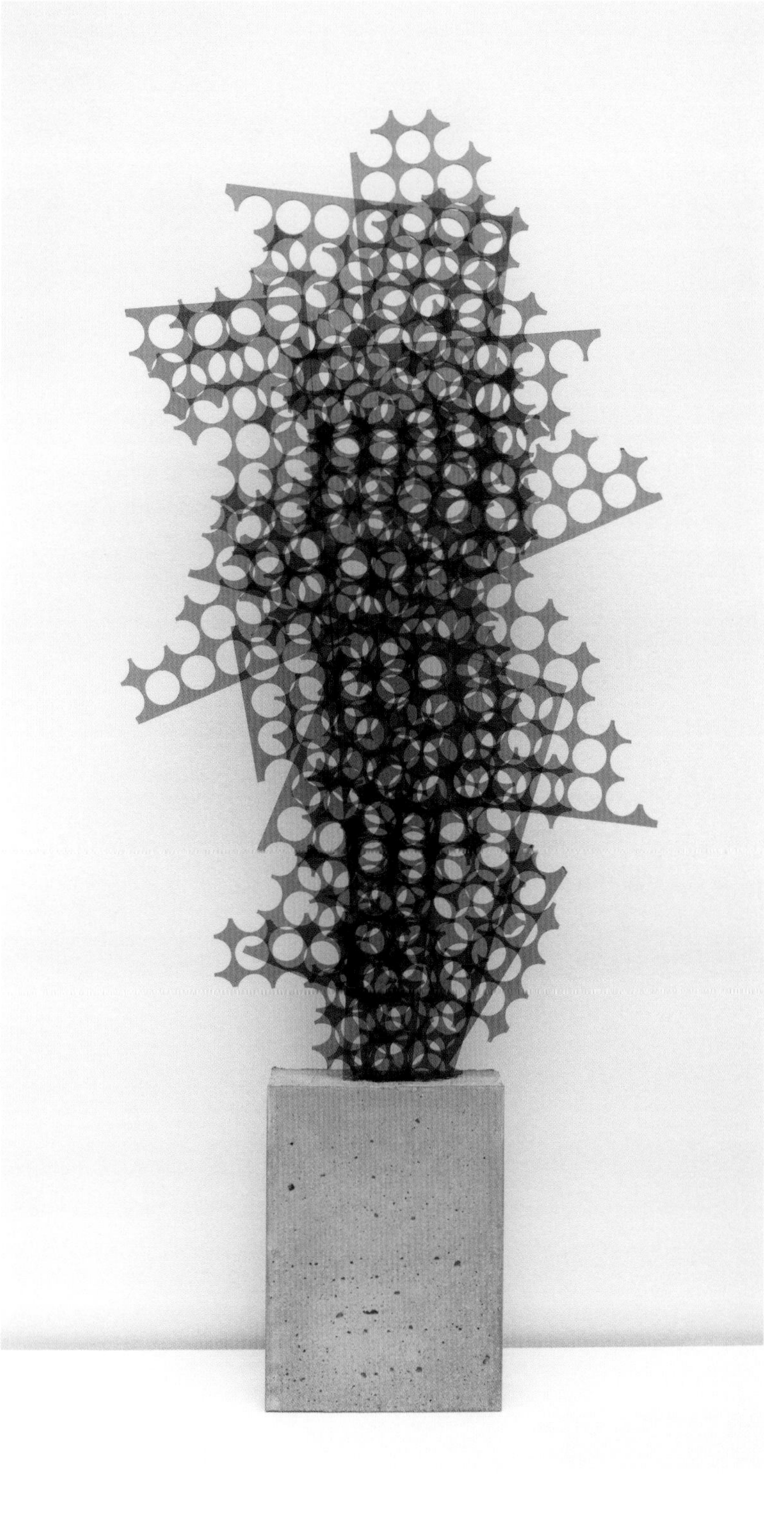

Extra-Concreto 02, 2020
Cast acrylic, concrete
167 x 76 x 10 cm

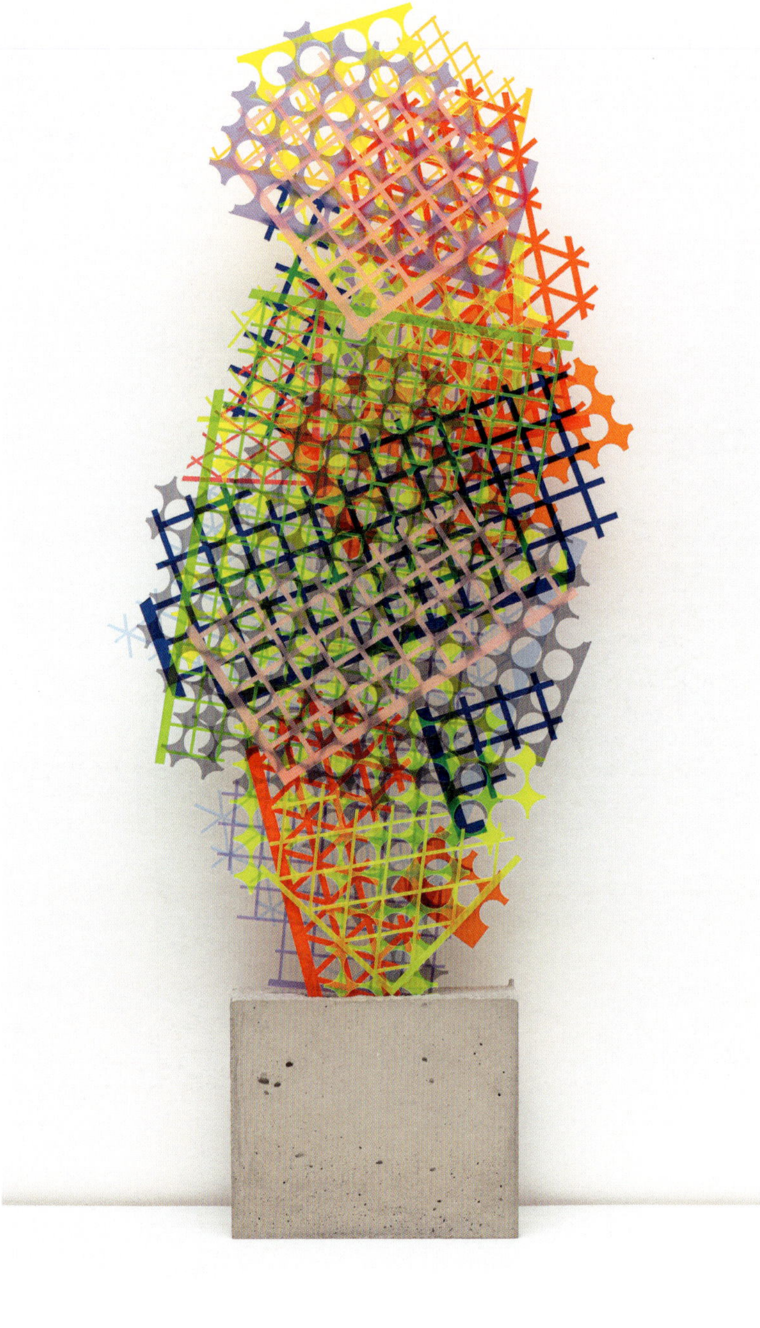

Extra-Concreto 03, 2020
Cast acrylic, concrete
181 x 79 x 13 cm

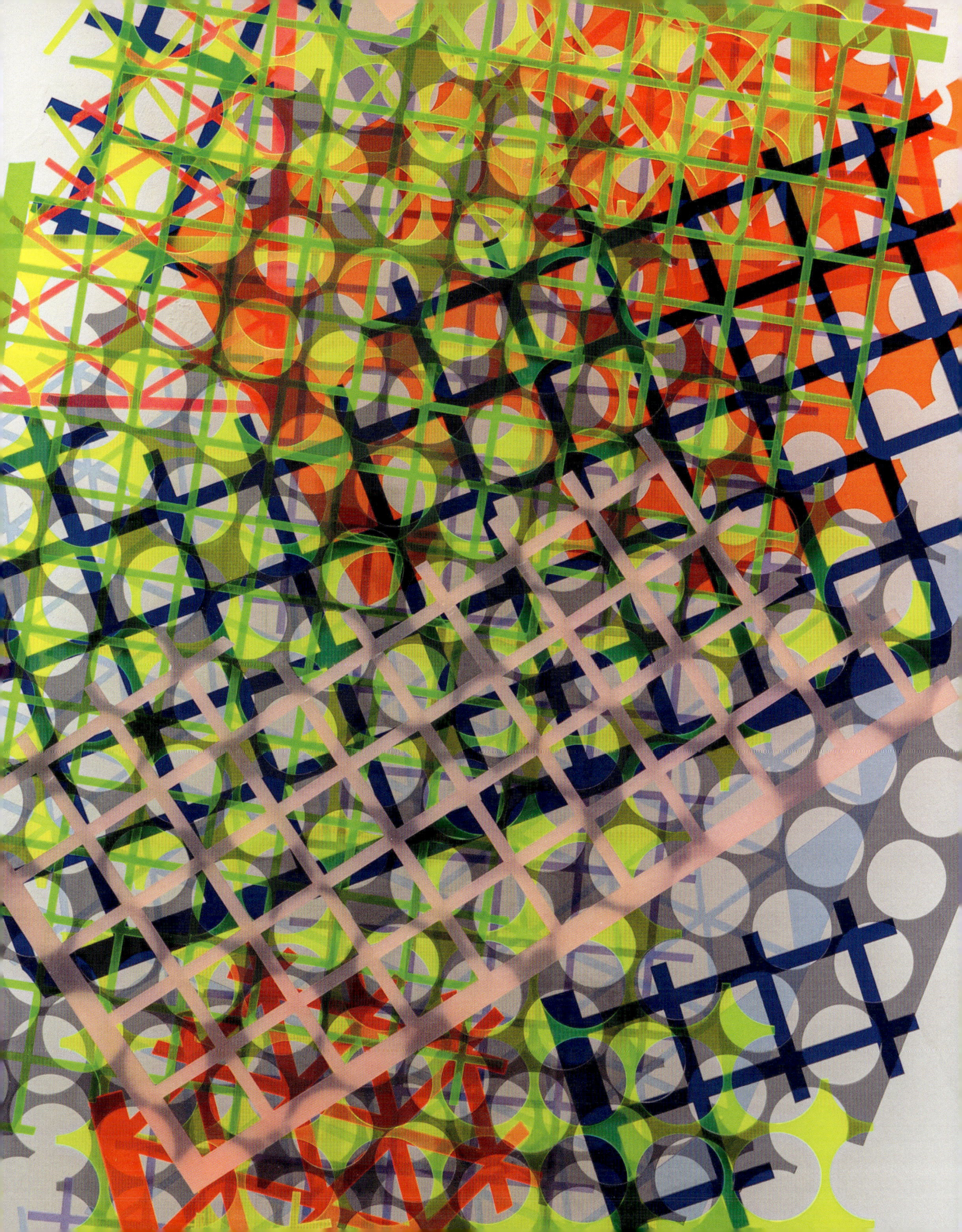

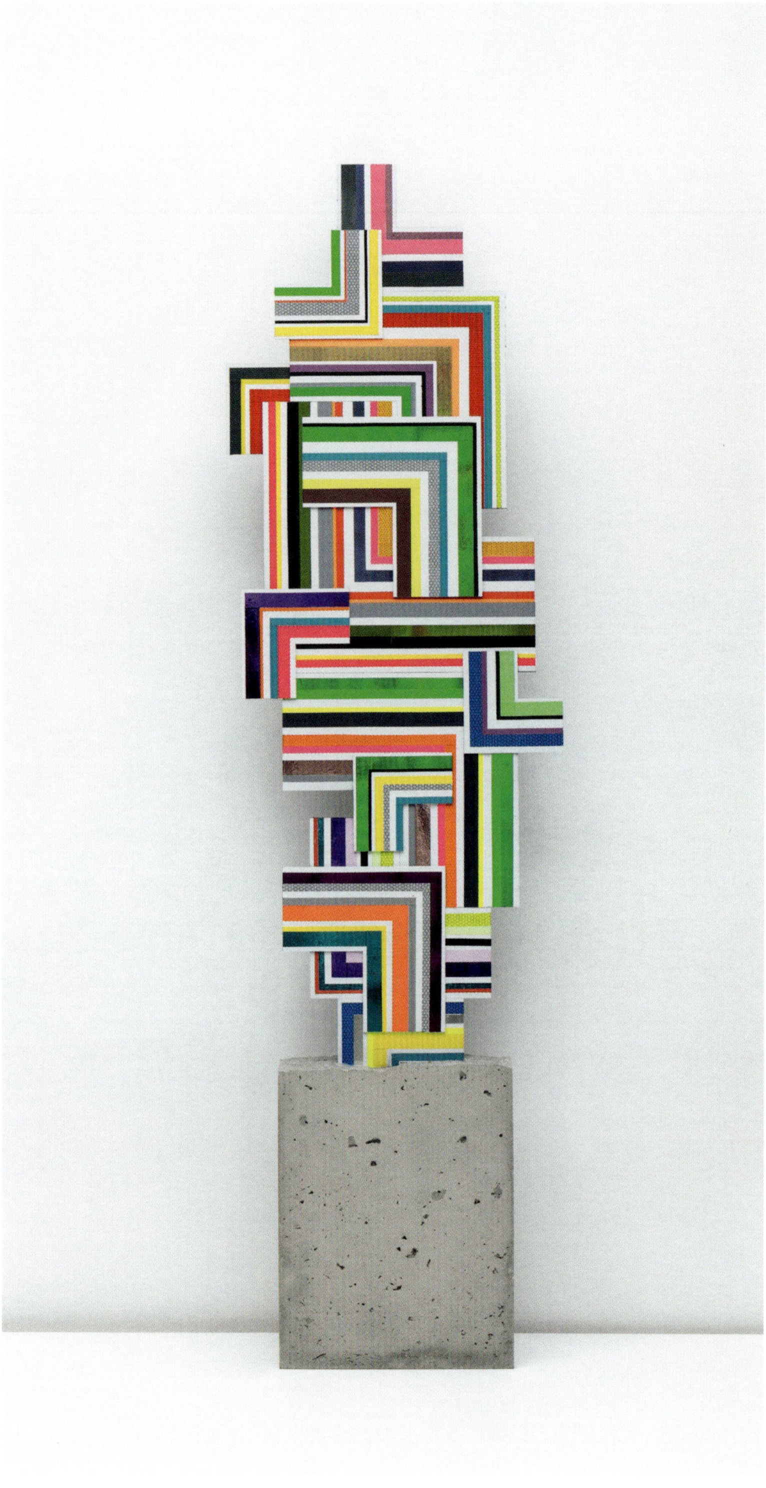

Extra-Concreto 05, (front) 2022
Adhesive tape, composite panel, concrete
199 x 55.5 x 10 cm

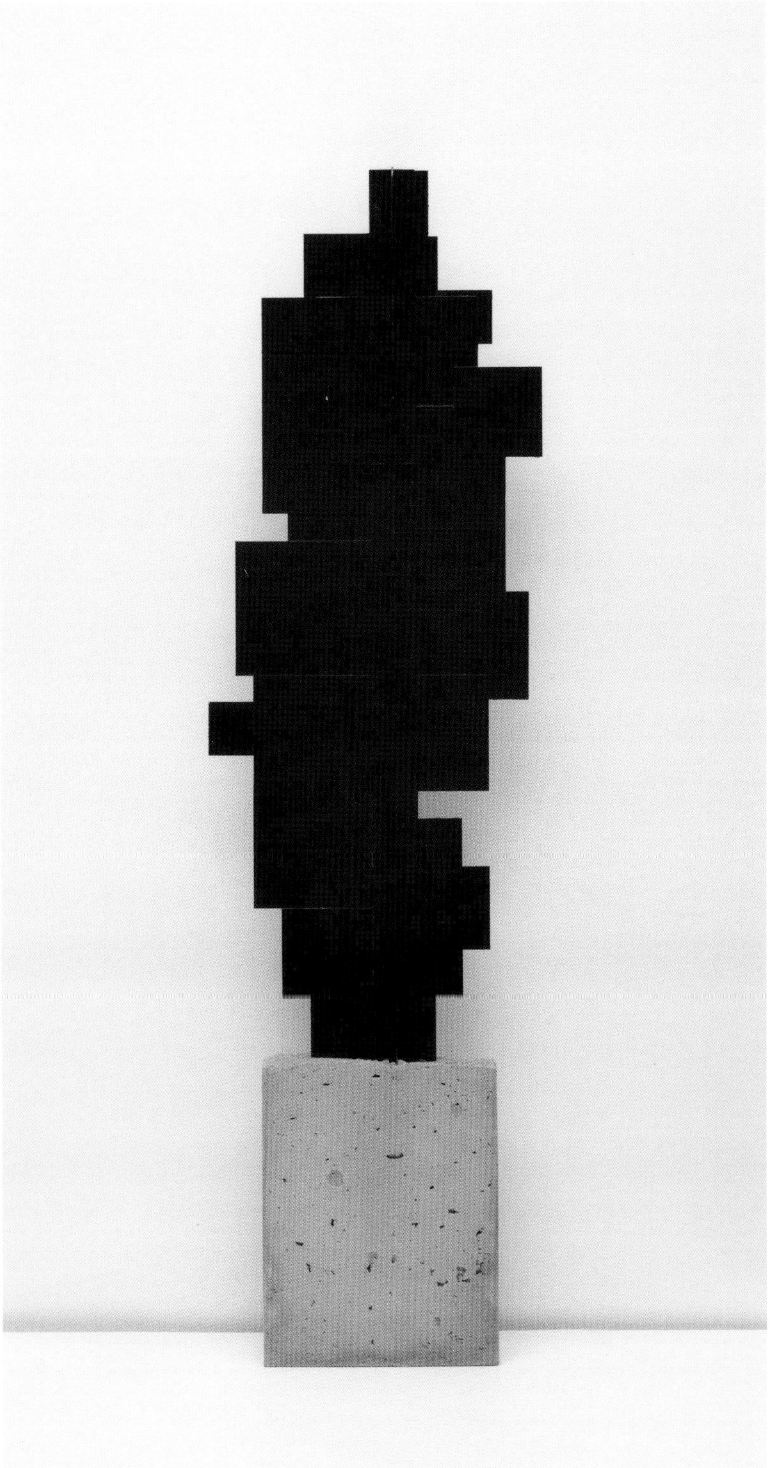

Extra-Concreto 05, (back) 2022
Adhesive tape, composite panel, concrete
199 x 55.5 x 10 cm

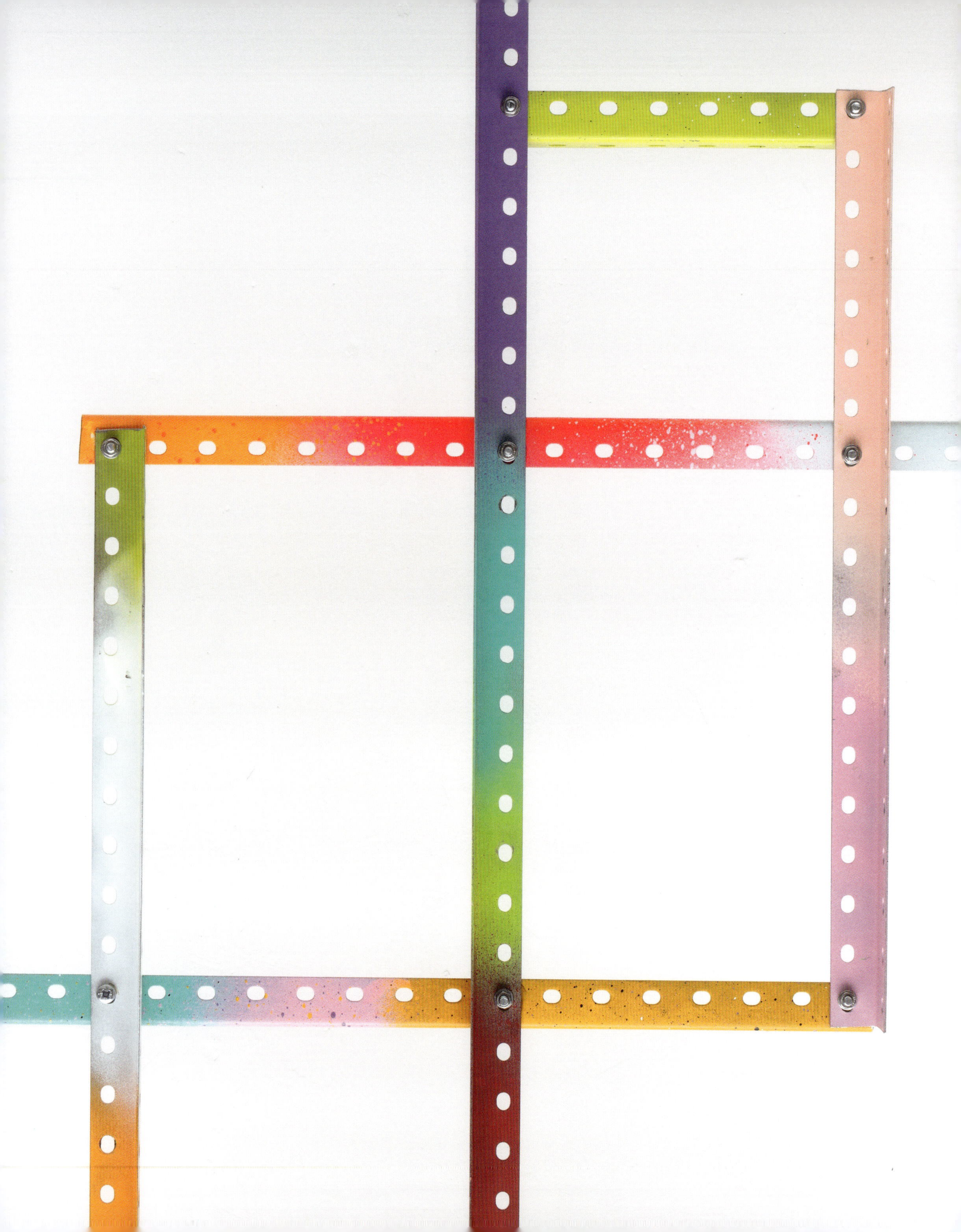

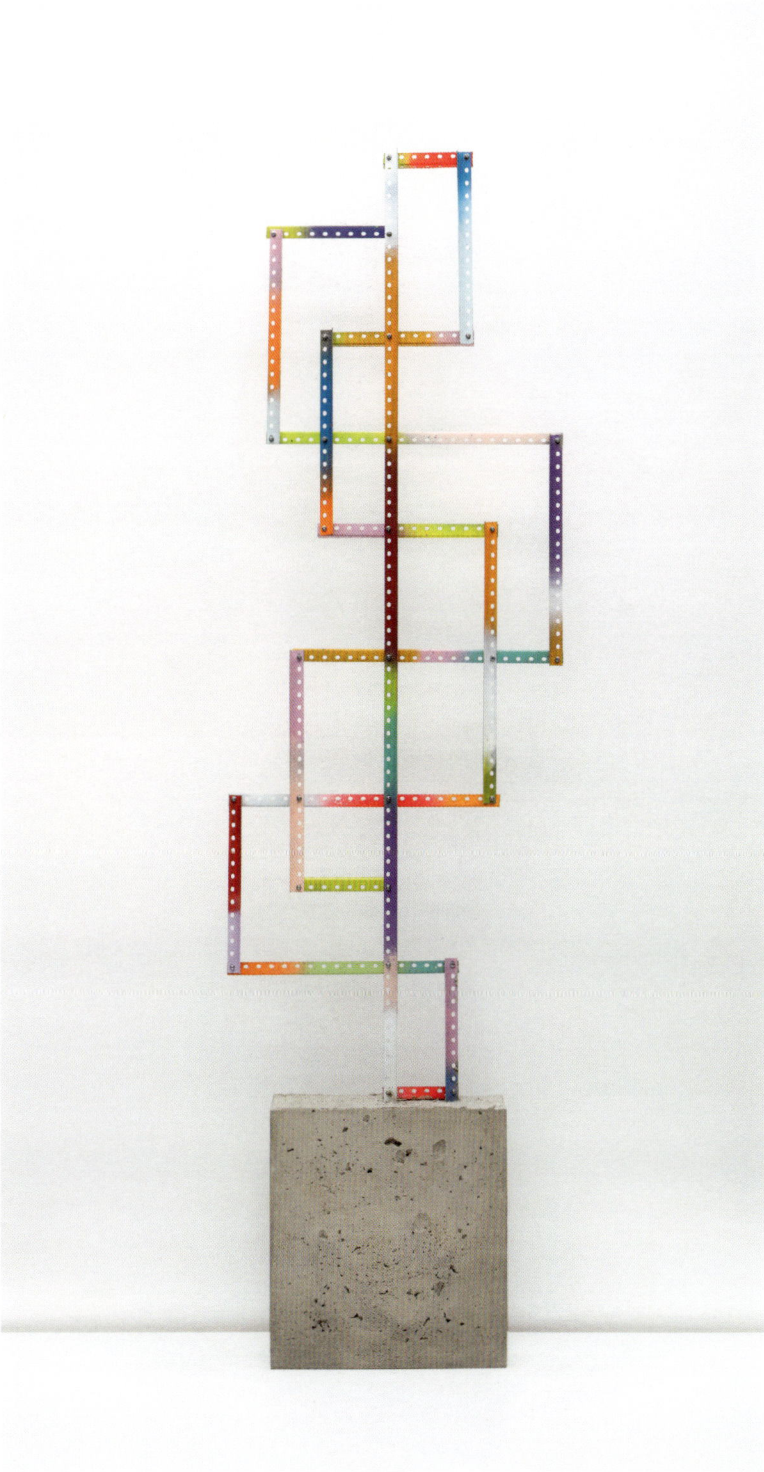

Extra-Concreto 06, 2022
Perforated steel, spray paint, concrete
235 x 57.5 x 15 cm

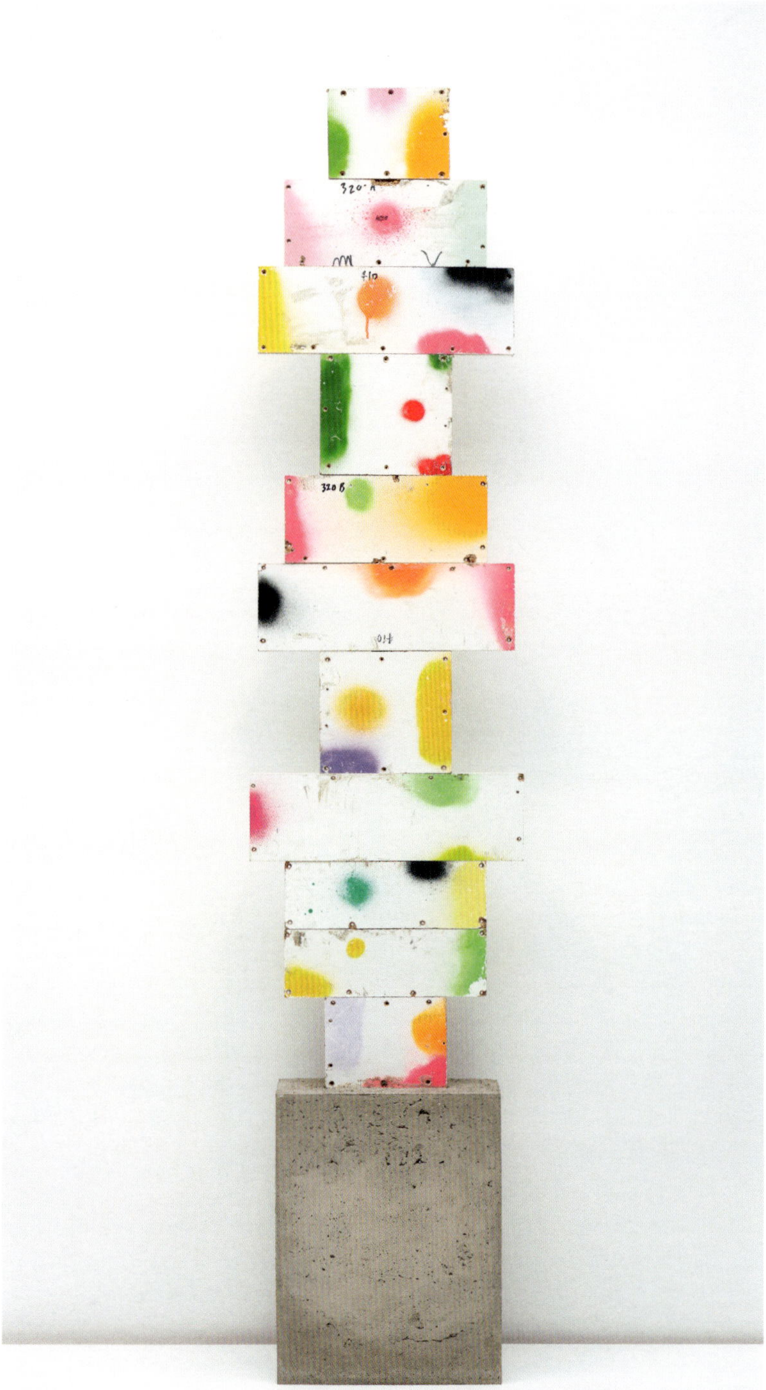

Extra-Concreto 07, 2022
Used *Concreto* moulds, aluminium, concrete
225 x 47.5 x 15 cm

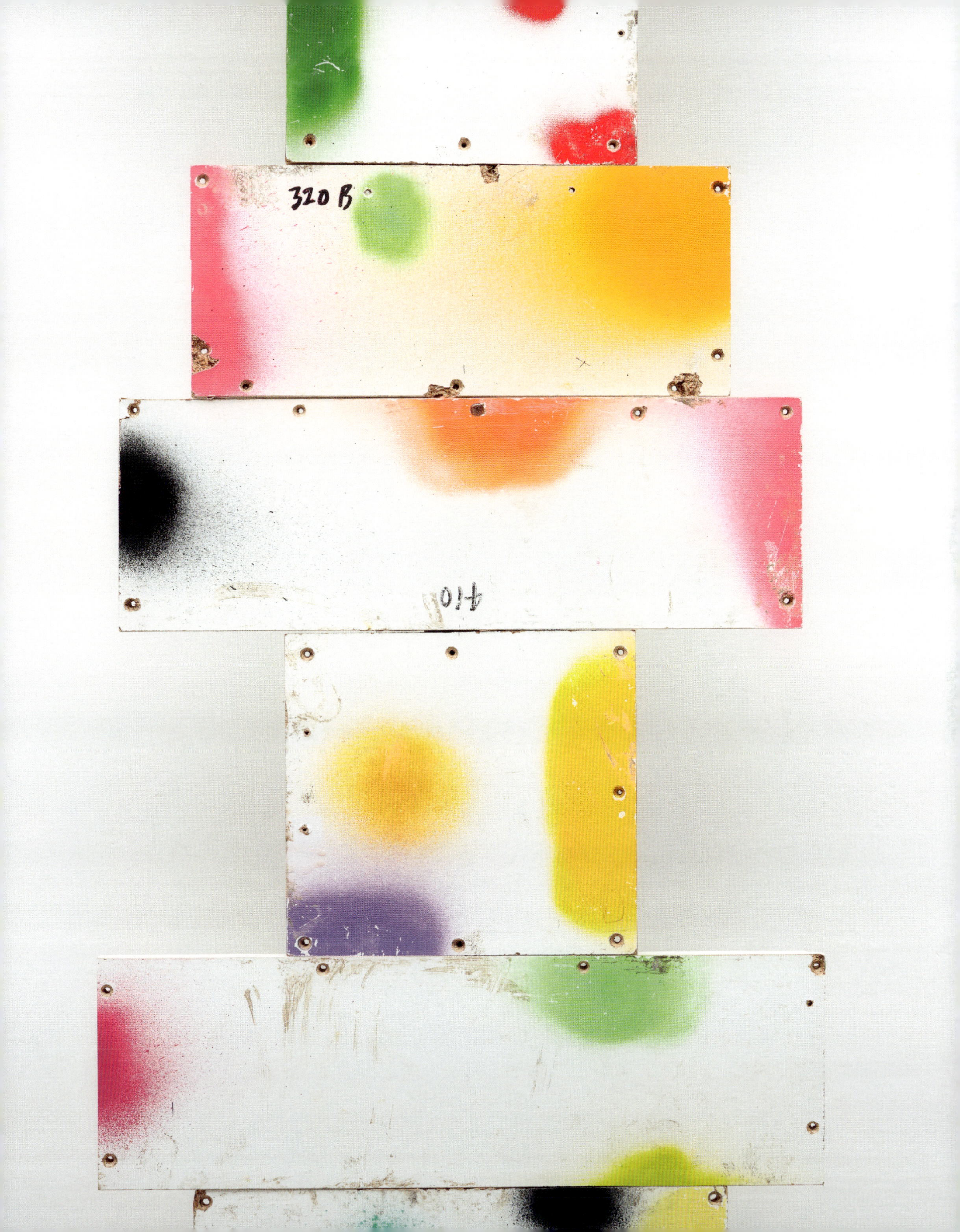
320 B

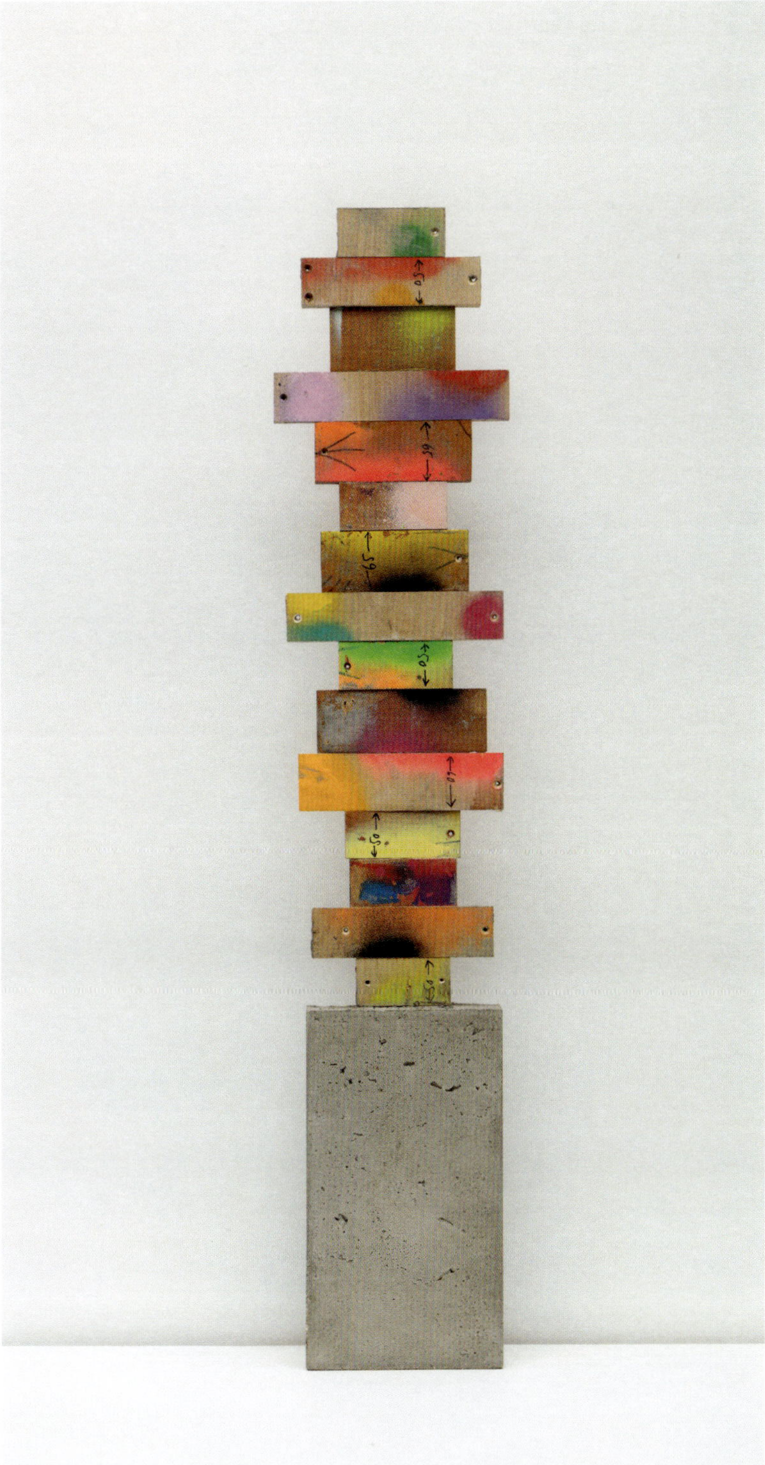

Extra-Concreto 08, 2022
Used *Concreto* moulds, aluminium, concrete
120.5 x 22.5 x 9.5 cm

The Pleasure Principle
Eleanor Nairne

'i kept having this hunch that pleasure was a philosophy   but i couldn't explain it
    peach juice   going down   my cheek' Rebecca Tamás, *Palermo*[1]

They make me think of a bouquet. Perhaps by Margaret Mellis or Winifred Nicholson, or an opulent seventeenth-century Dutch still life; that careful poise between top and bottom, the ordered spread of selected blooms above a vase of just the right size and shape. But there is also something more disorderly: a collision of unrelated elements and surprising forms, just the sort of thing to get the Surrealists excited about a date between an umbrella and a sewing machine.

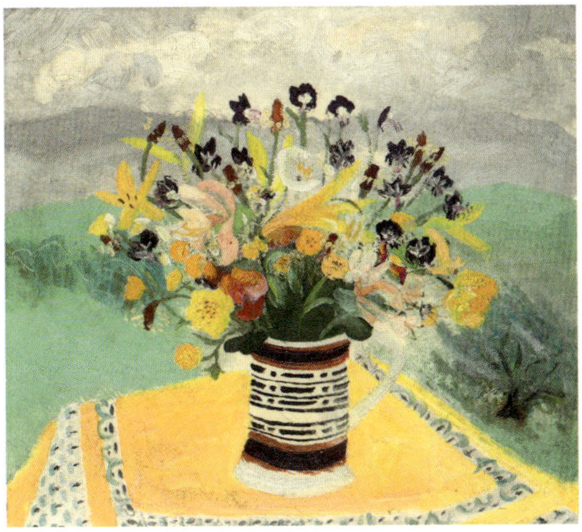

Winifred Nicholson, *Cumberland Flowers*, 1946, oil on board, 43.8 x 48.2 cm

The much-quoted line from the Comte de Lautréamont's *Les Chants de Maldoror* (1868–9) is rarely given its original context:

> He is fair as the retractility of the claws of birds of prey; or again, as the uncertainty of the muscular movements in wounds in the soft parts of the lower cervical region [...] and above all, as the chance meeting on a dissecting-table of a sewing machine and an umbrella![2]

You can see why the Surrealists admired the Comte's inventive writing as he strung together visceral images that speak to the connective tissue binding the phenomenal world – perhaps best visualised by Marcel Duchamp in his web of string for the New York opening of *The First Papers of Surrealism* in October 1942. What is a simile if not a literary device to remind us that we all swim in the same universal soup?

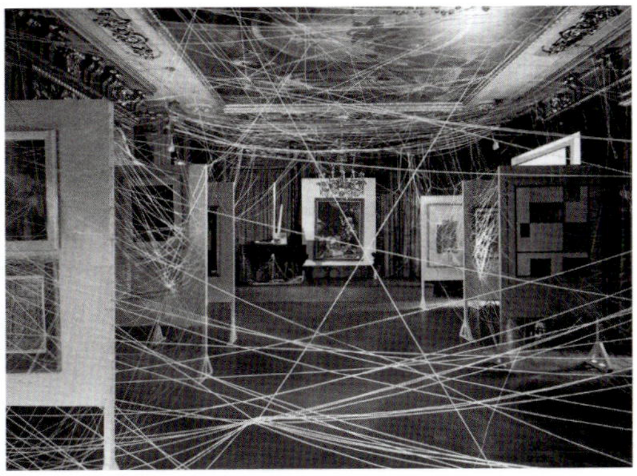

John D. Schiff, installation view of the exhibition *First Papers of Surrealism*, showing Marcel Duchamp's *Sixteen Miles of String* installation, 1942. Gelatin silver print.

'Concreto' is Portuguese for 'concrete' – one of the few languages, apart from English, in which the term refers both to the physical mixture of cement, sand and water, and to a more abstract notion of the physical or material. In Brazil, where Batchelor has regularly made and exhibited work over the last two decades, the *Concreto* and *Neo-Concreto* movements were vital parts of Latin American post-war abstract art.

Do these sculptures make tangible the flotsam of late capitalism that we don't normally bother to see? Like the 'Hang it all' coat racks, designed by Charles and Ray Eames in 1953 but popularised internationally by cheap plastic knock-offs, which have been repurposed here to swarm over a concrete base. There is such pleasure in the caption line, like a recipe listed beneath a cake: *Inter-Concreto 10*, 2019, painted steel coat hangers, painted wood, plastic and concrete.

For me, the word 'Concreto' brings to mind nothing so much as a Cornetto, and seeing them arranged along a shelf carries the delight of eyeing a line of ice-cream cones on a counter. Especially given the synthetic candy colours. Perhaps we should think of Batchelor's recent series of adapted postcards, each embellished with an explosion of colourful dots, as a scattering of hundreds of thousands onto a sacred scene – be it a fifteenth-century Fra Angelico or a Giorgio Morandi still life. The analogy points to that which is delectable in each of Batchelor's collisions.

The *Concretos* were begun in 2011, inspired by a wall in Palermo, in which slivers of blue glass had been pressed into the cement top to ward

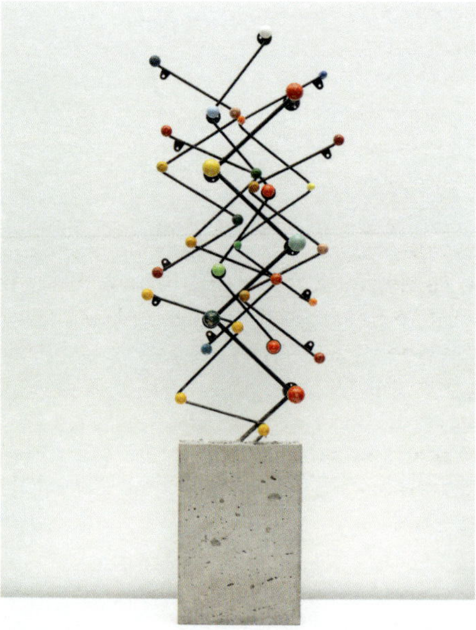

David Batchelor, *Inter-Concreto 10*, 2019, steel coat hangers, paint, wood, plastic, concrete, 125.5 x 43 x 11 cm

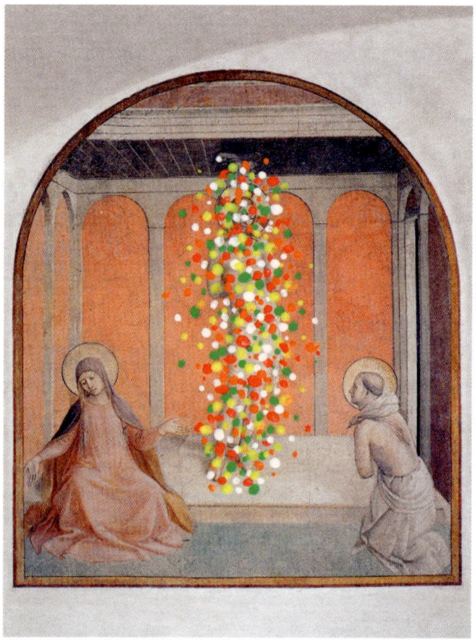

David Batchelor, *Luminous Explosion in Space 03 (Fra Angelico)*, 2021, postcard, acrylic paint, 17 x 12 cm

off trespassers. Has there ever been a more beautiful deterrent device? (In my naivety I thought the gesture was anti-pigeon, but of course it's anti-person.) The decorated wall reflects the drive in each of us towards idle pleasures – seen with a new intensity over the past two years. As Zadie Smith wrote in a pandemic-induced text:

> In each generation, a few too many people will feel moved to pen an essay called, inevitably, 'Why I Write' […] and none of them (including my own) see fit to mention the surest motivation I know, the one I feel deepest within myself, and which, when all is said, done, stripped away – as it is at the moment – seems to be at the truth of the matter for a lot of people, to wit: *it's something to do.*[3]

Many of the *Concretos* were born of happy accidents, and their energy feeds off the 'chance' in Lautréamont's 'encounter'. As Batchelor explains with some glee: 'at a certain point, what you're throwing away feels more interesting than what you're making and you need to address that'.[4] I am particularly fond of the pink Perspex offcut that was found when moving studios and slipped into a concrete base, moulded on a single brick [see p.40], like a shard of glittering light from a disco ball, cast onto an industrial floor. Some of the *Concretos* have panels of coloured fabric pinned to the wall behind them, to offset their conjunction of parts. Batchelor tells me the history of positioning marble statues in niches draped with red velvet, to bathe their stone flesh in an erotic pink light.

What we are cycling around here is play. I have the uncanny sensation that if I turn my back on the folding carpenter's ruler (the type so common in Germany), it will spring into life, *like the retractility of the claws of birds of prey*. Jean Dubuffet was obsessive about the work of children, and learned from their games that life-force could be injected into his work by putting the things he loved in peril. Look at his *Petites statues de la vie précaire* (Little statues of precarious life) and you witness humble materials (driftwood, rusty nails, burnt tyres) transform into extravagant beasts. And of course the materials have their own rules: for Batchelor, there is a thirty-minute window while the concrete is malleable before the game is up. Alfred Jarry tells us that 'it is conventional to call "monster" any blending of dissonant elements… [but] I call "monster" every original, inexhaustible beauty.'[5]

I borrow this line from Dick Hebdige's *Subculture: The Meaning of Style* (1979), where it features as an epigraph to his section on 'style as *bricolage*'. I've pulled his book off the shelf because something about Batchelor's cast of toys has the flavour of punk poetry. In the text, Hebdige traces how *bricolage* has come to be described as a 'science of the concrete', a means for untrained artists to order, classify and arrange 'into structures the *minutiae* of the physical world' according to their own improvised logic.[6]

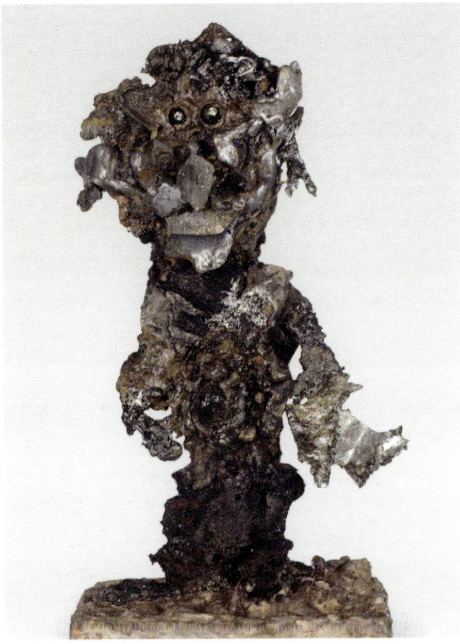

Jean Dubuffet, *Personnage aux yeux de strass* (Character with rhinestone eyes), April 1954, remnants of a burnt car, 25.5 cm high

And then he cites John Clarke from the Centre of Contemporary Cultural Studies at Birmingham University, where Batchelor once studied, and I begin to feel that the world is laced with references to these *Concretos*: 'when the bricoleur re-locates the significant object in a different position within the discourse [...] or when that object is placed within a different total ensemble, a new discourse is constituted, a different message conveyed.'[7]

Which is to say: this is a game that defamiliarises our everyday world and re-enchants the banal. Most children overflow with this instinct to disrupt, but it has to be cultivated in adults. The poet Ben Lerner writes with warm humour about how...

> If you are an adult foolish enough to tell another adult that you are (still!) a poet, they will often describe for you their falling away from poetry; *I wrote it in high school; I dabbled in college*. Almost never do they write it now [...] These familiar encounters – my most recent was at the dentist, my mouth propped open while Dr. X almost gagged me with a mirror, as if searching for my innermost feelings – have a tone that's difficult to describe. There is embarrassment for the poet – couldn't you get a real job and put your childish ways behind you? – but there is also embarrassment on the part of the non-poet, because having to acknowledge one's total alienation from poetry chafes against the early association of poem and self.[8]

(I mention this anecdote to Batchelor, who replies that on a recent visit to an optician, a bright light peering into his left eye – as if looking for his innermost thoughts – he was asked what he did for a living. On saying he was an artist, the optometrist asked, 'Do you have any other hobbies?')

Batchelor's concrete poems return us to our primal instinct to play, conjuring a cacophony of voices, and connections; a breathless story told by a child with a run of conjunctions instead of full stops: *and then, and then, and then*. I could go on and on, because when the signifier is displaced, the possibilities for the signified become endless. Like the implied ellipsis of the title for his exhibition at Compton Verney, *Colour Is*. And it is this spirit of invention, of free association, which makes the energy of these works so infectious and their final form so covetable.

1 Rebecca Tamás, 'Palermo', *London Review of Books*, Vol. 40, No. 19, 11 October 2018.

2 Comte de Lautréamont, *Maldoror*, Crowell, New York, 1972 edition, translated by Alexis Lykiard, quoted by the artist John Coulthart, http://www.johncoulthart.com/feuilleton/2020/06/24/chance-encounters-on-the-dissecting-table/, accessed 13 February 2022.

3 Zadie Smith, *Intimations: Six Essays*, Penguin Random House, London, 2020, p.19.

4 Conversation with the artist at his studio, 11 February 2022.

5 Alfred Jarry, quoted in Dick Hebdige, *Subculture: The Meaning of Style*, Methuen & Co., London, 1979, p.102.

6 Hebdige, p.103.

7 Hebdige, p.104.

8 Ben Lerner, *The Hatred of Poetry*, Fitzcarraldo Editions, London, 2016 edition, p.17.

The Neutral and the Active
Adrian Forty

Among the many features of concrete that people have found repellent, one may count its light-absorbing property. As early as 1946, a committee of British architects recognised that this was likely to be an obstacle to its future use in building:

> The aesthetic disadvantages of exposed concrete are mainly those of colour and texture. The natural grey of Portland cement is cold and depressing, and time and weather, which give mellowness to brick and stone, make untreated concrete more dirty, dark and untidy, and rapidly lower its initially low power of reflecting light.[1]

Compared to the shine and sparkle of most of the materials of modernity – aluminium, stainless steel, plastics of all kinds, the countless products containing titanium – concrete lacks lustre. Along with asphalt, tarmac (or blacktop in the US), the surface finish of stealth bombers, concrete is one of the very few products of modernity that does not contribute to the lustrousness that is so much a part of the contemporary urban landscape. Concrete's failure to conform to the look expected of modern things is one more example of its awkward relationship to modernity. Although a product of scientific industrial processes (Portland cement, its binding agent, was invented in the 1820s), there are many ways in which concrete does not entirely fit within the expectations of a modern product – it is never perfect, it is reliant upon a significant quotient of unskilled labour, it is messy, and while it is a synthetic substance, it shares chemical and geological similarities with naturally occurring stones, calling into question its often stated 'unnaturalness'. Concrete's ambiguous relation to modernity – too modern, and not modern enough – has been a long-running theme, and its light-absorbent properties are but one aspect of this wider picture.

Over the course of the twentieth century, concrete specialists, only too aware of the negativity attaching to concrete, developed ways of making it more lustrous. White cement, instead of the standard grey Portland cement, creates a brighter surface. An example of white-cement concrete, well known to the art world, is the Nordic Pavilion in the Giardini of the Venice Biennale. Alternatively, the use of crushed stone as an aggregate in place of sand can give a more reflective surface, as also may certain surface treatments – bush hammering, acid washing – to remove the film of grey cement that covers cast concrete, and expose the aggregates beneath. Experiments with these techniques preoccupied concrete technologists and architects for much of the twentieth century, but all involved additional expense, and for general purposes the surface of standard concrete remained uniformly grey.

Not everyone has regarded concrete's greyness as a drawback. In the latter part of the twentieth century, some architects became absorbed in the search for a neutral medium that would allow the material properties of buildings to recede so that other qualities, most often 'form', might stand out. In some cases this ambition involved the pursuit of transparency. In others, it meant finding a medium that would not signify, that would pass unnoticed. Although the current revival of interest in Brutalism has focused on the way Brutalist buildings apparently celebrated concrete, this was not always the intention at the time they were built: in some cases, the architects were looking for a way to make the material of which the building was made disappear, in so far as this was possible. To this end, concrete became employed as a 'neutral' material – in Peter Eisenman's early houses, as the next best structural equivalent to the cardboard of which the models were made. Concrete seemed to lend itself to this kind of neutral, non-signifying role, letting other qualities in the architecture emerge more clearly. One may see this ambition in terms similar to Roland Barthes's discussion of the 'neutral', in which he explored the possibilities of the 'unmarked', the 'indistinct'.[2] Barthes's interest in the neutral originated in his desire for a literature that would not be 'literary', 'to create a colourless writing freed from all bondage to a pre-ordained state of language [...] a style of absence which is almost an ideal absence of style'.[3] If this was the aim of certain post-war writers, a similar ambition lay behind the work of at least some architects in the 1960s. Concrete appealed as a means to make matter lose its substance, its seeming neutrality an asset, not a disadvantage. More recently, the Australian architect Thomas Daniell, working in Japan, describes this effect:

Despite the opacity and weight of concrete, its neutrality makes it easier to perceptually 'dematerialize' than truly lightweight and translucent materials: concrete is ordinary enough to become effectively invisible, emphasizing the experience of the space rather than the qualities of its container.[4]

Similar motives are present in the work of the Japanese architect Tadao Ando.

Ando likes to use concrete because it is a neutral material. The main elements from Ando's designs are light and space. A neutral material is then very suitable because it does not distract people from the main ideas of the design. From this point of view concrete is preferable over other building materials such as steel, timber and masonry.[5]

How far this strategy has been successful, whether in the 1960s or in the more recent work of Ando, is another matter, given the propensity of concrete to attract meaning – but the intention that lay behind the architects' choice of the medium is clear. In this context, light-absorbency is no defect, but a virtue.

When artists have used concrete – which has not been very often – it has rarely been for the sake of its neutrality. Mostly, the choice of concrete, unless it has been a direct substitute for some other material (explicitly so in Carl Andre's *Dog Turd Sculptures*), has been directed towards the tension that arises between its opacity as mute substance, and the desire to animate it, to make it communicate. This is a tension that exists with all materials, but with concrete it is somehow magnified because of its reputation as inert matter, more sullen and unresponsive than the other, seemingly more lively, substances out of which art gets made. Good examples of this are Isa Genzken's *World Receivers*, concrete casts of transistor radios, with metal aerials sticking out of them. In one way or another, most of the other instances of concrete in the art of the last forty or fifty years, going back to Bruce Nauman's *A cast of the space under my chair*, play on this conundrum: how can a substance so dumb at the same time be said to communicate? And what sort of communication is it capable of?

The concrete of David Batchelor's *Concretos* does not belong to this lineage. What began more or less accidentally as a solution to displaying the fragments of coloured material that Batchelor was collecting has now become a constant element

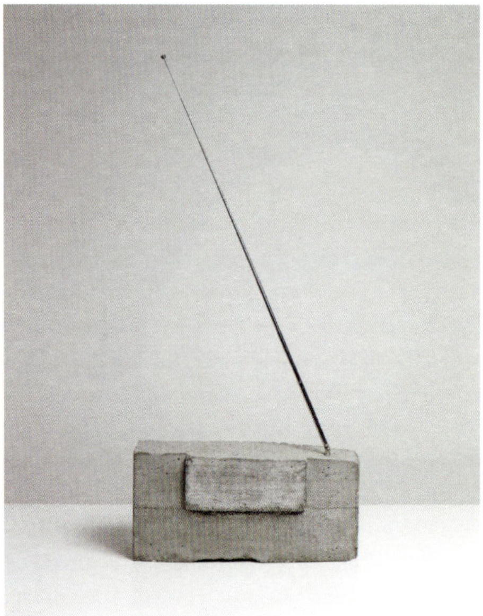

Isa Genzken, *Weltempfänger* (World Receiver), 2012, concrete, antenna, 19 x 40 x 15 cm (concrete), installation dimensions variable

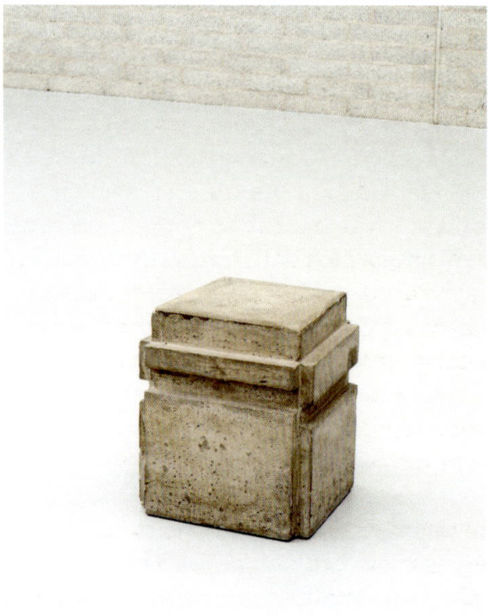

Bruce Nauman, *A cast of the space under my chair*, 1965-8, concrete, 45 x 39 x 37 cm

of the works. Are the concrete plinths, in fact, *the work* – to which the pieces of coloured plastic are simply an ornamental addition? Absurd though this suggestion is, it does at least focus the mind on what the concrete is doing in the assemblages – and whatever it is, it is very much closer to the 'neutral' exploited by twentieth-century architects than it is to what artists have done with concrete. The conjunction of two 'modern' products – fragments of brightly coloured material tinted with aniline dyes, luminous and light-reflective, and the utterly non-reflective, light-absorbing surface of the concrete – speaks to something fundamental in how we encounter both kinds of substance day to day. If Batchelor's purpose is to unmoor colour from its various supporting mediums, and to show it as near as possible in its pure, or raw, state, the concrete, sullen, non-signifying, has a part to play in this. The concrete bases are not inert, devoid of content, in the way that sculptural plinths are generally assumed to be. Walter Benjamin's response, quoted by Batchelor, to his own question comes to mind: 'What, in the end, makes advertisements so superior to criticism? Not what the moving red neon sign says – but the fiery pool reflecting it in the asphalt.'[6] Batchelor writes:

> By day or at night colour is usually accompanied by the less than colourful. It is supported by the contingencies of the street: it is literally bolted onto the sides of buildings, propped up on ledges and secured to roofs, and its reflections form in the potholes and gutters on the ground. These less-to-be-looked-at elements are nonetheless essential to the experience of colour in the city. This colour needs resistance and thrives on opposition. In the city the luminous is almost always accompanied by the grey: they cohabit and sustain one another in an often-unacknowledged relationship of interdependence. The grey makes the luminous more luminous and the luminous makes the grey so much greyer. But it is not an entirely equal relationship, for while grey can live alone, unsupported, unremarked and seemingly unchanging, the luminous can only be present in the presence of that which it is not, and then only for a while.[7]

As in some of the architecture of the second half of the twentieth century, where concrete acted as a recessive medium in order to allow other architectural properties to emerge, so too in the *Concretos* concrete plays a necessary part in allowing colour to be itself. Present, but at the same time part of the barely noticed, half-invisible infrastructure of the city, concrete's very neutrality performs an unexpectedly active part in these works.

1 *The Architectural Use of Building Materials*, Post-War Building Studies no.18, Ministry of Works, London, 1946, p.40, §257.

2 Roland Barthes, *The Neutral. Lecture Course at the Collège de France (1977-78)*, translated by Rosalind E. Krauss and Denis Hollier, Columbia University Press, New York, 2005.

3 Roland Barthes, *Writing Degree Zero*, translated by A. Lavers and C. Smith, Jonathan Cape, London, 1984 edition, p.64.

4 Thomas Daniell, 'Case Study I', *Japan Concrete*, Congress Proceedings November 12 2002, Brussels, organised by the Belgian Cement Industry and the Department of Architecture and Urban Planning, University of Ghent, A&S Books, Ghent, Belgium [n.d.], p.125.

5 Andre de Roo, 'Case Study II', *Japan Concrete*, p.151.

6 Walter Benjamin, 'One Way Street' in *One Way Street and Other Writings*, translated by Edmund Jephcott and Kingsley Shorter, Verso, London, 1979, pp.89-90.

7 David Batchelor, *The Luminous and the Grey*, Reaktion Books, London, 2014, pp.60-1.

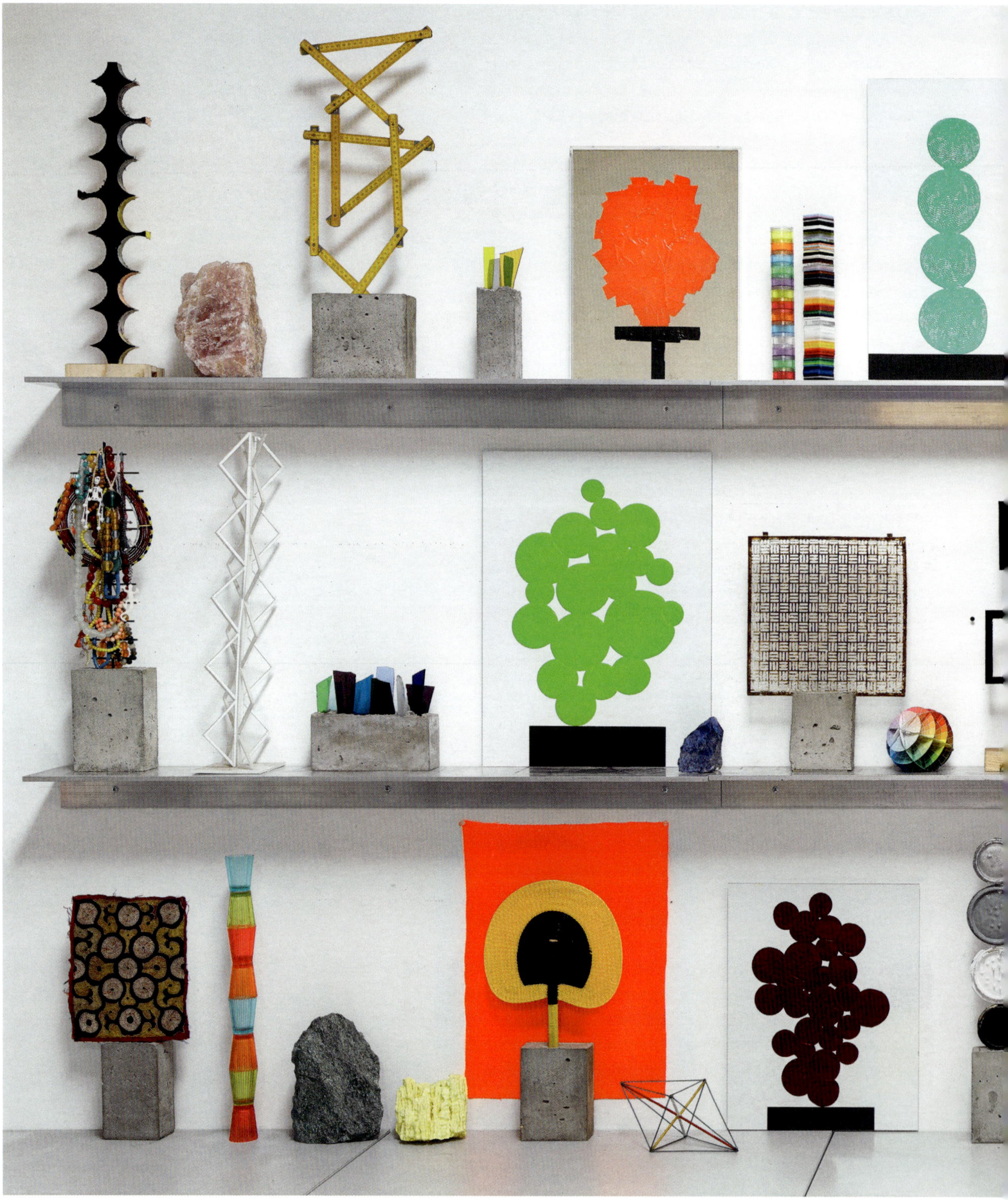

Studio wall, 2022

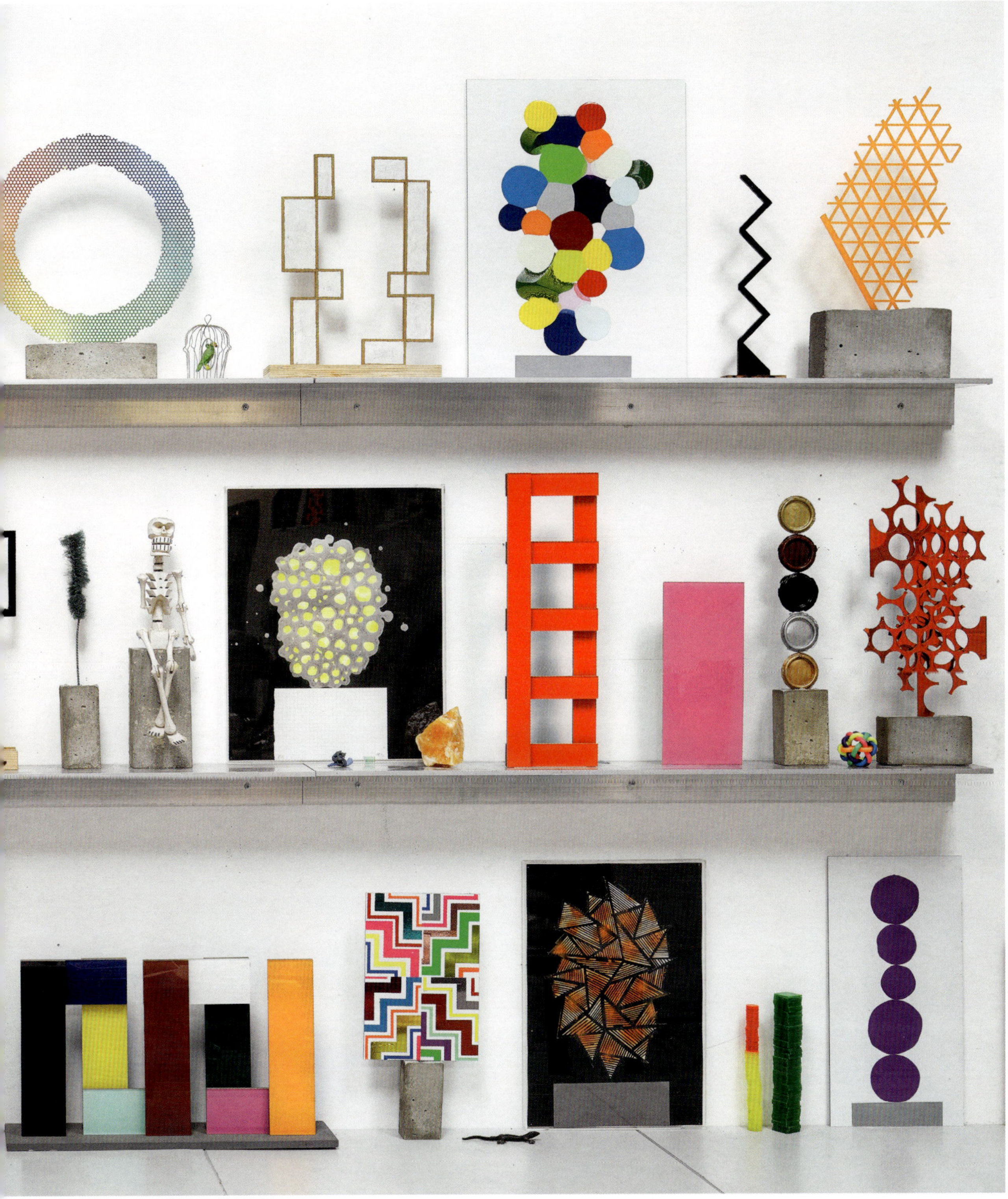

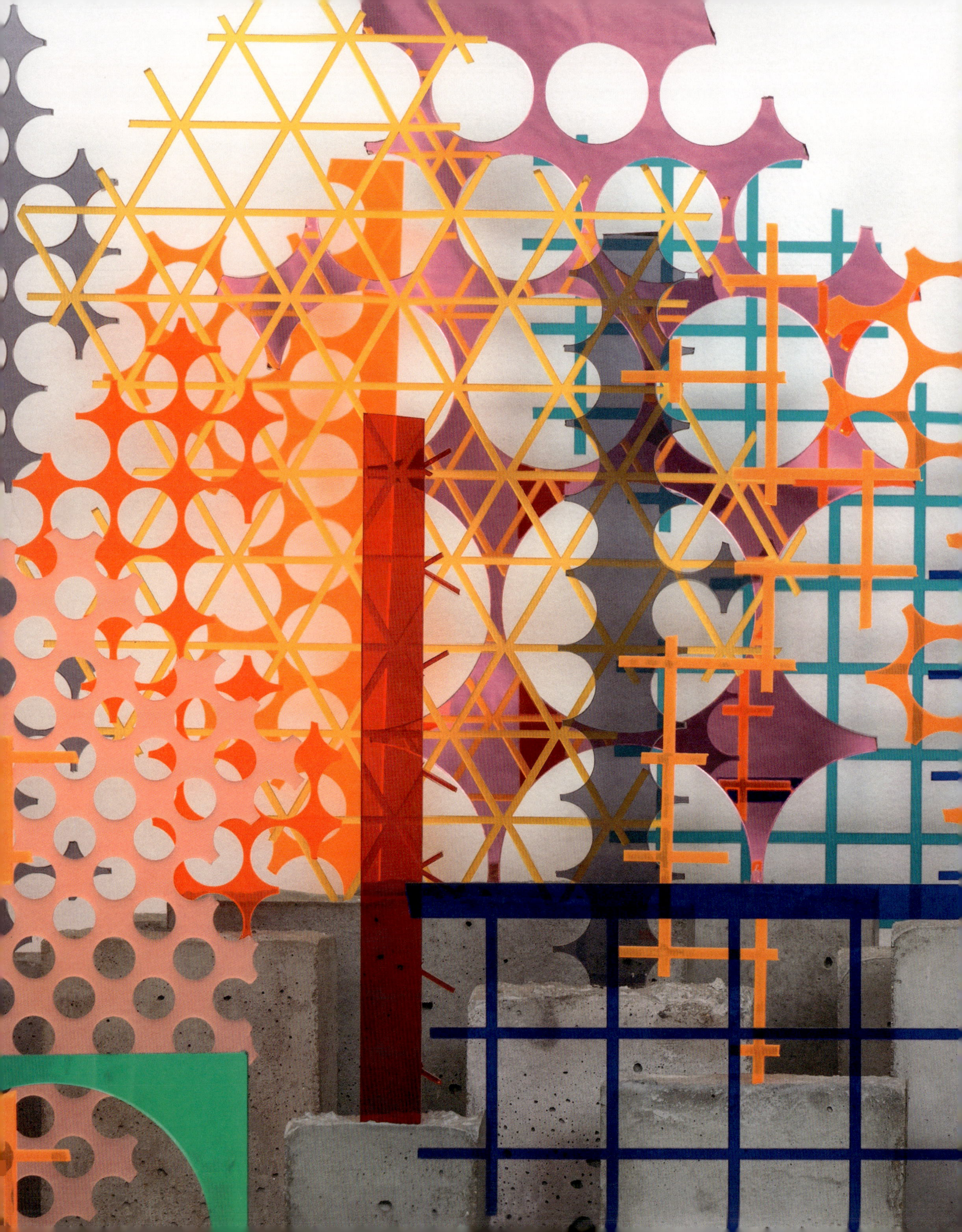

Acknowledgements

This book was published to coincide with *Colour Is*, the first large-scale survey of my work, at Compton Verney Gallery and Museum in Warwickshire. The exhibition opened on 25 June 2022 and contained many works from the early 1980s to the present day, including a range of *Concretos*.

The publication and the exhibition would not have been possible without the help and support of a great many people. Penny Sexton from Compton Verney first proposed the exhibition in early 2021; it was curated with Oli McCall with the help of many others from the museum. Matt Price of Anomie Publishing responded positively to my initial book proposal and has managed the process from start to finish. Kate Sclater and Tim Balaam from Hyperkit designed the book, and Lucy Dawkins photographed most of the works. I am grateful to Richard Deal and the team at DPM for their work on the reprography, and to Anna Powell, Rob Williams, Ross Pritchard and Perry Cella at Park. Eleanor Nairne and Adrian Forty both agreed to write texts on aspects of the *Concretos*, and my studio manager, Isabelle Bucklow, co-ordinated just about everything to do with the book and the exhibition. My heartfelt thanks to all and one, and to all of the following: Richard Ingleby, Florence Ingleby, Eduardo Leme, Fedja Klikovac, Madeleine Bessborough, Stephen Feeke, Mario Codognato, Tanya Barson, Cecilia Brunson, Doro Globus, Madeleine Ruggi, Tim Meaker, Tim Holmes, Angus Mill, Alan McFetridge and, not least, Ann Gallagher.

DB, May 2022

Detail from *Reef 02*, 2018, cast acrylic, concrete, dimensions variable

David Batchelor – Concretos

Published on the occasion of the exhibition
David Batchelor: Colour Is
Compton Verney, Warwickshire, UK
25 June – 2 October 2022

Designed by Hyperkit
Edited by David Batchelor and Matt Price
Proofreading by William Lambie
Repro by DPM
Printed and bound by Park, London

Photographer credits:
Lucy Dawkins: all works except those below
Angus Mill: pp.95, 96, 97, 99, 100, 101, 102, 103, 104, 105, 106, 107
Tom Nolan: pp.52-3
Alan McFetridge: pp.140-1

Published in 2022 by Anomie Publishing, London
www.anomie-publishing.com

A catalogue record for this book is available from the British Library

ISBN: 978-1-910221-38-9

Distributed by Casemate Art

This publication has received financial support from Goldsmiths' College, University of London, and Arts Council England.

Supported using public funding by
ARTS COUNCIL ENGLAND

Image credits:

p.13 John Cooper Clarke: Photo © Paul Wolfgang Webster.

p.13 Bob Ross: Bob Ross, *The Joy of Painting*, 1983-94. © Bob Ross Inc.; ® Bob Ross name and images are registered trademarks of Bob Ross Inc.

p.14 Arrange Whatever Pieces Come Your Way: Courtesy Sheelagh Boyce and Annabelle Harty, Arrange Whatever Pieces Come Your Way. Photo: Susie Lowe.

p.133 Winifred Nicholson: © Trustees of Winifred Nicholson. Photo © Christie's Images / Bridgeman Images.

p.133 John D. Schiff: Courtesy of Philadelphia Museum of Art, Library and Archives: Gift of Jacqueline, Paul and Peter Matisse in memory of their mother Alexina Duchamp, Leo Baeck Institute Photograph Collection. © Alexina and Marcel Duchamp Papers, Philadelphia Museum of Art, Library and Archives.

p.135 Jean Dubuffet: Private collection, New York. Courtesy Fondation Dubuffet, Paris. © ADAGP, Paris and DACS, London, 2022.

p.138 Isa Genzken: Courtesy Galerie Buchholz. Photo: Nick Ash. © VG Bild-Kunst, Bonn / DACS, London, 2022.

p.138 Bruce Nauman: Collection Kröller-Müller Museum, Otterlo, the Netherlands, formerly in the Visser collection, acquired with support from the Mondriaan Foundation. Photo: Cary Markerink. © Bruce Nauman / Artists Rights Society (ARS), New York and DACS, London 2022.